SOCIALLY SAVVY:

An Assessment and Curriculum Guide for Young Children

James T. Ellis, Ph.D., BCBA-D and Christine Almeida, M.S.Ed., Ed.S., BCBA
Edited by: Nancy Ferrari

SOCIALLY SAVVY:
An Assessment and Curriculum Guide for Young Children

Copyright © 2014 James T. Ellis, Ph.D., BCBA-D
                      Christine Almeida, M.S.Ed., Ed.S., BCBA

Published by: Different Roads to Learning, Inc.
                           12 West 18th Street, Suite 3E
                           New York, NY 10011
                           tel: 212.604.9637 | fax: 212.206.9329
                           www.difflearn.com
                           http://www.facebook.com/difflearn
                           http://blog.difflearn.com/
                           www.drlbooks.com

Editor: Nancy Ferrari, H.E. Saunders
Art Director: Samantha Yanow

Library of Congress Control Number: 2014947003
ISBN: 978-0-9910403-0-8

Dedicated to the many children with whom we have worked
and from whom we have learned so much.

CONTENTS

List of Activities vi

Introduction 1

CHAPTER 1: The Socially Savvy Checklist 7

    Socially Savvy Checklist 9

    Socially Savvy Checklist Summary Report 19

CHAPTER 2: Description of Skills 31

CHAPTER 3: Sample IEP Objectives 47

CHAPTER 4: Teaching Strategies 57

    Direct Teaching 57

    Modeling 58

    Rule-Based Teaching 59

    Activity-Based Teaching 60

    Commercially Available Curricula 61

    Incidental Teaching 63

    Reinforcement 63

    Social Stories 64

    Visual Supports 65

    Self-Monitoring 65

    Peer-Mediated Intervention 66

    Structuring Groups 66

CHAPTER 5: Activities for Teaching Social Skills 105

CHAPTER 6: Data Collection 167

CHAPTER 7: Case Studies 177

    Case 1 177

    Case 2 195

Appendix 1: Lesson Plans 213

Appendix 2: Visual Supports 241

Appendix 3: Social Stories 259

LIST OF ACTIVITIES

ACTIVITY 1: Duck-Duck-Animal 106

ACTIVITY 2: Guess What's Different? 107

ACTIVITY 3: Monkey Under the Blanket 108

ACTIVITY 4: Charades 109

ACTIVITY 5: Who Am I? 111

ACTIVITY 6: Operator 112

ACTIVITY 7: Head Honcho Directions 113

ACTIVITY 8: Roll the Ball 114

ACTIVITY 9: Freeze Tag 116

ACTIVITY 10: Bubble Gum River 117

ACTIVITY 11: Simon Says 118

ACTIVITY 12: Bubbles 119

ACTIVITY 13: It's All About You! 120

ACTIVITY 14: Silly Face 122

ACTIVITY 15: Mystery Story 123

ACTIVITY 16: Alphabet Name Game 124

ACTIVITY 17: Going to the Moon 125

ACTIVITY 18: Red Rover 126

ACTIVITY 19: Hello My Friend 128

ACTIVITY 20: Blob Tag 129

ACTIVITY 21: Pass the Wink 130

ACTIVITY 22: Partner Hokey Pokey 131

ACTIVITY 23: Spider Web Questions 132

ACTIVITY 24: What Do You Think? 133

ACTIVITY 25: Wonderball 134

ACTIVITY 26: 20 Questions 135

ACTIVITY 27: Category Game 136

ACTIVITY 28: Mystery Rules 138

ACTIVITY 29: Obstacle Course 139

ACTIVITY 30: Sharing News 140

ACTIVITY 31: I Spy 141

ACTIVITY 32: One Elephant 142

ACTIVITY 33: Children, Children, Who Do You See? 144

ACTIVITY 34: Fill in the Story 145

ACTIVITY 35: Partner Twister 146

ACTIVITY 36: Peek-A-Who 147

ACTIVITY 37: Animal Playdate 148

ACTIVITY 38: Follow My Eye! 150

ACTIVITY 39: Show and Tell 151

ACTIVITY 40: List Walk 153

ACTIVITY 41: Self-Monitoring Checklist 154

ACTIVITY 42: The Good Friend Book 156

ACTIVITY 43: The Emotion Book 157

ACTIVITY 44: The Waiting Book 158

ACTIVITY 45: Ice Breaker 159

ACTIVITY 46: Whose is That? 160

ACTIVITY 47: Animal Pass 161

ACTIVITY 48: Conversation Chain 162

ACTIVITY 49: In the Woods 163

ACTIVITY 50: How Does that Rate? 165

ACKNOWLEDGMENTS

This social-skills manual is the result of our many years working with children who have social deficits and the incredible teachers and professionals whose dedication is shown through the many creative ideas and teaching strategies outlined in this manual. We would like to express our gratitude to the many children, teachers, professionals, and parents who inspired us to write this social-skills manual. It is truly a blessing to spend each day helping children learn how to play and interact with one another, while at the same time learning so much ourselves.

We have been blessed to work with many creative and talented professionals who have shared many brilliant ideas to make learning social skills more fun for children. Although it is impossible to individually thank every person who has contributed to this book in some way, we would like to acknowledge the following people: Katie Towle, Victoria Willis, Phoebe Forsley, Daniel Cohen, Katie Perniola, Reiko Shiota, Cristina Ross, Rebecca Maxfield, Elisa DiCarlo-Piskura, Cassandra Marcucci, Kristin Hovis, Barbara Cannon, Jessica Everett, and Dan Almeida. We would also like to thank Curt Hagenlocher and Tim Carroll for providing us with their expert technical guidance.

We are extremely indebted to DRL, especially Julie Azuma. We are grateful for her willingness to work with us when we presented her with our idea for this social-skills manual and for her ongoing encouragement and subtle nudging.

We are also grateful to Heather Saunders for her attention to detail in editing the manuscript and clearly understanding the type of book we were trying to create.

As novices to writing a book, we did not know how important the layout and design of a book is, and we are extremely grateful to Samantha Yanow for her incredible ideas and expertise in making the educational content so appealing.

There is no doubt that this social-skills manual would never have been completed and published without the incredible wisdom and guidance of Nancy Ferrari. Nancy helped edit the manuscript, connected us with the right resources and people, provided advice with the design and layout of the book, and offered constant support and encouragement. Nancy—you are a godsend!

Finally, we would like to thank our families:

I would especially like to thank my partner, Ken Brooks, for his ongoing support, encouragement, and patience.

—Jim

"My love is like a ring that has no beginning or ending:" words that can only be said about and to my tolerant family, T.L. and T.Z., without whom I would never have tried.

—Christine

INTRODUCTION

Far too often, children with social impairments are left to flounder in a confusing world of social nuances and expectations without explicit and consistent rules or support to guide them. Impairments in social skills can present in many different ways. A child may show little to no interest in other children, may have difficulty initiating and/or sustaining interactions with others, or may have difficulty following expected rules in group or social situations. In many cases, social-skills deficits may result in a child withdrawing from social interaction and appearing disinterested in activities or interacting with other people. In other cases, there can be a cascade of difficult behaviors (pushing others, knocking over materials, meltdowns) toward other children, in certain situations, or both.

Today, schools, teachers, and parents often focus intensely on young children's academic skills at the expense of adequate attention to social skills (many of which develop from play). This emphasis begins as early as preschool, and this is shortsighted for a number of reasons. First, academic success requires a foundation of strong social skills. Second, if a child can read and perform basic math at 5 years old, but cannot negotiate social situations, that child is unprepared for many situations in which she must interact and collaborate with others. Finally, social skills are the currency of a "happy" childhood. Social competencies pave the way for a child to have fun at birthday parties, resolve conflicts with friends, feel heard, stand up for oneself, and ask for help when needed. We would argue that, particularly for a very young child, developing effective social skills is as important, or perhaps more important, than exceling academically. Additionally, many children will not develop the necessary social skills unless direct instruction is provided.

Social-skills training in public schools is often woefully inadequate. Most often, it takes the form of a "social-pragmatics group" for thirty minutes to an hour a week, with the hope that these skills will generalize throughout the school day. However, to be successful in this format, children need a minimum repertoire of social skills to function well within the group. To be truly effective, group leaders must begin with a detailed and precise assessment of each child's individual skills.

This manual relies on the principals of Applied Behavior Analysis (ABA) to assess and conceptualize social-skills deficits and to design effective interventions. Decades of research show that ABA, which relies on the systematic use of evidence-based procedures to teach skills and make changes in behavior, can yield socially valid changes that can have a significant impact in a child's life and functioning. ABA requires that teachers, therapists, and aides collect data regularly to measure the effectiveness of intervention and to enable mindful and strategic changes to the plan.

When we break down broad areas of social functioning into concrete skills, we can determine a child's specific strengths, and weaknesses. Once a child's specific situation has been assessed, it is much easier for teachers and parents to prioritize the skills most in need of intervention, to develop strategies to address them, and to monitor the success of those strategies. Working on social skills becomes less overwhelming for both the adults and children involved. By working on one or two specific skills through planned and naturally occurring opportunities throughout the course of the day, teachers and parents become less overwhelmed at the prospect of working on "social skills." We developed this manual because we have seen this approach be so successful for so many children, families, and teachers, and because we would like to serve more young children who struggle with social impairments.

The purpose of this manual is to provide an assessment and tracking tool, based on the principles of ABA, for the social skills of young children, as well as a guide for interventions.

Effective teaching and behavior change through ABA relies on the basic learning paradigm of antecedent–behavior–consequence (A–B–C), or stimulus–response–consequence. That is, to understand why certain behaviors occur, or when a social skill is absent or deficient, we need to look at what happens before the behavior (antecedent or stimulus) and what happens after the behavior (consequence). To reduce or eliminate a challenging behavior, we need to change the antecedent and the consequence. Similarly, to teach a new skill effectively, we must pay careful attention to how we deliver an instruction, the environmental conditions before a skill occurs, and how we (and others) respond when a child demonstrates that skill. Each component may have a variety of factors that affect the occurrence of a skill or behavior.

Let's look at one example using the A–B–C learning paradigm for an expected stimulus and response.

A	B	C
Person says "Hi"	Child responds "Hi"	Person starts a conversation

Now let's investigate, using this paradigm, why a child might not respond when someone says hello. There may be a variety of factors at each component that affect whether the child exhibits the expected skill (i.e., responding "Hi").

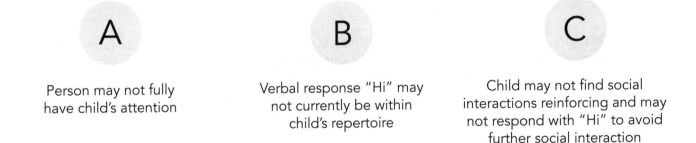

A	B	C
Person may not fully have child's attention	Verbal response "Hi" may not currently be within child's repertoire	Child may not find social interactions reinforcing and may not respond with "Hi" to avoid further social interaction

Understanding the reason why a child does not demonstrate a social skill should guide the choice of intervention.

A	B	C
Teacher ensures she has the child's full attention before initiating a greeting or other social interaction. The teacher should also work on increasing the child's attention when others approach.	Teach the verbal response "Hi" or an alternative physical response, such as a wave.	Provide individualized reinforcement to increase and sustain the child's motivation to respond to a greeting or other social initiation. Initially, do not place additional social demands after a child responds to a greeting.

Thus, to be most effective in teaching new social skills and in increasing the independent use of a social skill by a child, we need to consider each component of the learning paradigm and potentially make changes to each in order for a child to demonstrate the targeted social skill consistently.

This manual focuses on the social skills that are important for a child preparing to transition into kindergarten. This is a time when many children present with deficits or impairments with social skills. It is based on our experience helping children in an integrated preschool program, but the tools and strategies can be applied to children with a range of impairments in social skills. Even though many of the social-skills interventions outlined in the manual take place in a play-based and language-rich setting, the assessment tool itself does not focus on play or language skills. There are other good instruments with which to evaluate those skill areas, such as the Assessment of Basic Language and Learning Skills-Revised (ABLLS-R)[1] or the Verbal Behavior Milestones Assessment and Placement Program (VB-MAPP).[2]

The assessment tool is easy to use. It includes a description of each item and an explanation of its importance to help ensure consistency among those completing the assessment and to help less familiar evaluators understand the items/skills. The assessment can be individualized to include additional skills that a teacher, parent, or team might find important for a particular child or in a particular environment. The manual also includes a sample criterion-based objective for each skill to assist teachers and parents in developing goals for a child's Individualized Educational Program (IEP).

Specific teaching strategies are provided for each skill. We describe fifty different activities that can serve as contexts to teach a variety of different social skills. We also give detailed teaching plans, examples of visual supports, and/or sample social stories. The central methodology of the program is that social-skills intervention best takes place in a social environment (i.e., a group) within typical, age-appropriate, and fun activities. Finally, we offer guidance on how to measure a child's progress with targeted skills, along with specific data collection procedures and data sheet examples.

CHAPTER 1: THE SOCIALLY SAVVY CHECKLIST

The Socially Savvy Checklist is a social-skills assessment that provides a structured way for a teacher or parent to determine a child's strengths and areas most in need of intervention. The assessment is divided into seven areas of social development: Joint Attending, Social Play, Self-Regulation, Social/Emotional, Social Language, Classroom/Group Behavior, and Nonverbal Social Language. Within each area, we identify a number of specific skills, which are typically ordered in sequence of developmental progression.

CHAPTER 2: DESCRIPTION OF SKILLS

This chapter provides a brief description of each area of the assessment and a description of each individual skill.

CHAPTER 3: SAMPLE IEP OBJECTIVES

This chapter offers sample criterion-based objectives for each skill to help teachers and parents identify and articulate specific IEP goals and benchmarks for a child.

CHAPTER 4: TEACHING STRATEGIES

This chapter offers specific teaching strategies for targeted skills. These include general considerations for targeted skills, references to potential games or activities to serve as a context for learning, ways to use social stories or visual supports, or detailed step-by-step teaching plans.

CHAPTER 5: ACTIVITIES FOR TEACHING SOCIAL SKILLS

This chapter provides fifty specific games and activities that can serve as a context for teaching targeted social skills. Instructions include targeted social skills for each activity, a detailed description of each activity, the required materials, and sample visual supports when appropriate. We also offer ideas on how to vary or generalize the activity and helpful suggestions.

CHAPTER 6: ASSESSMENT AND DATA COLLECTION

This chapter offers specific ideas regarding how to assess the child, including the types of data to collect, as well as the most efficient ways to gather this data. Sample data sheets are provided.

CHAPTER 7: CASE STUDIES

To illustrate the process from initial assessment to intervention and data collection, we provide two case studies based on a compilation of children for whom we have provided social-skills intervention involving a variety of formats, including one-on-one, dyad, and group formats.

APPENDIX 1: LESSON PLANS

Sample lesson plans are provided for some of the targeted social skills.

APPENDIX 2: VISUAL SUPPORTS

Sample visual supports are provided for some of the activities and intervention strategies.

APPENDIX 3: SOCIAL STORIES

Sample social stories are provided for some of the targeted social skills.

The key to helping a young child learn any new skill is to provide a learning context that is seen as enjoyable, not as "work." Interacting with others is meant to be a fun experience, and learning social skills for a child struggling in this area should be fun. One way to make learning fun is to provide the adult, whether a teacher or a parent, with a manageable and less overwhelming way to assess and teach social skills. This manual can serve as a resource for parents and educators to make both learning and teaching social skills a fun experience.

CHAPTER 1:
The Socially Savvy Checklist

The Socially Savvy Checklist serves multiple purposes. It identifies children's strengths and challenges in each social-skills area, highlights specific skills in need of intervention, and assesses social-skills growth over time. The checklist is divided into seven general areas:

1. **JOINT ATTENDING:** Skills that involve showing shared interest or enjoyment

2. **SOCIAL PLAY:** Skills related to engaging in various levels of interactive play with other children

3. **SELF-REGULATION:** Skills related to demonstrating flexibility and the ability to regulate behavioral reactions in response to unexpected changes, making mistakes, being given corrective feedback, or other difficult situations

4. **SOCIAL/EMOTIONAL:** Skills related to identifying and appropriately responding to different emotions in oneself and others

5. **SOCIAL LANGUAGE:** Skills related to using language to respond to, initiate, and maintain various levels of social interaction

6. **CLASSROOM/GROUP BEHAVIOR:** Skills related to following the rules and meeting expectations put in place by adults or that are necessary for group activities

7. **NONVERBAL SOCIAL LANGUAGE:** Skills related to reading and using nonverbal communication as part of social interactions

Within each of the seven areas, the skills are generally considered to present in a progressive order, but this is not necessarily the case for all skills. In some cases, skills that are further along in each area do not have prerequisite skills that children must first develop. It should be noted that there is not always clear differentiation among the skills in these seven areas, as some skills overlap across areas. A number of resources were referenced in developing the Socially Savvy Checklist, with an emphasis on identifying those skills considered important for children in a preschool environment.[3-7] Many of the social-skills interventions outlined in the manual assume a play-based and language-rich setting; however, the assessment tool does not focus on play or language skills, with the expectation that other tools are available to evaluate these skills.

The Socially Savvy Checklist can be completed by a teacher, parent, or any person with a firsthand understanding of a child's overall social functioning. The expectation is that the evaluator completing the Socially Savvy Checklist would have observed the child in a social setting for at least a two-week period and that the ratings are based on observations of the child over that period. The Socially Savvy Checklist uses a four-point rating system: 0 = rarely or never demonstrates this skill; 1 = has demonstrated this skill but only on a few occasions; 2 = can demonstrate this skill but does not do so consistently; 3 = consistently demonstrates this skill; and N/A = not applicable due to setting or because child compensates in other ways.

Young children participate in a wide variety of preschool and social environments. We acknowledge that the critical social skills will vary across these settings and that skills not identified in this checklist might be relevant in other settings. Thus, the Socially Savvy Checklist is designed to be modified to meet the needs of each setting, child, or group of children. At the end of each of the seven areas, there are spaces to add additional skills that might be relevant for the individual child being assessed or for the environment in which the child is being evaluated.

The Socially Savvy Checklist can be referenced and updated as often as required to help assess a child's progress and to identify new skills in need of intervention. A child's scores can be graphed on the grid provided at the end of this chapter to give a visual representation of progress. Each time a child is assessed with the Socially Savvy Checklist, a different color pen or pencil should be used to record the child's scores on the graph. We have assigned colors to each assessment period, but any color pen or pencil can be used, provided that the colors used are different across each assessment point and the color used for each assessment point is clearly delineated. For example, the first time a child is assessed, a pencil or a grey pen should be used to shade in scores. The next time the child is assessed (whether in several months or in a year), a black pen should be used. If the child does not have the skill, put a colored dot next to the number corresponding to the skill in the correct column. For example, if the child does not have Joint Attending 2, put a colored dot next to *JA 2*. If the child scores a 1, 2, or 3 on a particular skill, color in the same number of boxes corresponding to the skill number (one box for a 1, two boxes for a 2, and three boxes for a 3).

The next time that the child is assessed, no changes should be made to the boxes that have previously been shaded unless the child is no longer showing that skill at the same level. If there has been growth with a specific skill, the appropriate number of additional boxes should be shaded to reflect this. For example, if a child had a score of 1 (with one box shaded) at the initial assessment, but has now completely mastered the skill, the additional two boxes should be shaded so that all three boxes are shaded, the first box with one color and the second and third boxes with a second color. Progress can thus be clearly depicted by the different colors. If for some reason, a child's skill level has decreased at a follow-up assessment, this is best depicted by placing an "X" through the corresponding box(es) using the color assigned to that assessment period.

In some situations, it is also helpful to provide a summary report when the Socially Savvy Checklist is completed. A sample report template is provided at the end of this chapter. Using this report format, if a child receives a score of 0, the skill is indicated as "Not Yet in Repertoire" by placing an "X" in that column. If a child receives a score of 1 or 2, the skill is indicated as "Emerging Acquisition" by placing an "X" in that column. Similarly, if the child receives a score of 3, an "X" is placed in the "Mastered" column next to the corresponding skill. If a child receives a score of "N/A," it is not marked on the report.

SOCIALLY SAVVY CHECKLIST

OBSERVATION	DATE	EVALUATOR	OBSERVATION SETTING(S)	LENGTH OF OBSERVATION(S)
1				
2				
3				
4				

For each item, use the following rating scale to indicate the strength of each skill. Ratings should be based on direct observation of the child in small- and large-group social situations. The evaluator completing the Socially Savvy Checklist should have observed the child in a social setting for at least a two-week period and the ratings should be based on observations of the child in this environment.

Rating System: 0 = rarely or never demonstrates this skill; 1 = has demonstrated this skill but only on a few occasions; 2 = can demonstrate this skill but does not do so consistently; 3 = consistently demonstrates this skill; and N/A = not applicable due to setting or because child compensates in other ways.

	JOINT ATTENDING	1	2	3	4
JA 1	Orients (e.g., looks or makes a related response) when an object is presented				
JA 2	Repeats own behavior to maintain social interaction				
JA 3	Repeats action with toy to maintain social interaction				
JA 4	Uses eye gaze to maintain social interaction (i.e., looks directly at the other person's face for at least one second multiple times throughout the interaction)				
JA 5	Follows point or gesture to objects				
JA 6	Follows eye gaze to objects				
JA 7	Shows others objects and makes eye contact to share interest				
JA 8	Points to objects and makes eye contact to share interest				
JA 9	Comments on what self or others are doing (e.g., "I am (action).")				

	SOCIAL PLAY	1	2	3	4
SP 1	Engages in social interactive games (e.g., Peek-a-Boo, tickling game)				
SP 2	Plays parallel for five to ten minutes, close to peers with close-ended toys (e.g., puzzles, shape sorters)				
SP 3	Plays parallel for five to ten minutes, close to peers with open-ended toys (e.g., blocks, trucks, LEGOs)				
SP 4	Shares toys/materials (e.g., allows others to play with materials, gives materials when asked)				
SP 5	Plays cooperatively (gives and takes directions from peer) for five to ten minutes with close-ended toys (e.g., puzzles, shape sorters)				
SP 6	Plays cooperatively (gives and takes directions from peer) for five to ten minutes with open-ended toys (e.g., blocks, trucks, LEGOs)				
SP 7	Takes turns as part of a structured game and sustains attention until completion of the game				
SP 8	Plays outdoor games with a group until the completion of the activity (e.g., Duck-Duck-Goose, Red Rover)				
SP 9	Stops action when requested by a peer				
SP 10	Ends structured play/game with peer appropriately				
SP 11	Takes a role in an imaginative play theme and sustains it, both verbally and nonverbally, for up to three to five actions (e.g., restaurant, doctor, firefighter)				
SP 12	Trades toys/materials (e.g., participates in negotiation to swap paint colors during an art project)				
SP 13	Invites peer to play in a preferred activity				
SP 14	Approaches peers and appropriately joins in the ongoing activity				
SP 15	Accepts invitation to play in an activity of peer's choice				
SP 16	Accepts losing games or getting called "out"				

Social Play continued on next page

	SOCIAL PLAY (continued)	1	2	3	4
SP 17	Remains appropriately engaged during unstructured times (e.g., moves to new activity once completes first; engages in age-appropriate play)				
SP 18	Follows changes in play ideas of others and sustains the changes during open-ended play (e.g., changes in play scheme/scenario)				
SP 19	Appropriately plays games involving a person being "It"				
SP 20	Demonstrates flexibility in following changes in the rules of a game or in accepting novel ideas from peers				
SP 21	Plans a play scheme with a peer and follows it through (e.g., decides to build a house out of blocks and then builds it)				
SP 22	Identifies children who are their friends and can give a simple explanation why				
SP 23	Appropriately accepts that others' likes and interests may be different from their own				
SP 24	Wins without making bragging comments/gestures				
	SELF-REGULATION	1	2	3	4
SR 1	Demonstrates flexibility with new tasks/activities				
SR 2	Appropriately handles denied requests				
SR 3	Raises hand and waits to be called before speaking				
SR 4	Responds to calming strategies prompted by an adult				
SR 5	Identifies when upset/frustrated and appropriately asks for a break or a calming item/activity				

Self-Regulation continued on next page

	SELF-REGULATION (continued)	1	2	3	4
SR 6	Follows classroom expectations and demonstrates flexibility during transitions				
SR 7	Demonstrates flexibility when things are different than planned				
SR 8	Demonstrates flexibility when preferred activities are interrupted				
SR 9	Responds to feedback/correction without exhibiting challenging behaviors				
SR 10	Responds to mistakes made by self or others without exhibiting challenging behaviors				
SR 11	Demonstrates awareness of own and other's space (e.g., not stepping on other's feet when walking in a line, not crowding a person during Circle Time, keeping an arm's distance when interacting with others)				
SR 12	Modifies behavior in response to feedback				
SR 13	Uses appropriate words and voice tone to turn down requests from others				
SR 14	Advocates for oneself (e.g., "I didn't get one." "I can't see." "Please move." "Stop.") without exhibiting challenging behaviors (e.g., bullying, teasing, aggression)				
SR 15	Asks for help during novel or challenging activities				
SR 16	Waits for help, for a requested item, or when directed to for up to one minute without exhibiting challenging behaviors				
SR 17	Avoids perseveration on a topic or question				
SR 18	Uses conversational voice level and tone when speaking				

SOCIAL/EMOTIONAL		1	2	3	4
SE 1	Recognizes emotions in others and self (e.g., happy, sad)				
SE 2	Gives a simple explanation for the emotional state of self and others (e.g., happy, sad) when asked				
SE 3	Shows empathy toward others (e.g., says, "Are you okay?" to peer who falls on playground; hugs a peer who is crying)				
SE 4	Expresses negative emotions without exhibiting challenging behaviors				
SE 5	Expresses appropriate level of enthusiasm about the actions or belongings of others				
SE 6	Anticipates how a peer might respond to his behavior (e.g., knocking down a tower might make a peer mad; helping a peer might make her happy) and responds accordingly				

SOCIAL LANGUAGE		1	2	3	4
SL 1	Responds to greetings/partings				
SL 2	Follows directions involving named adults or peers				
SL 3	Initiates greetings/partings				
SL 4	Addresses peers by name				
SL 5	Answers social questions (e.g., name, age, family names, pet names)				
SL 6	Asks social questions (e.g., name, age, family names, pet names)				
SL 7	Asks concrete questions about an item or information shared by others (e.g., name of object, location of object, who has something)				

Social Language continued on next page

	SOCIAL LANGUAGE (continued)	1	2	3	4
SL 8	Requests attention (e.g., "Look at what I made." "Watch how far I can jump.")				
SL 9	Gains listener attention appropriately (e.g., calls name, taps shoulder)				
SL 10	Responds to initiations from others				
SL 11	Answers questions about ongoing activities				
SL 12	Shares information about self, family, and major events (e.g., school day, holidays, family events)				
SL 13	Answers more than five questions on a preferred topic				
SL 14	Makes reciprocal comments (e.g., child responds to peer: "I like that movie too!" "I don't have (that), I have (this)")				
SL 15	Shares information about immediate past or future events				
SL 16	Answers questions, asks questions, or makes comments to maintain conversation for three to four exchanges				
SL 17	Responds appropriately when a peer changes topic				
SL 18	Directs body and eyes toward social partner when speaking				
SL 19	Directs body and eyes toward social partner when listening				
SL 20	Speaks using polite phrases (e.g., "Please," "Thank you," "Sorry," "Excuse me," "You're welcome")				
SL 21	Accepts people who are different (e.g., does not make negative comments)				
SL 22	Seeks to repair or clarify breakdowns in social interactions				
SL 23	Converses on age-appropriate topics (i.e., talks about topics similar and of interest to peers)				
SL 24	Uses contextually appropriate language/introduces topic				

Social Language continued on next page

SOCIAL LANGUAGE (continued)	1	2	3	4

	CLASSROOM/GROUP BEHAVIOR	1	2	3	4
CG 1	Follows schedule and classroom rules (including playground rules)				
CG 2	Follows verbal directions as part of classroom routines or activities (e.g., get materials, put away lunch)				
CG 3	Recognizes belongings of own, others, and group				
CG 4	Keeps toys/materials in designated locations				
CG 5	Responds to teacher by looking or coming when directly or indirectly cued				
CG 6	Imitates a peer who is leading songs/activities (e.g., Simon Says)				
CG 7	Responds to indirect cueing (e.g., "Where are your friends?" when child needs to line up)				
CG 8	Uses playground equipment appropriately				
CG 9	Helps others, both spontaneously and when asked				
CG 10	Remains in place in a group until called by teacher (e.g., staying in seat until called to line up)				
CG 11	Prepares for activity by locating area/materials (e.g., chair, coat)				
CG 12	Follows directions during novel activities				
CG 13	Gives directions during novel activities				
CG 14	Stays in place when walking in line and maintains pace with group				

Classroom/Group Behavior continued on next page

CLASSROOM/GROUP BEHAVIOR		1	2	3	4
CG 15	Repeats words/actions from a song, book, or play activity				
CG 16	Accepts that some peers may follow different rules or schedules				
CG 17	Asks permission to use others' possessions				
CG 18	Attends to small-group, teacher-led, hands-on activity for ten minutes				
CG 19	Sits quietly in circle for ten minutes				
CG 20	Attends to small-group, teacher-led listening activity for ten minutes				
CG 21	Responds together with group to teacher or peer leading activity				
CG 22	Follows basic two- to three-step verbal directions in a group				
CG 23	Passes items to peers (e.g., passing out materials, taking turns looking at a shared object and passing to next person)				

NONVERBAL SOCIAL LANGUAGE		1	2	3	4
NV 1	Reciprocates nonverbal interactions (e.g., high five, wave, thumbs-up, fist bump, smile)				
NV 2	Initiates nonverbal interactions (e.g., high five, wave, thumbs-up, fist bump, smile) with appropriate adults and peers				
NV 3	Identifies basic actions without words (e.g., Charades)				
NV 4	Demonstrates an appropriate level of affection based on history, relationship, and familiarity with the person (e.g., hugs parent, gives high five to friend, does not initiate with unfamiliar person)				

Nonverbal Social Language continued on next page

NONVERBAL SOCIAL LANGUAGE (continued)	1	2	3	4
NV 5	Follows basic gestures and nonverbal cues (e.g., stops when person holds up hand, comes when person motions with hand)				
NV 6	Modifies own behavior based on the body language, actions, or eye gaze of others				

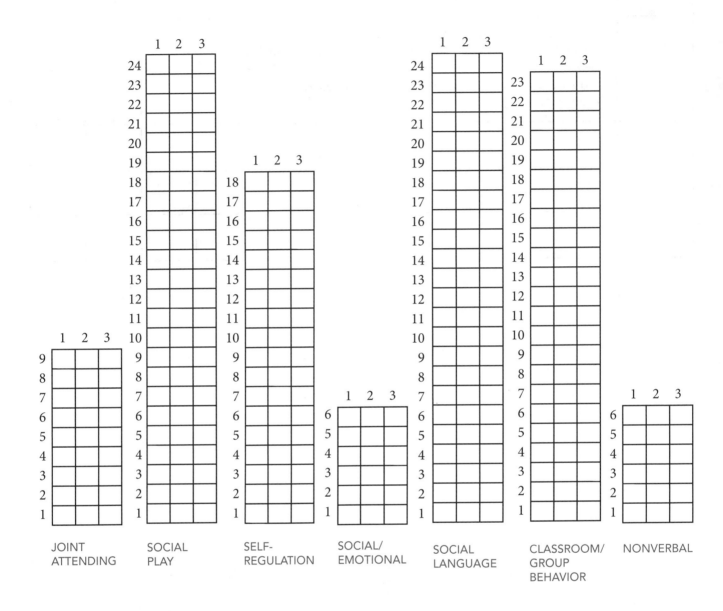

	1	2	3
9			
8			
7			
6			
5			
4			
3			
2			
1			

JOINT ATTENDING

SOCIAL PLAY

SELF-REGULATION

SOCIAL/ EMOTIONAL

SOCIAL LANGUAGE

CLASSROOM/ GROUP BEHAVIOR

NONVERBAL

	OBSERVATION	DATE	EVALUATOR	OBSERVATION SETTING(S)	LENGTH OF OBSERVATION(S)
●	1				
●	2				
●	3				
●	4				

SOCIALLY SAVVY CHECKLIST SUMMARY REPORT

Child: .... Age: ....

Date of Evaluation: .... Evaluator: ....

The Socially Savvy Checklist evaluates the social skills of preschool and early elementary school children. It provides a picture of a child's social skills in a variety of areas, specifically Joint Attending, Social Play, Self-Regulation, Social/Emotional, Social Language, Classroom/Group Behavior, and Nonverbal Social Language. Specific skills are identified within each of the seven areas for a total of 127 separate social skills. Within each section, skills generally move from simpler to more complex and are in the order in which a typically developing child would master them. In each section, the lower numbered skills are simpler or may be prerequisites for later skills.

Any person with firsthand experience or understanding of a child's overall social functioning can complete the Socially Savvy Checklist—this includes, but is not limited to, teachers and parents. The evaluator should have observed the child in a social setting for at least a two-week period and ratings should be based on observations of the child in this environment. The Socially Savvy Checklist consists of a four-point rating system:

0 = rarely or never demonstrates this skill; 1 = has demonstrated this skill but only on a few occasions; 2 = can demonstrate this skill but does not do so consistently; 3 = consistently demonstrates this skill; and N/A = not applicable due to setting or because child compensates in other ways. For the purpose of completing the report, skills receiving a score of either 1 or 2 are combined within the category of Emerging Acquisition, a score of 3 is Mastered, and a score of 0 is Not Yet in Repertoire.

The Socially Savvy Checklist helps identify a child's specific strengths and challenges. By evaluating these general areas and specific social skills with fine granularity, teachers and parents can prioritize the specific skills most in need of intervention.

JOINT ATTENDING

SKILL	MASTERED	EMERGING ACQUISITION	NOT YET IN REPERTOIRE
JA 1 Orients (e.g., looks or makes a related response) when an object is presented			
JA 2 Repeats own behavior to maintain social interaction			
JA 3 Repeats action with toy to maintain social interaction			
JA 4 Uses eye gaze to maintain social interaction			
JA 5 Follows point or gesture to objects			
JA 6 Follows eye gaze to objects			
JA 7 Shows others objects and makes eye contact to share interest			
JA 8 Points to objects and makes eye contact to share interest			
JA 9 Comments on what self or others are doing			

Socially Savvy: An Assessment and Curriculum Guide for Young Children

SOCIAL PLAY

SKILL	MASTERED	EMERGING ACQUISITION	NOT YET IN REPERTOIRE
SP 1 Engages in social interactive games			
SP 2 Plays parallel for five to ten minutes, close to peers with close-ended toys			
SP 3 Plays parallel for five to ten minutes, close to peers with open-ended toys			
SP 4 Shares toys/materials			
SP 5 Plays cooperatively for five to ten minutes with close-ended toys			
SP 6 Plays cooperatively for five to ten minutes with open-ended toys			
SP 7 Takes turns as part of a structured game and sustains attention until completion of the game			
SP 8 Plays outdoor games with a group until the completion of the activity			
SP 9 Stops action when requested by a peer			
SP 10 Ends structured play/game with peer appropriately			
SP 11 Takes a role in an imaginative play theme and sustains it, both verbally and nonverbally, for up to three to five actions			
SP 12 Trades toys/materials			
SP 13 Invites peer to play in a preferred activity			
SP 14 Approaches peers and appropriately joins in the ongoing activity			
SP 15 Accepts invitation to play in an activity of peer's choice			

Social Play continued on next page

SKILL	MASTERED	EMERGING ACQUISITION	NOT YET IN REPERTOIRE
SP 16 Accepts losing games or getting called "out"			
SP 17 Remains appropriately engaged during unstructured times			
SP 18 Follows changes in play ideas of others and sustains the changes during open-ended play			
SP 19 Appropriately plays games involving a person being "It"			
SP 20 Demonstrates flexibility in following changes in the rules of a game or in accepting novel ideas from peers			
SP 21 Plans a play scheme with a peer and follows it through			
SP 22 Identifies children who are their friends and can give a simple explanation why			
SP 23 Appropriately accepts that others' likes and interests may be different from their own			
SP 24 Wins without making bragging comments/gestures			

SELF-REGULATION

SKILL	MASTERED	EMERGING ACQUISITION	NOT YET IN REPERTOIRE
SR 1 Demonstrates flexibility with new tasks/activities			
SR 2 Appropriately handles denied requests			
SR 3 Raises hand and waits to be called before speaking			
SR 4 Responds to calming strategies prompted by an adult			
SR 5 Identifies when upset/frustrated and appropriately asks for a break or a calming item/activity			
SR 6 Follows classroom expectations and demonstrates flexibility during transitions			
SR 7 Demonstrates flexibility when things are different than planned			
SR 8 Demonstrates flexibility when preferred activities are interrupted			
SR 9 Responds to feedback/correction without exhibiting challenging behaviors			
SR 10 Responds to mistakes made by self or others without exhibiting challenging behaviors			
SR 11 Demonstrates awareness of own and other's space			
SR 12 Modifies behavior in response to feedback			
SR 13 Uses appropriate words and voice tone to turn down requests from others			
SR 14 Advocates for oneself without exhibiting challenging behaviors			

Self-Regulation continued on next page

SELF-REGULATION (continued)

SKILL	MASTERED	EMERGING ACQUISITION	NOT YET IN REPERTOIRE
SR 15 Asks for help during novel or challenging activities			
SR 16 Waits for help, for requested item, or when directed to for up to one minute without exhibiting challenging behaviors			
SR 17 Avoids perseveration on a topic or question			
SR 18 Uses conversational voice level and tone when speaking			

SOCIAL/EMOTIONAL

SKILL	MASTERED	EMERGING ACQUISITION	NOT YET IN REPERTOIRE
SE 1 Recognizes emotions in others and self			
SE 2 Gives a simple explanation for the emotional state of self and others when asked			
SE 3 Shows empathy toward others			
SE 4 Expresses negative emotions without exhibiting challenging behaviors			
SE 5 Expresses appropriate level of enthusiasm about the actions or belonging of others			

Social/Emotional continued on next page

SOCIAL/EMOTIONAL (continued)

SKILL	MASTERED	EMERGING ACQUISITION	NOT YET IN REPERTOIRE
SE 6 Anticipates how a peer might respond to his behavior and responds accordingly			

SOCIAL LANGUAGE

SKILL	MASTERED	EMERGING ACQUISITION	NOT YET IN REPERTOIRE
SL 1 Responds to greetings/partings			
SL 2 Follows directions involving named adults or peers			
SL 3 Initiates greetings/partings			
SL 4 Addresses peers by name			
SL 5 Answers social questions			
SL 6 Asks social questions			
SL 7 Asks concrete questions about an item or information shared by others			
SL 8 Requests attention			
SL 9 Gains listener attention appropriately			
SL 10 Responds to initiations from others			

Social Language continued on next page

SOCIAL LANGUAGE (continued)

SKILL	MASTERED	EMERGING ACQUISITION	NOT YET IN REPERTOIRE
SL 11 Answers questions about ongoing activities			
SL 12 Shares information about self, family, and major events			
SL 13 Answers more than five questions on a preferred topic			
SL 14 Makes reciprocal comments			
SL 15 Shares information about immediate past or future events			
SL 16 Answers questions, asks questions, or makes comments to maintain conversation for three to four exchanges			
SL 17 Responds appropriately when a peer changes topic			
SL 18 Directs body and eyes toward social partner when speaking			
SL 19 Directs body and eyes toward social partner when listening			
SL 20 Speaks using polite phrases			
SL 21 Accepts people who are different			
SL 22 Seeks to repair or clarify breakdowns in social interactions			
SL 23 Converses on age-appropriate topics			
SL 24 Uses contextually appropriate language/introduces topic			

CLASSROOM/GROUP BEHAVIOR

SKILL	MASTERED	EMERGING ACQUISITION	NOT YET IN REPERTOIRE
CG 1 Follows schedule and classroom rules			
CG 2 Follows verbal directions as part of classroom routines or activities			
CG 3 Recognizes belongings of own, others, and group			
CG 4 Keeps toys/materials in designated locations			
CG 5 Responds to teacher by looking or coming when directly or indirectly cued			
CG 6 Imitates a peer who is leading songs/ activities			
CG 7 Responds to indirect cueing			
CG 8 Uses playground equipment appropriately			
CG 9 Helps others, both spontaneously and when asked			
CG 10 Remains in place in a group until called by a teacher			
CG 11 Prepares for activity by locating area/materials			
CG 12 Follows directions during novel activities			
CG 13 Gives directions during novel activities			
CG 14 Stays in place when walking in line and maintains pace with group			
CG 15 Repeats words/actions from a song, book, or play activity			

Classroom/Group Behavior continued on next page

CLASSROOM/GROUP BEHAVIOR (continued)

SKILL	MASTERED	EMERGING ACQUISITION	NOT YET IN REPERTOIRE
CG 16 Accepts that some peers may follow different rules or schedules			
CG 17 Asks permission to use others' possessions			
CG 18 Attends to small-group, teacher-led, hands-on activity for at least ten minutes			
CG 19 Sits quietly in circle for at least ten minutes			
CG 20 Attends to small-group, teacher-led, listening activity for at least ten minutes			
CG 21 Responds together with group to teacher or peer leading activity			
CG 22 Follows basic two- to three-step verbal directions in a group			
CG 23 Passes items to peers			

NONVERBAL SOCIAL LANGUAGE

SKILL	MASTERED	EMERGING ACQUISITION	NOT YET IN REPERTOIRE
NV 1 Reciprocates nonverbal interactions			
NV 2 Initiates nonverbal interactions with appropriate adults and peers			
NV 3 Identifies basic actions without words			
NV 4 Demonstrates an appropriate level of affection based on history, relationship, and familiarity with the person			
NV 5 Follows basic gestures and nonverbal cues			
NV 6 Modifies own behavior based on the body language, actions, or eye gaze of others			

Socially Savvy: An Assessment and Curriculum Guide for Young Children

CHAPTER 2:
Description of Skills

This addendum to the Socially Savvy Checklist provides a brief description of the intent and importance of each identified skill. Having a clearly defined understanding of each skill is critical to an accurate assessment. In our experience, when a checklist skill is unclear, evaluators may not score an item or may score it incorrectly. We have also found that this can lead to variation in scores for the same item across evaluators because they interpret the item differently. The following descriptions for the targeted skills should help limit potential inconsistencies in completing the Socially Savvy Checklist. This is especially important for parents and other individuals who may be less familiar with social skills and their significance. These item descriptions can also help professionals explain the results of the Socially Savvy Checklist to parents and other professionals.

JOINT ATTENDING

JA 1. Orients (e.g., looks or makes a related response) when an object is presented

This is a very basic Joint Attending skill that typically developing children generally demonstrate at 3–6 months. This skill does not necessarily require the child to look at the person presenting the object but simply to look and orient toward the object that is presented.

JA 2. Repeats own behavior to maintain social interaction

This very basic Joint Attending skill requires the child to repeat or continue a specific behavior that has resulted in social attention from another person. For example, after receiving social attention for exhibiting a behavior (e.g., clapping hands, knocking a toy off a table, or making a certain sound), the child repeats the action in anticipation of a response from another person. The child may also physically guide the other person to continue their behavior, perhaps by taking the other person's hands and putting them together to clap. This usually happens between 4–8 months.

JA 3. Repeats action with toy to maintain social interaction

This skill is similar to *JA 2* but requires the child to repeat or continue an action with a toy that has resulted in social attention from another person. For example, after receiving social attention for exhibiting an action with a toy (e.g., banging on a drum or pushing a button on a toy), the child repeats the action in anticipation of a response from another person. This also usually happens between 4–8 months.

JA 4. Uses eye gaze to maintain social interaction (i.e., looks directly at the other person's face for at least one second multiple times throughout the interaction)

This skill requires the child to look at another person to communicate that he wants a social interaction or activity to continue. For example, the child might look toward an adult to continue a Peek-a-Boo game or to let an adult know that he wants another push on a swing. Eye contact might also be paired with repeating certain behaviors or play actions or with responding to the presentation of an object or materials. During more complex social interactions, this skill involves the child maintaining eye gaze during interactive games or conversations. This usually happens between 3–6 months.

JA 5. Follows point or gesture to objects

A child with this skill will follow another person's point or gesture to look toward an object or area. For example, if a person points toward the sky and says, "Look," the child will look toward the sky to see an airplane. This usually happens between 6–9 months.

JA 6. Follows eye gaze to objects

This is similar to *JA 5*, except the child is expected to follow another person's eye gaze to an object. For example, when a person shows enthusiasm and looks toward something, the child looks in the same direction (e.g., a person says, "Oh no," and looks under the table, and the child also looks under the table). This also usually happens between 6–9 months.

JA 7. Shows others objects and makes eye contact to share interest

This more advanced Joint Attending skill requires the child to bring objects to another person paired with looking at the person. This skill also requires that the child makes sure that the other person can see the object. The child may or may not pair verbal language with this interaction. This skill can be difficult for children who do not seem interested in sharing (i.e., the attention that is a typical consequence for this type of interaction may not be reinforcing for the child). This usually happens between 9–12 months.

JA 8. Points to objects and makes eye contact to share interest

This skill is similar to *JA 7* and requires the child to point to objects, paired with looking at the person. The child may or may not pair verbal language with this interaction. This skill can be difficult for some children who are not motivated to share (i.e., the attention that is a typical consequence for this type of interaction may not be reinforcing for the child). This can also happen around 9–12 months.

JA 9. Comments on what self or others are doing (e.g., "I am (action).")

This skill requires the child to attend to her own behavior and that of other people in the environment and to make comments that are clearly directed toward other people in the environment. As with *JA 7* and *JA 8*, this skill requires that the child be motivated by the reciprocal social response that occurs when the child makes a comment. This skill typically develops around 24–27 months.

SOCIAL PLAY

SP 1. Engages in social interactive games (e.g., Peek-a-Boo, tickling game)

This basic form of Social Play typically begins at about 8–9 months. A child shows engagement by providing an expectant look, showing signs of excitement, or verbally or nonverbally indicating that he wants more.

SP 2. Plays parallel for five to ten minutes, close to peers with close-ended toys (e.g., puzzles, shape sorters)

One of the first steps toward interacting with peers is for a child to remain in close proximity to peers, playing with similar toys. Children usually do best with more close-ended toys first. There is not necessarily an expectation for the child to interact with other children but simply to play in proximity to a peer or peers with similar toys and materials. This usually happens around 27–30 months.

SP 3. Plays parallel for five to ten minutes, close to peers with open-ended toys (e.g., blocks, trucks, LEGOs)

This is similar to *SP 2*, except the expectation is for the child to play parallel to peers in open-ended activities. There is not necessarily an expectation for the child to interact with other children but simply to play in proximity to a peer or peers with similar toys and materials. This usually also happens around 27–30 months.

SP 4. Shares toys/materials (e.g., allows others to play with materials, gives materials when asked)

This skill involves the child offering toys to other children, sharing toys when asked, and/or allowing other children to play with their personal toys or with highly preferred toys. The biggest challenge for many children is allowing others to play with toys with which the children show a high, or possibly perseverative, interest. As children approach 4 years old, they begin to share more readily.

SP 5. Plays cooperatively (gives and takes directions from peer) for five to ten minutes with close-ended toys (e.g., puzzles, shape sorters)

Once a child is consistently playing parallel to other children, the next goal is for the child to play cooperatively with close-ended activities. For example, will the child build a puzzle with a peer, taking turns giving, and following directions to put in the pieces? This form of play occurs among children 5 years old and older.

SP 6. Plays cooperatively (gives and takes directions from peer) for five to ten minutes with open-ended toys (e.g., blocks, trucks, LEGOs)

This is similar to *SP 5* except the expectation is for the child to play cooperatively with peers in open-ended activities. For this skill, the expectation is still for the child to play cooperatively with manipulative toys, rather than toys of a pretend nature. This could involve two children working together to build a structure with blocks or LEGOs. This type of play is more likely to occur with children 5 years old and older.

SP 7. Takes turns as part of a structured game and sustains attention until completion of the game

It is important to remember that the skill of turn taking is not simply to say, "My turn/Your turn," but to follow the game, take a turn at the appropriate time, pass game pieces or materials as appropriate, and wait while another's turn is completed. In the beginning, turn-taking games do not need to involve verbal interactions. Simple turn taking can start as young as 24 months; however, depending on the complexity of the game and the number of peers, expect to work on turn taking for a long time. It is common to work on turn taking well into when a child is 5 years old.

SP 8. Plays outdoor games with a group until the completion of the activity (e.g., Duck-Duck-Goose, Red Rover)

These traditional playground games usually involve at least four or five children. Children should be able to sustain their attention and follow the rules of the game. As with *SP 7*, outdoor games may involve the child taking a turn at the appropriate time, interacting with and passing or sharing materials, and waiting for other children to have a turn. This is a more complicated type of turn taking and should usually be targeted after a child is able to take turns with simpler games and activities.

SP 9. Stops action when requested by a peer

Children can have trouble stopping a variety of behaviors when asked, and the reasons why can vary (e.g., they do not understand the direction or the behavior is reinforced by the negative attention). A child who has mastered this skill will stop a behavior when asked to by a peer.

SP 10. Ends structured play/game with peer appropriately

It isn't unusual for some children to end a game or interaction with another person simply by leaving. Even children with typically developing social skills do not necessarily announce when they are leaving an activity. What is appropriate in terms of ending a game or activity should be based on observation of what typically developing children are doing in the environment.

SP 11. Takes a role in an imaginative play theme and sustains it, both verbally and nonverbally, for up to three to five actions (e.g., restaurant, doctor, firefighter)

Before a child can be expected to engage in imaginative play with another child, it is generally necessary that the child can engage in imaginative play by herself. This skill involves the child staying focused on a play theme, including following the actions or comments of another child and making reciprocal or complimentary actions or statements. Between the ages of 3 and 4, children start to take on roles in imaginative play. Often one child will assign roles to other children and then they all play together, acting their "parts."

SP 12. Trades toys/materials (e.g., participates in negotiation to swap paint colors during an art project)

This is in some ways a more advanced form of sharing toys. However, for this skill, the child must negotiate with another child by exchanging something she has for something she wants from the other child. Trading toys is a sophisticated skill and is usually not seen until 5 years old.

SP 13. Invites peer to play in a preferred activity

This skill requires the child to approach a peer and ask the peer to join him in an activity that is preferred to the child, even if not to the peer. Difficulties may arise in that some children may prefer to play alone, may not approach other children, or may not clearly initiate a verbal request to another child. Starting at around 4 years old, children begin to invite others to play with them, depending on the child's personality and their level of comfort with those particular peers.

SP 14. Approaches peers and appropriately joins in the ongoing activity

This skill is similar to *SP 13* but requires the child to join in the activity of a peer. This might involve joining a peer in a play area in the classroom or on the playground. What is appropriate in terms of how a child joins other children in play should be based on observations of what typically developing children are doing. As with *SP 13*, difficulties may arise if a child prefers to play alone, does not show the same interests as other children, or has difficulty approaching and clearly making a request to another child.

SP 15. Accepts invitation to play in an activity of peer's choice

Some children find it particularly challenging to participate in a play activity that is not their choice. This skill involves the child accepting an invitation from a peer, even if the peer is engaged in an activity that is not a preferred one for the child.

SP 16. Accepts losing games or getting called "out"

Many children have a difficult time losing a game or getting called out of the game. This skill requires the child to accept losing or being called out of the game without protesting, crying, or engaging in inappropriate behaviors.

SP 17. Remains appropriately engaged during unstructured times (e.g., moves to new activity once completes first; engages in age-appropriate play)

This skill requires the child to remain engaged appropriately during Free-Play, moving from one activity to another and engaging in play activities as intended, as well as refraining from wandering or engaging in any inappropriate behaviors.

SP 18. Follows changes in play ideas of others and sustains the changes during open-ended play (e.g., changes in play scheme/scenario)

During Free-Play that involves symbolic or dramatic play, children frequently shift the play theme or idea (e.g., "Now let's pretend it's a rocket." "The Mommy is going to the store."). This can be a very difficult skill for some children. The child needs to be able to shift the play theme when other children do by adapting play actions accordingly.

SP 19. Appropriately plays games involving a person being "It"

Many children's games involve one person being "It," such as the person who is tagging others during Freeze Tag. Some children have difficulty differentiating the role of being "It" versus trying not to get tagged or caught, whereas others may have difficulty following changes with who is "It."

SP 20. Demonstrates flexibility in following changes in the rules of a game or in accepting novel ideas from peers

For some children, once they have learned to play a game or activity in a particular way, it is difficult for them to play the game differently. However, typically developing children will frequently make changes to games or activities as they are playing, and it is important for a child to be able to shift and play the game/activity following the new rules or novel ideas proposed by other children.

SP 21. Plans a play scheme with a peer and follows it through (e.g., decides to build a house out of blocks and then builds it)

This skill requires both that the child plans a play scheme with a peer and that she then follows the activity through to completion. For example, this could involve the child and a peer planning to pretend that they are at a restaurant and then taking roles and acting out the restaurant theme. Difficulty with this skill may present in a number of ways, including challenges when verbally initiating or negotiating with a peer, when engaging in reciprocal play interactions, or with sustaining attention until the activity is completed.

SP 22. Identifies children who are their friends and can give a simple explanation why

Some children may simply name children that they know or children who are present in their immediate environment, so it is important that a child be able to give a reason why a child is his friend. For a young child, the explanation may be as simple as "because she plays with me."

SP 23. Appropriately accepts that others' likes and interests may be different from their own

A child's ability to accept that others' likes and interests are different from their own is best determined by whether the child demonstrates inappropriate comments or behaviors when a peer expresses likes or interests that differ from the child's likes or interests. For example, if the child likes fire trucks, but a peer says that they do not like them, the child accepts this without exhibiting any inappropriate behaviors.

SP 24. Wins without making bragging comments/gestures

Of course, we expect children to show excitement over winning. Acceptable ways to do so depend on the environment. However, it is important for a child not to brag excessively or make negative comments about other children not winning.

SELF-REGULATION

SR 1. Demonstrates flexibility with new tasks/activities

Some children have difficulty participating in new tasks or activities, especially when doing so involves changes in previously established routines. Children who have difficulty demonstrating flexibility may refuse to participate in activities or exhibit inappropriate behaviors. A child's ability to be flexible with new tasks/activities is best demonstrated by the absence of interfering behaviors when these situations occur.

SR 2. Appropriately handles denied requests

Appropriately handling situations in which they are told "No" is a skill that all young children need to learn. Children may verbally protest or exhibit other inappropriate behaviors when told "No." Appropriate ways to handle denied requests may include simply complying, asking for something different, or using a coping strategy (e.g., counting to 10, asking for a break).

SR 3. Raises hand and waits to be called before speaking

Mastery of this skill requires the child to refrain from calling out during group activities, with the appropriate behavior being either sitting appropriately while waiting for a turn or raising his hand and waiting for the teacher to call on him.

SR 4. Responds to calming strategies prompted by an adult

For this skill, the expectation is both that the child uses the strategy when prompted, and that using the strategy results in the child calming down. The calming strategies should be specific to the child and the environment. This skill may not be relevant for some children who can already regulate their emotions and bodies.

SR 5. Identifies when upset/frustrated and appropriately asks for a break or a calming item/activity

This is an extension of *SR 4* and requires that the child recognizes when he needs to use calming strategies and independently initiates these strategies. The applicable calming strategies should be specific to the child and the environment. Again, this skill may not be relevant for some children who can already regulate their emotions and bodies.

SR 6. Follows classroom expectations and demonstrates flexibility during transitions

Some children have difficulty making transitions between activities or across environments. Transitions can especially be difficult for some children when they are going from highly preferred activities or to less preferred activities. A child's ability to accept and make transitions is best demonstrated by the absence of interfering behaviors during transitions.

SR 7. Demonstrates flexibility when things are different than planned

For many children, unexpected changes in the schedule or in activities can be very challenging. Children may verbally protest or exhibit other inappropriate behaviors or may refuse to participate in the activity. A child's ability to accept when things are different than planned is best determined by the absence of any interfering behaviors during these situations.

SR 8. Demonstrates flexibility when preferred activities are interrupted

For many children, interruptions in the expected schedule or activities can be very difficult. Children may verbally protest, exhibit other inappropriate behaviors, or may refuse to leave or stop the preferred activity. A child's ability to accept interruptions during preferred activities is best determined by the absence of interfering behaviors during these situations.

SR 9. Responds to feedback/correction without exhibiting challenging behaviors

Some children become very upset (e.g., crying, verbally protesting, refusing to comply) when corrected. A child's ability to accept feedback, correction, or redirection is best determined by the absence of interfering behaviors during these situations.

SR 10. Responds to mistakes made by self or others without exhibiting challenging behaviors

Some children become very upset (e.g., crying, repeatedly trying to correct a mistake, refusing to move on with an activity) over even minor mistakes, or things that they perceive as mistakes (e.g., coloring outside of the lines). The difference from *SR 9* is that the child is not being given corrective feedback but simply perceives that she has made a mistake. A child's ability to handle mistakes is best determined by the absence of any interfering behaviors during these situations.

SR 11. Demonstrates awareness of own and other's space (e.g., not stepping on other's feet when walking in a line, not crowding a person during Circle Time, keeping an arm's distance when interacting with others)

Mastery of this skill is determined by the child maintaining an appropriate distance from others, especially during transitions, when sitting in close proximity to others in group situations, or during conversations.

SR 12. Modifies behavior in response to feedback

Some children have difficulty adapting their behavior when given feedback by an adult—for example, being asked to speak up or speak more softly, to sit appropriately, or to increase distance from others. This is different from *SR 9* in that the difficulty is not with the child exhibiting challenging behaviors but with the child not modifying his behavior.

SR 13. Uses appropriate words and voice tone to turn down requests from others

Though the goal is generally to have children accept requests from others, it is also important that children appropriately turn down requests (e.g., with words spoken in an appropriate tone, not just ignoring the request or walking away).

SR 14. Advocates for oneself (e.g., "I didn't get one." "I can't see." "Please move." "Stop.") without exhibiting challenging behaviors (e.g., bullying, teasing, aggression)

In situations in which a child is presented with a conflict, barrier, or inappropriate interaction from a peer, she needs to learn to respond appropriately and defend herself. For some children, they may either do nothing to advocate for themselves or may exhibit challenging behaviors in these situations. The goal is for children to use words and an appropriate tone of voice to defend their "rights" and advocate for themselves.

SR 15. Asks for help during novel or challenging activities

Some children are reluctant to try new or challenging activities or simply will not participate in unfamiliar or challenging situations, rather than asking for help. Other children may exhibit challenging behaviors. It is important that children learn to recognize situations in which they need help and request assistance.

SR 16. Waits for help, for a requested item, or when directed for up to one minute without exhibiting challenging behaviors

Children are often required to wait—for example, waiting for a requested item, during transitions, or for a turn in a game. For many young children, having "to wait" leads to challenging behaviors. Many young children need practice learning to wait.

SR 17. Avoids perseveration on a topic or question

Some children, especially those on the autism spectrum, repeat the same comment or question repeatedly or more broadly fixate on one specific topic. The goal is for children to be aware of when they have talked to a particular person about a topic, to be able to limit their conversation on that topic, and to expand the topics they will talk about.

SR 18. Uses conversational voice level and tone when speaking

Some children may use a very loud voice or a whining or negative tone, whereas others might speak so quietly that they cannot be heard. The expectation is that a child uses a voice volume and tone that matches the environment and is consistent with what others in that environment use.

SOCIAL/EMOTIONAL

SE 1. Recognizes emotions in others and self (e.g., happy, sad)

For a child to be able to handle emotional situations appropriately, she needs to be able to identify these emotions. Determining whether a child can recognize emotions can be based on comments that the child makes or by asking the child to tell you how she feels (or others feel) when faced with certain emotional situations.

SE 2. Gives a simple explanation for the emotional state of self and others (e.g., happy, sad) when asked

In addition to being able to identify emotional states, children need to be able to identify why they or others are experiencing these emotions. Children may first learn to explain why they are feeling certain emotions (e.g., "I am mad because I lost the game.") but may have more difficulty taking the perspective of others and being able to explain why another person is feeling certain emotions.

SE 3. Shows empathy toward others (e.g., says, "Are you okay?" to peer who falls on playground; hugs a peer who is crying)

This is an extension of *SE 1* and *SE 2* in that this skill requires the child to be able to identify that another person is showing a strong emotion, determine why that person is showing that emotion, and then be able to express empathy appropriately through words or gestures. Between the ages of 2 and 3 children are capable of showing empathy but may not have the language to express it.

SE 4. Expresses negative emotions without exhibiting challenging behaviors

Many young children have difficulty appropriately expressing anger, sadness, or other strong negative emotions, or they have an exaggerated response to minor frustrations. In these situations, children may throw a tantrum for an extended period, refuse to comply with teacher (or parent) directions, try to break or destroy things, or may even be aggressive toward another person. The goal is for children to recognize these negative emotions and express them appropriately and/or use a calming strategy.

SE 5. Expresses appropriate level of enthusiasm about the actions or belongings of others

Children may have difficulty with this skill either because they do not show enthusiasm for others' positive behaviors or because their enthusiasm does not match the situation (e.g., the enthusiasm is extreme). This skill requires first that a child attends to and recognizes what others are doing, sharing, or talking about and then provides a positive comment or gesture that fits the situation.

SE 6. Anticipates how a peer might respond to his behavior (e.g., knocking down a tower might make a peer mad; helping a peer might make her happy) and responds accordingly

The critical component of this skill is that the child learns to take the perspective of another and understands how his own behavior might affect that person. A child demonstrates this skill when his actions are intended to get a positive response from a peer (e.g., picking up something that a peer dropped, holding a door for another person) or when he avoids behaving in a way that might elicit a negative response from a peer (e.g., not getting in front of peer who is waiting in line).

SOCIAL LANGUAGE

SL 1. Responds to greetings/partings

This skill simply requires that a child consistently responds when others greet her. For many children, this serves as a natural cue that a social interaction has begun, and they need to attend, or that a social interaction has ended. The expectation should also include the child orienting her body and eyes toward the other person. A child should be consistently responding to greetings and partings by 12 months.

SL 2. Follows directions involving named adults or peers

This skill requires that a child knows teachers and other children by name (e.g., by following directions that involve giving something to a peer). The expectation for this skill is not that a child be able to expressively identify others.

SL 3. Initiates greetings/partings

Many children find it more difficult to initiate greetings and understand the naturally occurring cues of when it is appropriate to greet others (e.g., when they arrive to school, when they pass a person in the hall). The expectation is not for the child to be able to sustain an interaction, but simply to initiate and end. Some children who find social interactions uncomfortable may first learn to say "Bye" as a way to end an interaction.

SL 4. Addresses peers by name

This skill requires a child to use peers' names when initiating interactions with them. This skill is important when a child is starting an interaction and needs to get the other person's attention. Some children may be better at using adults' names, simply because they are more comfortable with adult interactions.

SL 5. Answers social questions (e.g., name, age, family names, pet names)

Before a child can begin to initiate social questions or conversations with others, it is helpful if they are first able to provide basic social information about themselves Many early social questions are rote, in that the answer is always the same (e.g., name), while later questions are more complex and variable in nature. For example, the answer to "What do you like to play with?" will change as a child's interests change. By the age of 3, most typically developing children can answer a variety of basic social questions.

SL 6. Asks social questions (e.g., name, age, family names, pet names)

This is an extension of *SL 5* and requires that the child begin to ask social questions of peers. These inquiries often occur during structured situations (e.g., sharing times), but the expectation is that a child can formulate questions in these situations without needing prompts.

SL 7. Asks concrete questions about an item or information shared by others (e.g., name of object, location of object, who has something)

This beginning conversational skill for many children requires simply that they ask other people questions to gather information (e.g., about the location of things, more details about things shared by others). In many preschool classrooms, this skill is often seen during Show and Tell times. Initially, children will likely be better at asking questions about tangible items that are within their sight, but should also be able to ask simple questions based on the verbal information shared by others.

SL 8. Requests attention (e.g., "Look at what I made." "Watch how far I can jump.")

This skill is related to the Joint Attending skills *JA 7* and *JA 8*. This skill requires the child to request others to attend to her, to something she is doing, or to something she has made or done. Children generally demonstrate this skill first with adults, but it is important that they also begin to ask for peers' attention as well.

SL 9. Gains listener attention appropriately (e.g., calls name, taps shoulder)

Many children have difficulty ensuring that they have their listener's attention before making a request or comment and will simply begin to talk. It is important that children learn to recognize whether another person is attending to them, either by the nonverbal signs of the listener or by intentionally gaining the listener's attention.

SL 10. Responds to initiations from others

It is important that a child consistently responds to initiations from others. Peers may stop initiating with a child if he does not respond to their initiations. Additionally, it is important that an initiation from another person always serves as a cue for the child to respond. A child may first show the ability to respond with nonverbal responses (e.g., passes materials when asked). However, to fully demonstrate this skill, a child must also be able to provide verbal responses as well (e.g., respond to questions or comments from others).

SL 11. Answers questions about ongoing activities

This skill requires the child to answer questions from adults and peers about things that are currently taking place. To be able to answer questions about ongoing activities, a child does not need to recall information, but does need to be attentive to the activities going on around her. A child should be able to answer questions about both tangible things in the ongoing environment, as well as questions about her actions or the actions of others or about verbal information shared by others.

SL 12. Shares information about self, family, and major events (e.g., school day, holidays, family events)

Many parents want their child to be able to share what he did at school with them. Sharing about life events is also often a part of a structured sharing time in a preschool classroom. To share information with peers, teachers, or parents, a child must be able to remember things that have happened in the past without relying on cues in the current environment. The requirement is not that the child initiates sharing information, but that he can answer questions and share information when asked. Children begin to share information about themselves between the ages of 3–5 years.

SL 13. Answers more than five questions on a preferred topic

This skill does not require the child to facilitate a conversation, only that she answers a variety of questions on a topic. This skill is the first step toward learning how to participate in a reciprocal conversation and talk about topics that are less preferred or not the child's choice. A child should be able to answer questions on at least five or more different topics.

SL 14. Makes reciprocal comments (e.g., child responds to peer: "I like that movie too!" "I don't have (that), I have (this).")

Once a child can respond to questions, he needs to learn to respond to comments from peers (e.g., "I like peanut butter too.") and to make follow-up comments or questions (e.g., "I like that movie too. Did you like the part where they went to the circus?").

SL 15. Shares information about immediate past or future events

This skill requires the child be able to talk about things that are not in his immediate environment. The child must be able to relate past or future experiences about a person or an activity to a peer for which there are likely no reference cues in the current environment. The requirement is not that the child initiates, but that he can answer questions and share information when asked (e.g., "What did you do in art?" "What are you doing after school?").

SL 16. Answers questions, asks questions, or makes comments to maintain conversation for three to four exchanges

Once a child is able to answer a variety of questions on a topic and to make reciprocal comments, the expectation should increase so that she puts those skills together to maintain a conversation on a topic by providing a variety of relevant comments or questions.

SL 17. Responds appropriately when a peer changes topic

Some children have difficulty shifting topics and will continue to talk on the same topic even after the other person has moved on. Once a child can talk about a variety of topics, it is important that he recognizes when another person has shifted topics and can shift with them.

SL 18. Directs body and eyes toward social partner when speaking

Some children can perform the verbal part of social interactions but have difficulty with the nonverbal components. Talking to others also involves the child orienting her body and face toward her social partner. It is not necessary that the child sustain eye contact during the entire interaction, only that she makes eye contact every few seconds.

SL 19. Directs body and eyes toward social partner when listening

In addition to looking at a person when speaking, it is important that the child look and orient when listening, showing his social partner that he is attending. This skill is important for both group listening and one-on-one listening situations. It is not necessary that the child sustain eye contact during the entire interaction, but that he makes eye contact every few seconds.

SL 20. Speaks using polite phrases (e.g., "Please," "Thank you," "Sorry," "Excuse me," "You're welcome")

This is a skill that is more important to adults than to peers. These phrases are some of the building blocks of social etiquette that gain importance as the child becomes older. A child demonstrates this skill by using these phrases at appropriate times without needing cues from adults.

SL 21. Accepts people who are different (e.g., does not make negative comments)

Many children have difficulty filtering what they say from what they think. One indicator that a child accepts people who are different is that she can be near and participate in interactions with children who are different than she is in appearance, interests, or abilities without making negative comments. Negative comments should be differentiated from a child asking questions about differences that are not familiar to her (e.g., asking why someone is in a wheelchair or has different skin color).

SL 22. Seeks to repair or clarify breakdowns in social interactions

Children who have difficulty in social interactions may find it particularly hard when a social interaction does not go as planned (e.g., they do not understand what a person said, they don't know how to respond). In these situations, some children may engage in inappropriate behaviors (e.g., repeating what the other person said) or may simply not respond at all. A child with this skill might, for example, modify what he has said or ask for help.

SL 23. Converses on age-appropriate topics (i.e., talks about topics similar and of interest to peers)

Some children may have difficulty engaging in conversations with peers because they can talk about only a few topics that are of high interest to them or have interests that are different than those of their peers. A child's ability to converse on age-appropriate topics is determined by whether she knows the topics other children are talking about and whether she participates in these conversations when they occur.

SL 24. Uses contextually appropriate language/introduces topic

Some children initiate a conversation without clearly introducing the topic or may make comments unrelated to the current context. There is a variety of ways in which a child can demonstrate this skill. These include making comments about the ongoing topic or initiating a conversation with a topic-relevant comment or question.

CLASSROOM/GROUP BEHAVIOR

CG 1. Follows schedule and classroom rules (including playground rules)

For a child to participate independently in a group setting, it is important that he follows the schedule and rules of the group. A child's ability to follow a schedule or classroom rules is determined based on his ability to meet the specific expectations of the classroom or environment.

CG 2. Follows verbal directions as part of classroom routines or activities (e.g., get materials, put away lunch)

An important independence skill for a young child entering kindergarten is that she be able to follow general instructions provided to the group during routine activities and transitions, such as during lunch, snack, and Circle Time.

CG 3. Recognizes belongings of own, others, and group

Young children may have difficulty understanding what is "mine," "yours," and "ours." This important prerequisite skill is necessary in order for children to learn to care for their belongings, to share, and to ask before using the belongings of others. This skill is demonstrated by a child caring for and putting away his things, not taking what belongs to someone else without first asking, and sharing group belongings (e.g., classroom materials, playground toys).

CG 4. Keeps toys/materials in designated locations

Each classroom has rules and expectations regarding where toys and materials are kept. It is important that a child learns these rules and expectations. This skill is demonstrated when a child knows where things belong and puts materials in the appropriate place when cleaning up.

CG 5. Responds to teacher by looking or coming when directly or indirectly cued

It is important that a child responds to a variety of directions or signals and attends to the teacher (e.g., name being called, light being turned off as cue to stop and look, group direction). It is also important that a child be able to exhibit this skill across a variety of contexts.

CG 6. Imitates a peer who is leading songs/activities (e.g., Simon Says)

Some children can have difficulty attending during group activities/games and others may attend but not be actively engaged. This skill requires that a child not only attends but also actively participates in group activities/games by imitating the ongoing actions of a leader.

CG 7. Responds to indirect cueing (e.g., "Where are your friends?" when child needs to line up)

A child's growing independence within a classroom depends on her ability to read the environment (e.g., see what her peers are doing when she has gotten off-task or is not clear on a direction) or to rely on past experience (e.g., remembering that when she doesn't understand a direction, she can look at what her friends are doing or can raise her hand for help). However, many children have difficulty using these strategies. Teaching the child indirect cueing can help her learn to use the actions of peers as a guide. This skill requires that a child responds appropriately when indirect questions or cues are provided (e.g., cues to respond to peer interactions or to make requests).

CG 8. Uses playground equipment appropriately

Some children have difficulty accessing all areas of the playground. They may tend to engage in nonfunctional play (e.g., walking the perimeter of the playground, throwing wood chips). Learning to use playground equipment appropriately serves as a context for social interactions. A child demonstrates this skill by remaining actively engaged when on the playground by accessing and appropriately using a variety of equipment.

CG 9. Helps others, both spontaneously and when asked

It is typically easier for a child to learn to help others when he is specifically asked to do so. However, it is also important that a child learns to identify naturally occurring situations in which it is appropriate to provide help (e.g., when a peer drops something or has difficulty opening a container). The expectation is that a child provides help in a variety of these situations or reaches out to an adult to let them know that a peer needs help.

CG 10. Remains in place in a group until called by teacher (e.g., staying in seat until called to line up)

Many children have difficulty waiting during group activities without calling out or jumping out of their seat. This skill requires that a child attends to teacher directions and to what other children are doing and uses this information to guide her behavior and actions.

CG 11. Prepares for activity by locating area/materials (e.g., chair, coat)

An important independence skill for a young child entering kindergarten is the ability to get materials for an activity without being specifically directed to do so. For example, rather than being told to get his placemat and lunchbox, a child starts to get these materials when told it is time for lunch.

CG 12. Follows directions during novel activities

In addition to being able to follow directions as part of routine activities, it is also important that children learn to follow directions during less familiar activities. This includes following directions during non-routine small- and large-group activities (e.g., new games, novel art activities).

CG 13. Gives directions during novel activities

Not only are children required to follow directions during novel activities, but they are also sometimes required to give directions during novel activities. This includes being asked to give directions during new or less familiar games or activities.

CG 14. Stays in place when walking in line and maintains pace with group

When children have difficulty with this skill, it is often because they do not attend to the cues of where they need to be or because they have difficulty recognizing other people's space. There are many times during the course of a typical preschool or kindergarten day when children are asked to walk in line. The expectation is that a child stay an appropriate distance behind the child in front of him without falling too far behind and without bumping into other children.

CG 15. Repeats words/actions from a song, book, or play activity

Many preschool activities involve repeating words or actions. This alone builds the skill in many children. However, some children do not actively participate. The expectation is both that a child repeats words or actions immediately as part of ongoing activities, and that he can do so when familiar activities are presented at a later time.

CG 16. Accepts that some peers may follow different rules or schedules

While most rules and expectations should apply to all children in a group or classroom, the individual needs of some children dictate different rules or schedules. As much as possible, teaching staff should work to minimize the appearance of these variations. However, it is also important for children to learn that not all children are the same, and that some children learn differently and therefore may need to do things a little differently. It is appropriate for a child to ask why other children might follow different rules or schedules, but the expectation is that she accepts the explanation provided by an adult and follows the rules and expectations put in place for her.

CG 17. Asks permission to use others' possessions

For some children, even when they begin to understand what belongs to them, to others, or to the group, they may still take other people's things without asking permission. The expectation for this skill is that children do not take or use the belongings of others without first asking.

CG 18. Attends to small-group, teacher-led, hands-on activity for at least ten minutes

Many children have difficulty sustaining attention during group activities—some have more success with hands-on activities rather than activities that primarily involve listening. The expectation is that a child be able to actively participate without exhibiting disruptive behaviors.

CG 19. Sits quietly in circle for at least ten minutes

Most preschool classrooms include a Circle Time routine that typically follows a set procedure and includes activities such as calendar, weather, and a greeting. The expectation is that a child be able to sit without being disruptive, but also be able to actively participate.

CG 20. Attends to small-group, teacher-led listening activity for at least ten minutes

This is an extension of *CG 18* but requires that a child sustains attention in an activity that is primarily auditory. The expectation is that a child be able to attend without exhibiting disruptive behaviors and be able to follow directions or respond to questions from the teacher leading the activity.

CG 21. Responds together with group to teacher or peer leading activity

A number of group activities involve the teacher leading activities, such as reading familiar stories or poems and pausing from time to time to let the children fill in responses. The expectation is that a child be able to respond along with the other children.

CG 22. Follows basic two- to three-step verbal directions in a group

This is an extension of *CG 2* and *CG 12*. In addition to following one-step directions during routine or novel activities, children need to work toward being able to follow multi-step directions. The expectation is that children first follow multi-step directions during routine activities and then during novel or less familiar activities.

CG 23. Passes items to peers (e.g., passing out materials, taking turns looking at a shared object and passing to next person)

Many activities require the use of different materials (e.g., paper and crayons during art projects, napkins during lunch), and children often take a part in passing out these materials to their peers. The expectation is that a child is able to make sure that a peer is attending and passes materials to him following the expectation of the activity.

NONVERBAL SOCIAL LANGUAGE

NV 1. Reciprocates nonverbal interactions (e.g., high five, wave, thumbs-up, fist bump, smile)

Children need to respond to nonverbal interactions appropriately. The response can be either a reciprocation of the nonverbal initiation (e.g., high five back to other person) or a request for the person to stop (e.g., if other person hugs the child, and they do not like this).

NV 2. Initiates nonverbal interactions (e.g., high five, wave, thumbs-up, fist bump, smile) with appropriate adults and peers

In addition to being able to respond to nonverbal interactions, children must also be able to initiate nonverbal interactions. Children who struggle with this skill may not initiate nonverbal interactions or may initiate interactions that are not appropriate (e.g., handshake with a peer rather than a high five or wave). The expectation is that a child both initiates appropriate nonverbal interactions, either during naturally occurring times or during structured activities (e.g., greeting time during morning circle), and that he refrains from initiating inappropriate nonverbal interactions.

NV 3. Identifies basic actions without words (e.g., Charades)

In addition to being able to respond to verbal information provided by others, it is also important that a child understands activities and situations that involve no or limited verbal information. Structured Charades-like activities provide opportunities for young children to practice this skill. The expectation is that children can identify actions modeled by others without needing verbal information to do so.

NV 4. Demonstrates an appropriate level of affection based on history, relationship, and familiarity with the person (e.g., hugs parent, gives high five to friend, does not initiate with unfamiliar person)

Children who have difficulty with this skill may simply not initiate affection with others or may initiate inappropriate expressions of affection (e.g., hugging peers). The expectation is that a child both initiates an appropriate affection, either during naturally occurring times or during structured activities (e.g., greeting time during morning circle), and that he refrains from initiating an inappropriate level of affection.

NV 5. Follows basic gestures and nonverbal cues (e.g., stops when person holds up hand, comes when person motions with hand)

In addition to having difficulty responding to nonverbal interactions, many children also have trouble identifying and following gestures and nonverbal cues. A child with this skill can appropriately respond to gestures or nonverbal cues from others during naturally occurring or game-like activities.

NV 6. Modifies own behavior based on the body language, actions, or eye gaze of others

It is important that children learn to determine when it is appropriate to begin or engage in an activity (e.g., transition, open their lunch, start a new activity) based on the nonverbal behavior of others. The expectation is that a child be able to modify her behavior when presented with a communicative eye gaze, a head nod/shake, or other types of body language.

CHAPTER 3:
Sample IEP Objectives

Sample IEP objectives are provided below for each item on the Socially Savvy Checklist. These are only examples. Objectives must be individualized based on a child's needs, the environment, the teaching methodology, and the data collection procedures. Space is also provided at the end of each section to add other objectives if additional skills are identified as targets.

	JOINT ATTENDING
JA 1	When presented with an object, child will orient (e.g., look or make a related response) in 80% of opportunities across three objects.
JA 2	During a five-minute social interaction (e.g., clapping hands and looking with expectation at others), child will repeat her behavior at a frequency at least 50% above baseline across three behaviors.
JA 3	During a five-minute social interaction (e.g., dropping ball and looking with expectation at others), child will repeat her behavior with a toy at a frequency at least 50% above baseline across three toys.
JA 4	During a five-minute social interaction, such as Free-Play or a simple game, child will use eye gaze to maintain the interaction (i.e., look directly at other person's face for at least one second multiple times throughout the interaction) at a frequency at least 50% above baseline across three consecutive opportunities.
JA 5	Child will follow the point or gesture of an adult to an object in 80% of opportunities across three adults.
JA 6	Child will follow the eye gaze of an adult to look at an object in 80% of opportunities across three adults.
JA 7	During a fifteen-minute Choice Time or Free-Play, child will show objects to share interest to an adult or peer at a frequency at least 80% of a typical peer across two weeks.
JA 8	During a fifteen-minute Choice Time or Free-Play, child will point to objects to share interest with an adult or peer at a frequency at least 80% of a typical peer across two weeks.
JA 9	During Choice Time, Free-Play, or a Table Top activity, child will comment on her actions (e.g., "I'm coloring.") or the actions of others (e.g., "She's building.") at a frequency at least 80% of a typical peer across two weeks.

SOCIAL PLAY

SP 1	During the course of a two-minute social interactive game (e.g., Peek-a-Boo, being pushed by adult on swing), child will use his body, hands, eyes, or voice to show that he is engaged in the game at a frequency at least 50% above baseline across three consecutive opportunities.
SP 2	Child will play with a close-ended toy (e.g., shape sorter, puzzle) within three feet of peers for five to ten minutes, requiring no more than three prompts for three consecutive opportunities.
SP 3	Child will play with an open-ended toy (e.g., blocks, trucks, LEGOs) within three feet of peers for five to ten minutes, requiring no more than the same number of prompts as a typical peer across three toys.
SP 4	During a thirty-minute Free-Play, child will allow others to play with materials (e.g., gives materials when asked or allows a peer to play with materials she is using), requiring no more than the same number of prompts as a typical peer across two weeks.
SP 5	When jointly completing a puzzle, shape sorter, or other close-ended toy, child will take turns giving and following simple directions to complete the activity for four out of five opportunities.
SP 6	Given an open-ended activity (e.g., block building, marble toy construction) with one other peer, child will take turns giving and following simple directions to complete a structure of at least ten parts for four out of five opportunities.
SP 7	During a simple game with a peer, child will take turns nonverbally (waiting, taking turn, and passing materials) in three out of four turns across three sessions.
SP 8	Child will play outdoor games until the completion of the activity (e.g., Duck-Duck-Goose, Red Rover) with a group of up to five peers requiring no more than the same number of prompts as a typical peer across three activities.
SP 9	Child will stop a behavior when requested by a peer in four out of five consecutive opportunities.
SP 10	Child will end structured play or game with peers appropriately (e.g., says, "Let's play something else!") in four out of five consecutive opportunities.
SP 11	Child will take a role in an imaginative play theme (e.g., restaurant, doctor, firefighter) and sustain it for up to three to five actions (verbal or nonverbal) for three consecutive play sessions.
SP 12	During a structured turn-taking/sharing activity, child will trade toys when directed by an adult for 80% of opportunities across three consecutive sessions.
SP 13	At the start of Free-Play or Choice Time, child will invite a peer to play in a preferred activity for four out of five consecutive opportunities.
SP 14	With use of a visual activity schedule, child will approach peers and appropriately join in (e.g., "Can I play, too?") an ongoing activity for four out of five opportunities.

Social Play continued on next page

SOCIAL PLAY (continued)

SP 15	Child will accept an invitation to play in an activity of a peer's choice in four out of five consecutive opportunities.
SP 16	Child will accept losing games or getting called "out" in four out of five consecutive opportunities.
SP 17	During a fifteen-minute unstructured playtime, child will use free time appropriately (e.g., move to a new activity once she completes the first activity; engage in age-appropriate play), requiring no more than three prompts for three consecutive sessions.
SP 18	Child will follow changes in play ideas of others and sustain the changes during open-ended play (e.g., changes in play scheme/scenario), requiring no more than the same number of prompts as a typical peer across three play sessions.
SP 19	Child will appropriately play a game involving a person being "It" across three consecutive sessions for at least three different games.
SP 20	During structured games or activities, child will accept novel ideas or changes in the rules of the game in four out of five consecutive opportunities.
SP 21	Child will plan a play scheme with a peer and follow it through (e.g., decide to build a house out of blocks and then build it) requiring no more than the same number of prompts as a typical peer across three play schemes.
SP 22	When asked "Who are your friends?" child will identify children who are his friends and give a simple explanation why (e.g., "Because I eat lunch with them." "Because they are nice." "Because I sit next to them.") in four out of five consecutive opportunities.
SP 23	During structured activities that involve children sharing information about their likes or interests (e.g., teacher has children take turns saying what their favorite game is), child will refrain from making negative comments or gestures in four out of five consecutive opportunities.
SP 24	During games that involve a person winning, child will win gracefully (e.g., without making bragging comments) in four out of five consecutive opportunities.

SELF-REGULATION

SR 1	When presented with new tasks/activities, child will demonstrate flexibility by not exhibiting challenging behaviors in four out of five consecutive opportunities.
SR 2	When requests are denied, child will respond to "No" appropriately without exhibiting challenging behaviors in four out of five consecutive opportunities.
SR 3	Given a fifteen-minute small-group listening activity, child will raise her hand and wait to talk for four out of five consecutive opportunities.
SR 4	When directed by an adult to use a calming strategy (e.g., taking a walk, squeezing a ball), child will use the calming strategy in eight out of ten consecutive opportunities.
SR 5	Child will recognize when he is upset or frustrated and ask for a break or access to a calming item/activity, rather than exhibiting disruptive behavior, for eight out of ten consecutive opportunities.
SR 6	During naturally occurring transitions during the day, child will accept and make transitions without exhibiting challenging behaviors in 80% of opportunities for three consecutive days.
SR 7	When unexpected changes are made to the schedule or routine, child will accept changes without exhibiting challenging behaviors in four out of five measured opportunities.
SR 8	When preferred activities are interrupted, child will accept the interruption without exhibiting challenging behaviors in four out of five measured opportunities.
SR 9	When provided with corrective feedback or redirection, child will accept the feedback without exhibiting challenging behaviors in four out of five measured opportunities.
SR 10	When child makes a mistake or has difficulty with a task (e.g., colors outside of line, does not know answer to a question), he will ask for assistance appropriately and/or take redirection from an adult without exhibiting interfering behaviors (e.g., ripping paper, yelling, refusing to move on with activity) for four out of five measured opportunities.
SR 11	When walking in line or moving through a busy environment, child will demonstrate awareness of his or her own space as well as the space of others (e.g., not stepping on other's feet, keeping an appropriate distance) in 80% of intervals (two-minute time sample divided into ten-second intervals) for three consecutive days.
SR 12	When given direction by an adult to stop or change a specific behavior (e.g., sit crisscross during circle, use an inside voice), child will modify her behavior within five seconds in four out of five measured opportunities.
SR 13	When others make requests of child, he will either comply with the request or use appropriate words and voice tone to turn down a request (e.g., "Not right now.") in four out of five measured opportunities.
SR 14	During small-group activities, child will appropriately advocate for herself (e.g., "I didn't get one." "I can't see." "Please move." "Stop.") without exhibiting challenging behaviors in four out of five planned opportunities.

Self-Regulation continued on next page

	SELF-REGULATION (continued)
SR 15	Given novel or challenging activities, child will ask for help rather than exhibiting off-task behaviors in four out of five measured opportunities.
SR 16	Given a variety of naturally occurring situations (e.g., when directed by teacher, when requesting to use a toy), child will wait appropriately without exhibiting challenging behaviors for 80% of opportunities for three consecutive days.
SR 17	When told in advance a specific topic or question is off limits, child will require no more than two prompts per day to refrain from talking about the topic or question for four out of five consecutive days.
SR 18	Throughout the three-hour school day, child will use a conversational voice level and voice tone when speaking, requiring no more than three prompts per day for three consecutive days.
	SOCIAL/EMOTIONAL
SE 1	In naturally occurring situations throughout the day, child will be able to verbally identify the emotion being displayed (e.g., happy, sad, mad, scared) by herself or others in four out of five measured opportunities.
SE 2	Child will be able to verbally identify the emotion being displayed (e.g., happy, sad, mad, scared), first in pictures and then in naturally occurring situations, and provide a simple explanation for the emotion (e.g., she dropped her ice cream) in 80% of opportunities across three consecutive days.
SE 3	In a variety of targeted situations, child will make an empathic response (e.g., say, "Are you Ok?" to peer who falls on playground; hug a peer who is crying; pick up a toy that peer drops) in four out of five measured opportunities.
SE 4	During the school day, child will express negative emotions appropriately (e.g., say, "I'm mad!" or "Can I take a break?") as measured by the absence of targeted challenging behaviors for eight out of ten consecutive days.

Social/Emotional continued on next page

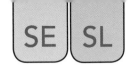

	SOCIAL/EMOTIONAL (continued)
SE 5	During situations in which another person makes either a neutral comment (e.g., shares what they had for breakfast) or an excited comment (e.g., presents a favorite toy or shares a completed art project), child will provide a related verbal response using an appropriate voice volume and tone in four out of five measured opportunities.
SE 6	During thirty-minute Free-Play situations, child will refrain from exhibiting behaviors that might make a peer mad (e.g., knocking over a tower) and will exhibit behaviors that might make a peer happy (e.g., sharing a toy) for eight out ten measured play situations.

	SOCIAL LANGUAGE
SL 1	When presented with a greeting or parting by an adult or peer, child will respond with an appropriate greeting in 80% of opportunities across three consecutive days.
SL 2	When one of his teachers or peers is present and he is given a direction (such as "Give this to Joey." or "Go to Ms. Smith's table."), child will follow the direction in 80% of opportunities across three consecutive days.
SL 3	When entering a classroom or a new activity, child will initiate greetings/partings with the adult or peer in that environment in 80% of opportunities across three consecutive days.
SL 4	In game-like activities in which children have to engage in turn taking that requires verbal interactions, child will address peers by name in 80% of opportunities across three consecutive opportunities.
SL 5	Given one of twenty different social questions, child will appropriately respond to each social question from a peer or adult for 80% of opportunities for three consecutive days.
SL 6	During planned activities or games, child will ask one of ten different social questions (e.g., name, age, family names, pet names) to an adult or peer in 80% of opportunities across three consecutive days.
SL 7	When presented with new or insufficient information (e.g., a novel object, a missing piece to a puzzle), child will ask for information (e.g. "What is that?" "Where is it?") in four out of five opportunities across three activities or situations.

Social Language continued on next page

SOCIAL LANGUAGE (continued)

SL 8	Given the completion of various activities (e.g., puzzles, artwork, picture schedule), child will use complete verbal statements and appropriate voice tone to solicit attention for completed activities (e.g., "I did it!" "Look what I made.") for four out of five opportunities across three different activities or situations.
SL 9	When requesting attention, child will gain listener attention appropriately (e.g., use verbal phrase, tap listener on the shoulder) in four out of five measured opportunities across three consecutive days.
SL 10	Child will respond to initiations (e.g., make space for peer in group, answer a yes/no question) from adults progressing to peers in 80% of opportunities across three consecutive days.
SL 11	During targeted activities (e.g., art activity, morning circle), child will answer questions about ongoing activities (e.g., "What comes after gluing?") for four out of five measured opportunities across three different activities.
SL 12	During structured activities, child will share information about school day, holidays, family, or other major events in 80% of opportunities across three consecutive days.
SL 13	When asked questions on a preferred topic (e.g., "What is your dog's name?" "Who feeds Rover?" "Where does Rover sleep?" "Where do you walk Rover?"), child will verbally answer more than five questions in four out of five consecutive opportunities across three topics.
SL 14	Child will make a reciprocal comment to a peer (e.g., child responds to peer: "I like that movie, too!" "I don't have (that), I have (this).") in 80% of opportunities across three peers.
SL 15	During lunch or snack time, child will make comments about events that just happened (e.g., "My Mom brought me to school today.") or are about to happen (e.g., "Martha is coming later for music.") at least two times for four out of five consecutive lunch/snack sessions.
SL 16	Child will maintain a conversation for three to four exchanges by answering questions, asking questions, or making comments in four out of five opportunities across three topics.
SL 17	During small-group interactive activities, child will respond appropriately when a peer changes topic, as shown by commenting on or asking questions related to the new topic in four out of five opportunities across three different settings.
SL 18	When talking to an adult or peer, child will turn toward listener in four out of five consecutive opportunities across three different settings.
SL 19	When given a two- to three-step direction, child will turn toward the speaker and make eye contact at least once at the beginning and once at the end of the request in four out of five opportunities across three different adults.
SL 20	In targeted situations (e.g., when given a toy, when trying to pass around a peer), child will use one of five different polite phrases (e.g. "Please," "Thank you," "Sorry," "Excuse me," "You're welcome") in four out of five measured opportunities.

Social Language continued on next page

	SOCIAL LANGUAGE (continued)
SL 21	Child will accept people who are different, as shown by not making negative comments (e.g., "He's ugly." "That lady is fat.") across the entire school day for ten consecutive days.
SL 22	When child is unable to complete a direction, he will ask for clarification ("Where do I put it?" "What's next?") in four out of five measured opportunities.
SL 23	During unstructured small-group activities, child will engage in three to four social exchanges on age-appropriate topics (i.e., topic of interest to peers) in four out of five measured opportunities.
SL 24	When initiating a new topic during unstructured small-group activities, child will use introductory or transition phrases to introduce the topic (e.g., "Oh, guess what?" "That reminds me..." "Want to hear something that is funny?") in four out of five measured opportunities.

	CLASSROOM/GROUP BEHAVIOR
CG 1	Child will follow the identified classroom rules (e.g., sit crisscross at circle, keep hands to self) with less than three adult prompts per day for eight out of ten consecutive days.
CG 2	During targeted classroom activities (e.g., Circle Time, art, snack), child will follow a teacher direction to get items or supplies in four out of five consecutive opportunities.
CG 3	During structured activities that involve sharing individual- and group-owned items/materials, child will be able to identify what belongs to her, to others, and to the classroom in four out of five measured opportunities.
CG 4	Across the school day, child will require no more than three adult prompts to keep toys/materials in designated locations in four out of five consecutive days.
CG 5	When called by name by the teacher, child will look or come to the teacher in 80% of opportunities across three consecutive days.
CG 6	During peer-led songs/activities, child will imitate a peer leader for at least five consecutive actions in four out of five consecutive days.
CG 7	When provided with indirect cues from an adult (e.g., "What do you need?" to finish something or make something), child will respond to the cue in four out of five measured opportunities.

Classroom/Group Behavior continued on next page

CLASSROOM/GROUP BEHAVIOR (continued)

CG 8	During thirty-minute periods on the playground, child will require no more than three adult prompts to use the playground equipment appropriately across three consecutive days.
CG 9	In situations in which a peer clearly needs help (e.g., drops materials, spills juice, cannot open package), child will offer to help for four out of five consecutive planned opportunities.
CG 10	Child will wait to be called on in a group (e.g., staying in seat until called to line up) in four out of five measured opportunities.
CG 11	During targeted activities (e.g., snack, art, end of day routine), child will get necessary materials and go to the designated area in four out of five measured opportunities.
CG 12	During novel activities (e.g., new game or song), child will follow known directions from an adult, progressing to following directions from a peer, in four out of five measured opportunities across three consecutive activities.
CG 13	During novel activities (e.g., new game or song), child will give known directions to others in four out of five measured opportunities across three consecutive activities.
CG 14	When walking in line during a transition, child will keep pace with his peers, requiring no more than three adult prompts for four out of five measured opportunities.
CG 15	During group activities involving repeating actions in songs, books, or play activities, child will repeat at least five consecutive actions in four out of five consecutive activities.
CG 16	Child will accept that some peers may follow different rules or schedules, as shown by not exhibiting challenging behaviors across the entire school day for ten consecutive days.
CG 17	During targeted activities (e.g., art activity when each child has a distinct set of materials, during Show and Tell time), child will ask permission to use other's possessions in four out of five measured opportunities across three different activities.
CG 18	Child will attend to small-group, teacher-led, hands-on activity for at least ten minutes, requiring no more than three prompts for three consecutive opportunities.
CG 19	Child will sit quietly in a Circle Time activity for up to ten minutes, requiring no more than two prompts for three consecutive opportunities.
CG 20	Child will attend to small-group, teacher-led, listening activity for at least ten minutes, requiring no more than two prompts for three consecutive opportunities.
CG 21	During targeted activities (e.g., songs, calendar, Simon Says), child will respond along with the group to the teacher or peer leading the activity, requiring no more than three prompts for three consecutive opportunities.

Classroom/Group Behavior continued on next page

CLASSROOM/GROUP BEHAVIOR (continued)

CG 22	During group activities, child will follow basic two- and three-step verbal directions (e.g., "Get your news book, sit next to the teacher, and open to your news page.") for four out of five measured opportunities.
CG 23	During targeted activities (e.g., art activity, Show and Tell, snack set up), child will independently pass items to peers for four out of five measured opportunities.

NONVERBAL SOCIAL LANGUAGE

NV 1	In response to nonverbal initiations (e.g., high five, wave) from a peer, child will respond appropriately in four out of five measured opportunities.
NV 2	During targeted activities/transitions (e.g., end of a game, when entering an activity, when a peer wins), child will initiate nonverbal interactions (e.g., high five, wave) with appropriate adults and peers in four out of five measured opportunities.
NV 3	During a Charades-like game, child will identify common actions, animals, or emotions demonstrated without words in four out of five measured opportunities.
NV 4	As measured throughout the course of the day, child will demonstrate appropriate level of affection with adults and peers within the school environment for ten consecutive days.
NV 5	During organized games (e.g., Obstacle Course, Red Light/Green Light), child will follow basic gestures (e.g., stop, open arms, finger shake "no") in four out of five measured opportunities.
NV 6	When exhibiting disruptive or off-task behavior and provided with nonverbal feedback from the teacher (e.g., head shake, finger to lips, eye gaze, point), child will modify his own behavior in four out of five measured opportunities.

CHAPTER 4:

Teaching Strategies

Children may demonstrate deficits or impairments in social skills for one or more reasons. These might include lack of motivation, an actual skill deficit, or other competing motivators (e.g., over-interest in a toy). Fortunately, there are a variety of effective ways to teach social skills. What approach (or approaches) to use depends in large part upon "why" a child is showing social-skills deficits. In choosing strategies to teach social skills, it is also important to determine a child's unique learning style. The following questions can help.

- Can the child learn in a group or does she need one-on-one instruction to start?
- What group size has worked best for the child?
- What skill areas or skills on the Socially Savvy Checklist need to be addressed?
- Does the child demonstrate behaviors that will interfere with participation in social-skills intervention?
- Are the child's social difficulties related to motivation or decreased interest in other children?
- Does the child learn from watching and imitating other children?

This chapter will describe the following methods of teaching social skills: Direct Teaching, Modeling, Rule-Based Teaching, Activity-Based Teaching, Commercially Available Curricula, Incidental Teaching, Reinforcement, Social Stories, Visual Supports, Self-Monitoring, and Peer-Mediated Intervention. Further, it will outline the types of children who will most likely benefit from them and offer advice on structuring groups.

DIRECT TEACHING

This method works well for children with very limited social skills or who have difficulty attending or learning in a group format.

Systematic instruction following detailed teaching plans is used by breaking down more complex social skills into smaller components and following specific prompting and reinforcement procedures. This type of instruction typically requires a one-on-one or one-on-two teacher to child ratio. Some children can participate and learn some social skills in structured group situations, but may require direct teaching for other skills.

For example, rather than working on conversation skills during snack time, a child might need to first be taught fundamental conversation skills one-on-one with an adult. This might begin with teaching the child how to respond to a variety of social questions that have static answers (e.g., "What's your name?" "Where do you live?" "How old are you?"). A teaching plan might include a time delay prompting procedure[8] that initially provides a verbal model of the correct answer and then builds in a prompt delay of two to four seconds until the child can respond correctly without prompting. Once the child is able to consistently respond to social questions that have static answers, more open-ended social questions can be targeted (e.g., "What's your favorite color?" "What do you like to eat?" "What do you like to do on the playground?"). Next, the child might be taught to answer the targeted social questions and respond with a follow-up question, for example:

Teacher: "What's your mom's name?"
Child: "Ann. What's your mom's name?"

At this point, the same teaching approach can be followed to teach the child to respond to comments from others, for example:

> Teacher: "I have an apple."
> Child: "I have grapes. Do you like grapes?"

Once a child has mastered discrete conversational skills, the next step is to generalize them into the classroom and group during activities like snack and lunch.

A number of different sample teaching plans are included in Appendix 1. Each teaching plan identifies the target skill and corresponding objective, the materials required to teach the skill, a general description of teaching strategies, the specific type of prompting procedure to be used (including how to fade the prompts), and the specific targets if appropriate. The teaching plans are only examples and will need to be individualized for each child. The other component that needs to be determined in teaching each skill is how to reinforce appropriate responses. As with all aspects of teaching, the type, amount, and frequency of reinforcement must be individualized for each child.

MODELING

This method works well for children with strong imitation skills and the ability to attend to modeled scenarios for one to two minutes. For video modeling, the child should be interested in videos.

Modeling can be used in a planned and systematic way to teach a variety of new social skills.[9] Creative modeling can engage an otherwise unmotivated child and hold his interest in areas that are challenging for him—particularly if he no longer needs intensive, direct instruction. Models can include adults, other children, and/or puppets. When possible, modeling of targeted social skills should occur just before the situation in which the skill is to be used. Additionally, it is often necessary to provide modeling of targeted skills multiple times and to also have the child role-play or practice the skill in a contrived situation.

We stumbled on a wonderful example one rainy day when the teachers in our social-skills group were looking for a fun indoor activity. Two talented and creative teachers (Katie and Katie) created a television show (The Katie and Katie Show) using a giant cardboard box in which they cut out a rectangle as the "TV screen." The teachers had the children pretend to turn on the television with a pretend remote control. When the TV "came on," the teachers acted out a social scenario (e.g., one of teachers not sharing with the other). The teachers had the children use the remote to pause the show and then asked them to suggest possible solutions to the problem. Once three or four solutions were identified, the children hit "rewind," and the teachers did the scene again, acting out one of the solutions (and leading to a better outcome). Over time, the children were less interested in the TV prop and more interested in the teachers' pretending. Once the children became very familiar with the format, the teachers started including the children in the "Show," which was a highlight for the class and often the first thing about the day that they shared with their parents. "Shows" covered a range of social challenges that the children were experiencing in ongoing social situations—for example, remembering to ask to go to the bathroom, not copying inappropriate behavior, taking responsibility for one's actions, keeping personal space, and being flexible when others have ideas. This made the exercise personal and directly applicable to the group.

Video modeling is also an effective way to teach a variety of skills.[10] This approach works well when children demonstrate strong imitation skills and enjoy videos. The first step is to either make a video or purchase a commercially available one. With modern technology, it is easier than ever to make a video of children playing or having an appropriate social interaction or of adults modeling specific social skills. Making videos can be time and resource intensive, but, fortunately, there is also a range of apps and videos on everything from conversational skills to play. However, commercially made videos cannot fulfill children's love of seeing themselves or familiar people onscreen. Using do-it-yourself videos makes the modeled social skill very personally relevant and potentially more reinforcing,[11] and they can be tailored to familiar environments and precise social skills better than generic commercial videos. Another advantage of videos is that they are not staff intensive once a video is made or purchased. The typical video modeling procedure in the research involves the child watching the video clip two times just prior to them entering the social situation.[12]

RULE-BASED TEACHING

This method works well for most children. Nearly all children benefit from clearly defined rules and expectations; however, children who are more concrete and "black and white" thinkers respond especially well to rule-based teaching.

It is often helpful to begin with identifying a few specific rules for the group (e.g., raise your hand, stay in your seat). When possible, ask the children to help create the rules. This will increase their sense of personal investment in following the rules. Visual representations of the rules can be a useful tool. For example, we often show a laminated picture of the children in the group sitting appropriately at the beginning of the group activity, and frequently reference it throughout to remind the children of what it looks like when they are following the rule(s) successfully. You can use a stock photograph or clip art, or if you have parental permission, you can take a picture of the children in the group sitting appropriately. Children enjoy seeing updated photos of themselves, so you might take a new photo each month. You can also (again with parent permission) use a tablet or smart phone to take the picture, which is faster than printing and laminating it.

Rule-based teaching can also help a child learn specific social skills. For example, to teach the child how to end a conversation about a particular topic, you might teach the child a rule (e.g., "When you are tired of talking about something, ask to talk about something else."). Another example would be specific rules a child can use when she needs help. You might begin by helping a child identify situations in which she might need help (e.g., can't make a toy work, does not know an answer). Next, you would introduce "rules" on who to ask for help (e.g., teacher, parent, friend). Finally, you can offer specific rules on how to ask for help (e.g., "Mary, can you help me build a tower?").

Whether you are working with group rules or rules for individual social skills, you'll want to (1) have a visual for each rule, (2) review the rules on a regular basis, (3) have children practice demonstrating the rules, and (4) provide reinforcement when a child follows the rules successfully.

ACTIVITY-BASED TEACHING

This method works well for all children, but is especially a good fit for children with some prerequisite skills, who are able to participate in a small-group setting, and who do not require one-on-one staffing.

Small-group instruction through games or activities is the primary approach used in this manual for teaching social skills, but many other strategies are used as well. Modeling, role-playing, and social stories are used either as part of, or in addition to, activity-based practice. We have also found that an activity-based approach can effectively be used with children who have more limited social skills. One option is to design a group of one to two children with significant social needs, and include two to three children with more typically developing social skills. Another option would be to work only with two to three children with more significant social needs. In that case, you want to modify the session as necessary. For example, shorten the activities or the total group time so that the children don't get too tired or overwhelmed.

There are a number of advantages to using activities or games as the context for teaching social skills. First, games or interactive activities provide more natural social situations and allow multiple children to participate. Second, activity-based practice can incorporate a number of other effective techniques, including role-playing and social stories. What makes activity-based learning particularly efficient is that it enables a range of social needs and target skills to be addressed at the same time. Games and interactive activities allow different skills to be targeted for different children within the same game or activity. For example, as part of an I Spy game, you could target *SR 3* (Raises hand and waits to be called before speaking) with one child and *JA 8* (Points to objects and makes eye contact to share interests with another). The number of children in the group can vary from two or three, up to five or six. In setting the size of your group, be mindful of the number of adults you will need for a successful exercise.

Many of our activities and projects are based on a theme that runs for several weeks to a month. One of our favorite projects is having the children make Friendship Books. This project can last for eight to twelve sessions, sometimes more, and can target a number of skills, including skills in the Social Play and Social/Emotional categories. For this activity, children create books about themselves. Each page describes something about the child; for example, favorite color, number of brothers and sisters, favorite foods, and pets. By making and sharing their Friendship Books, the children learn about what makes them different and how they are similar. Friendship Books are a wonderful tool to reference during other activities. For example, when Sophie brings in the Show and Tell box, we have the other children guess what is inside the box based on what they know about Sophie from her Friendship Book. The children might guess that she has brought in a picture of her younger sister, something yellow (which is her favorite color), or her Lalaloopsy doll.

COMMERCIALLY AVAILABLE CURRICULA

Various commercially available curricula can make learning social skills fun for all children. Because most commercially available curricula are rule based, children who respond well to a rule-based approach generally respond well to commercially available curricula. The specific social-skills needs of the child determine whether a particular curriculum will be a good fit.

A variety of commercially available curricula can be incorporated into group or individual social-skills lessons. Many of these programs are designed for older children but can be modified for use with preschool children. Most classrooms include children with a wide range of social-skills development needs, so it is important to use a mix of curricula, rather than rely solely on one specific product.

One curriculum we have used in our social-skills groups is *Circles: Intimacy and Relationships* by James Stanfield.[9] This curriculum can be useful to address skills in the areas of Self-Regulation, such as *SR 11* (Demonstrates awareness of own and other's space), and Nonverbal Social Language, such as *NV 4* (Demonstrates an appropriate level of affection based on history, relationship, and familiarity with the person). We have found the Circles curriculum very helpful for children who have a hard time with social boundaries (e.g., who is appropriate to hug or kiss, when to share personal information, and what information is okay to share). Although originally developed for k–12 classrooms, we have found this curriculum to be effective for some preschool children. The color system in the Circles curriculum has proved very successful in our groups. We make each color very concrete for children (e.g., blue = hug circle, green = sideways hug circle, yellow = high five circle, orange = wave circle, red = stranger circle). We also ensure that parents understand the color system and ask them to provide photos of people in their child's life who would correspond to each circle. Each child is given his own circle, practices matching the photos of people in his life with the correct color, and role-plays what behavior is okay with each person.

Another rule-based curriculum is Michelle Garcia Winner's *Thinking About You, Thinking About Me*.[14] We use this program for higher learners. We have found that some of her eye contact games have been very successful in our groups. One game we use often, which was inspired by the concept of "Thinking with Your Eyes," is asking children to take turns saying the letters of the alphabet or numbers. We give them a letter or number that we will end on (e.g., "Today, we are going to the letter 'T.'" or "Today, we are going to the number 25."). The group sits in a semi-circle. The group leader starts the game by saying the first letter or number. The group leader then looks at a child in the group. When that child returns the eye contact of the group leader, he is supposed to say the next letter or number in the chain. Once that child "fills in the blank," the group leader looks at another child, who will take the next turn. For the child to know when his turn is, he must look at the group leader. In addition to working on skills such as *JA 4* (Uses eye gaze to maintain social interaction) and *NV 5* (Follows basic gestures and nonverbal cues), this game also provides an excellent opportunity to work on skills such as *SR 7* (Demonstrates flexibility when things are different than planned). Many children have fixed ideas on when the game should stop, so varying the end point of the game (using different letters and numbers from day to day) can help children work on flexibility. Because this game does not require any materials, it is perfect for "down times" (while waiting during a transition or during an unexpected delay).

Another component of the *Thinking About You, Thinking About Me* curriculum, the Group Plan, can be more challenging for preschool children, but it is worth considering to address skills in the areas of Social Play, such as *SP 6* (Plays cooperatively for five to ten minutes with open-ended toys); Self-Regulation, such as *SR 9* (Responds to feedback/correction without exhibiting challenging behaviors); and Classroom/Group Behavior, such as *CG 20* (Attends to small-group, teacher-led listening activity for ten minutes). The idea behind the Group Plan is that the group, together, has a plan (completing a floor puzzle together). If a child is doing her own thing (say, reading a book), she is not following the

Group Plan. "Body"—the idea that a child's body needs to be "in the Group" for learning to happen—can be difficult for some children to understand. That is, if their bodies are not in the group, they are not ready to learn. We've been most successful teaching this by asking children to dance in marked spots so that they can visualize that they need to stay within a given space to be "in the group." Whole Body Listening refers to listening not just with ones ears, but with one's eyes and a still body. We use photos and refer to them often to illustrate the behavior we expect to see from a child when he is listening with his whole body (e.g., a child has his hands in his lap, a "quiet mouth," and eyes looking forward). Winner discusses "expected and unexpected" behaviors rather than having rules. For example, hitting someone would be "unexpected." Occasionally, we ask children in the group to help us describe what are "expected and unexpected" behaviors. We may have the children come up with their own set of expected behaviors, but depending on the group, we might list them as "Rules of our Group" or "Expectations."

While not formal curricula, many commercially available books can be integrated into social-skills teaching.

The Tobin Series (*Tobin Learns to Make Friends* by Diane Murrell) is a set of books about a train that has social challenges. The Tobin Series is useful in addressing skills in the area of Social Play area, such as *SP 4* (Shares toys/ materials). In each short story, Tobin resolves these challenges by sharing or using his words. When we use this series, we act out the stories with a few train tracks and two trains. We offer the children the opportunity to show how to handle a problem better by pretending to be Tobin and acting out the story on the train tracks (e.g., Tobin having trouble sharing). Although many preschoolers love trains, not all children find this series engaging.

How Full Is Your Bucket? by Tom Rath and Mary Reckmeyer is a children's version of the 2004 book that uses the principles of positive psychology and is a great resource in teaching skills in the areas of Social Play, such as *SP 15* (Accepts invitation to play in an activity of peer's choice); Social Emotional, such as *SE 3* (Shows empathy toward others); and Social Language, such as *SL 8* (Requests attention). The premise is that each person has a metaphorical "bucket." When we are kind to others, we not only fill their buckets, but our own bucket as well. When we are not kind, we not only dip into someone else's bucket, but we deplete our own bucket as well. This metaphor is particularly appealing to this age group. The illustrations are colorful and fun. You can make this concept more concrete by giving each child a bucket and putting some small tangibles (e.g., puff balls) into the bucket when the child shows targeted skills like sharing, waiting, being a good friend and so on. The child can then see in a very tangible way when she is filling another person's bucket as well as her own. Many activities can go along with this book. As a side note, we have found that there are many related activities—many created by teachers—that are free on the Internet.

To address skills within the area of Self-Regulation, such as *SR 5* (Identifies when upset/frustrated and appropriately asks for a break or a calming item/activity), we also use the *Incredible 5-Point Scale* (Kari Dunn Buron and Mitzi Curtis) along with *When My Worries Get Too Big* (Kari Dunn Buron)—although both need some modifications for preschoolers. The five-point scale is exactly that—a five-point scale with a number and a solution for each number. Typically, we use words that describe sound to introduce the scale (e.g., five is a tornado down to one is a whisper) because children usually can easily relate urgency and intensity with sound. The children come up with their own pictures for the sound. We practice it. We talk about what we can do at a five. Later, we move the scale to something more abstract, like having a "five" problem versus a "one" problem.

INCIDENTAL TEACHING

Incidental teaching of social skills in the classroom setting is a good option when a child does not require direct instruction in a more controlled environment, or if he has done well in an activity-based social-skills group. Addressing social skills incidentally within the classroom requires that the child either receives specialized support at specific times within the classroom setting or that all staff members are trained to systematically address any targeted social skills.

Incidental instruction involves taking advantage of teaching opportunities that arise organically during the course of the day. It often occurs during direct or activity-based instruction. For example, if two children are having difficulty sharing, for one child you might model how to ask for a toy, and for another you might model how to share. However, even when teachable moments arise, you'll still need to create opportunities to practice targeted social skills. If you are targeting *SR 8* (Demonstrates flexibility when preferred activities are interrupted), you might periodically interrupt a child during Free-Play activities so that she has more opportunities to practice being flexible. Art and craft projects are great activities in which to incidentally address a variety of social skills, including *JA 7* (Shows others objects and makes eye contact to share interest), *SP 4* (Shares toys/materials), *SR 10* (Responds to mistakes made by self or others without exhibiting challenging behaviors), or *SL 11* (Answers questions about ongoing activities). We frequently structure group arts and crafts so that the children will need to ask one another for necessary materials. At the beginning of groups, we may set up the environment so that one child is in charge of the glue, one child is in charge of the markers, and so on.

REINFORCEMENT

This method works well for children who are not strongly motivated to engage in appropriate social behavior.

Some children do not exhibit targeted social skills consistently because the consequences of doing so are not reinforced. In other words, a child might not demonstrate the skill of *SP 9* (Stops action when requested by a peer) because stopping the targeted behavior isn't rewarding for the child. In these situations, planned reinforcement greatly increases the chances that a child will respond appropriately. By definition, reinforcement must be individually determined for a child and might include verbal praise, a preferred toy or activity, or a token that can later be exchanged for a preferred toy or activity.

Building in reinforcement can be particularly helpful for children who struggle to control their behavior (e.g., not calling out, staying in their seat) We have found that using tokens to reinforce targeted group skills can be very useful in certain group situations and is not difficult to do. For example, the group leader would have a token board for each child and periodically reinforce a child when she appropriately demonstrates the targeted skill (e.g., raising her hand without calling out). When a child's token board is filled, she receives a small reward (e.g., a sticker, a piece of candy). Some children will require highly individualized reinforcement plans. For example, a child in one of our groups, Paul, was very anxious about making an incorrect verbal response, so he would whisper his answers or refuse to respond. We tried a variety of visual supports and social stories, but it was a simple token system that made the difference. Whenever Paul attempted to appropriately respond, regardless of his answer, his teachers would respond with, "That was great trying, Paul," and give him a token. After filling his token board, he was given a small piece of candy. Initially, he had to receive three tokens to earn the reward and later moved to five tokens. At one year into the social group, Paul was very chatty about all sorts of activities and topics.

SOCIAL STORIES

This method works well for children who are able to follow a verbal or visual sequence, as well as children who are able to delay reinforcement.

A social story is a short story written in the first person that describes what happens in specific social situations and what is expected of the child.[15] Social stories are typically very simple and include pictures to help the child easily follow along. Social stories can be individually designed for any social situation or any situation that is challenging for a child. For example, if a child is having difficulty coming into school in the morning, a social story might look like:

When I get to school, I say "Hi" to my teacher and say "Bye" to Mommy.

I put my home toy into my backpack.

I hang up my backpack in my cubby.

_____

I go to my classroom and pick a center to play in.

My home toy stays in my backpack all day. I know it will be safe there.

I can play with my home toy again when school is done.

Everyone is proud of me for remembering to keep my home toys in my backpack!

I am proud of me too!

Typically, we review a social story with the child in advance, maybe even several different times a day. Before entering the situation for which the social story was written, the social story should be reviewed again. Some children like to keep social stories with them so they can look at them throughout their day. For example, with the social story about coming to school, the parents might review the social story with the child at home, might go over it again in the car when they get to school, and then the teacher might review it with the child when he gets to school and keep it available throughout the school day.

Social stories are not going to solve every problem, but can be extremely helpful for some children and can also be used with the entire group when multiple children present with similar social challenges. It is not unusual to need to pair social stories with other strategies, such as planned reinforcement or practice during contrived or natural situations. It is important that adults follow along with what is outlined in the social story and model what is expected for the children. Social stories can be particularly helpful for social situations that have more open-ended outcomes or varied ways in which a child can respond. For example, social stories can be helpful for skills such as *SL 21* (Accepts people who are different) or *SR 5* (Identifies when upset/frustrated and appropriately asks for a break or a calming item/activity). Children with more delayed language and who are still working on basic requesting and labeling may have difficulty understanding a social story. For these children, it may be better to start with a simple first-then board. For example, a picture that represents leaving the playground for the "first" and a picture of the computer for the "then" can convey the targeted skill and reinforcement. For children who can wait for access to reinforcement, the social story previews what is about to happen *and* the reinforcement put into place (e.g., "When I walk off the playground with safe hands and feet, I can earn extra computer time back in the classroom.").

VISUAL SUPPORTS

All children benefit from the use of visual supports, but especially children with any impairment in language use or processing.

Visual supports, usually pictures, photographs, or commercially available icons such as Boardmaker[16], are an invaluable part of teaching social skills. The written word can also serve as visual support for children with some early reading skills. Visual supports can be used in a variety of ways to teach and support the development of social skills in young children. Pictures can be used to remind children of the rules of a group, game, or specific social skills or social situations. As mentioned earlier, visual supports are a key part of social stories, helping to make the expectations in social situations as simple and clear as possible for children. Visual schedules can be used to structure group sessions, and serve as a way to break down more complex activities (e.g., steps of an art project) or provide directions for how to complete an activity. Many children have difficulty with transitions or unexpected changes, and systematically using visual schedules can help children handle these changes. It can be helpful to have a set of visuals for situations that may come up unexpectedly, such as an alternative activity when it is raining on the playground, or a way to show when activities occur out of the expected order. Children are provided with many choices throughout the day, and visual supports can be a great resource to help children make a range of decisions—from which toys they want to play with, to which coping or calming strategy they want to use. Visual supports can also help children quickly name the emotion (or emotions) that they are feeling. For many children, visual directions or cues can be easier to follow than verbal or auditory cues. Many children who have social-skills deficits also have difficulty processing verbal information, and visual cues stay in place after verbal cues are gone. Visual cues or directions can reduce the need for verbal prompts, which increases a child's independence.

SELF-MONITORING

This method works well for children who respond well to corrective feedback and reinforcement and who are able to report on their own actions.

To increase children's ability to self-regulate and interact independently, we often introduce self-monitoring into our social groups. Extensive research supports the use of self-monitoring to increase prosocial behaviors and decrease challenging behaviors[17-19]. Self-monitoring offers children a way to self-regulate with diminished need for outside prompts and reinforcements. Although self-monitoring alone has been shown to lead to changes in behavior, it is typically necessary to also build in self-reinforcement. The steps to putting a self-monitoring system in place include (1) identifying the target behavior, (2) selecting a simple self-monitoring system, (3) identifying how and with what the child will be reinforced, (4) teaching the child how to use the system, and (5) fading out any adult support. For young children, it is important to target a behavior that can clearly be identified (e.g., sharing a toy) and a behavior that the child can recognize with adult help. Similarly, the actual system used needs to be very simple, likely including visuals of the targeted behavior. Once this is in place, we create opportunities for an adult to guide the child in using the system, eventually fading out the amount of support that is necessary.

With one of our groups, we taught the children to use self-monitoring to track their initiating and responding to peers during Free-Play. Prior to a planned Free-Play time, we reminded the children of the target behavior of "Talking to their friends." At the end of Free-Play, we had the children check off "Yes/No" with regard to these three questions (presented visually): (1) Did you play near your friends? (2) Did you talk to your friends? (3) Did you answer your friends? The children were provided with clipboards and a special form and seemed to enjoy this process.

PEER-MEDIATED INTERVENTION

Peer-mediated intervention is appropriate for all children, but can be especially helpful for children with limited social skills or who only focus on or interact with adults.

Research suggests that a variety of strategies involving typically developing children helping teach and facilitate social interaction skills in peers with limited social skills can be effective[20-22]. Many of these approaches include peers modeling, prompting, and/or reinforcing the social behaviors of children with social deficits. In integrated classroom settings, teachers have an excellent opportunity to build children's social skills through peer-mediated instruction and intervention. For example, this strategy is particularly successful in helping children learn how to respond appropriately (e.g., to questions or greetings) and how to see another person's point of view. These skills are relevant to a number of the competencies outlined in the Socially Savvy Checklist, such as, Social Play, Self-Regulation, Social/Emotional, and Social Language. Additionally, for children who do not spend time in an environment with typically developing children, we have used peer-mediated strategies through a reverse inclusion model. We may target one or two skills (e.g., taking turns, answering social questions) and set up specific, brief opportunities to have a child practice these skills with a typical peer.

In any situation, it is important to teach the typically developing child to follow the intervention procedures. For example, she must be able to clearly deliver questions and directions, provide an accurate model, allow time for the other child to respond, and give reinforcement. In some cases, one of the most important pieces is to have peers provide reinforcement to the target child, so that other children become more motivating to the target child. For children who tend to gravitate toward adults or do not find interactions with peers reinforcing, it can be helpful to pair peers with access to preferred activities or items. Additionally, it is also important to make sure that the typically developing peers are having fun, which often means providing some type of reinforcement for them also.

STRUCTURING GROUPS

The majority of our social groups include four to seven children and are approximately two hours in length. Ideally, we like to have children participate four days a week throughout the entire school year. We have found that children who take part in group four days a week progress significantly faster than those who participate only two days a week.

When placing children in social groups, we begin by completing the Socially Savvy Checklist on each child. We then look for common areas of need so that group activities and interventions address the target skills the children have in common. This makes instruction and data collection much easier. Not every child needs to be working on the same skills, but working on shared targets simplifies managing the groups. However, it is typically necessary to focus on some skills simply because they are more of a priority for one or two specific children. In these cases, it is often helpful if children who need to learn a skill see other children modeling it.

Next, we develop data sheets to be used during each group. If possible, we use one data sheet that includes all the children. Then, we plan a general structure for the group sessions. Although the activities don't need to be the same during each session, it does help if there is a standard structure to the group work. When selecting activities to include as part of the group, be sure that the identified skills can be targeted within the activities and that the exercises will be fun and engaging for the children. Children who are having fun during games and activities aren't even aware of the serious social-skills work they are doing. Even though your goal is to try to target the common needs of the children in the group, one of the great things about using an activity-based approach is that you can address different skills for different children within the same activity. For example, as part of Show and Tell, some children might be working on *JA 7* (Shows others objects and makes eye contact to share interest), while others are working on *SR 3* (Raises hand and waits to be called before speaking) or *SL 7* (Asks concrete questions about an item or information shared by others).

Well-structured social pragmatic groups tend to be the most successful. We have tried many schedules and formats and have provided a sample of one that works well for a two-hour social group.

15 MINUTES   COOPERATIVE PLAY

Have the children participate in a close-or open-ended activity, such as building a floor puzzle or playing with blocks. End project by playing I Spy on a floor puzzle or following eye gaze to take apart the block structure.

Potential Target Skills: *SP 5* (Plays cooperatively for five to ten minutes with close-ended toys); *SP 18* (Follows changes in play ideas of others and sustains the changes during open-ended play); *SL 8* (Requests attention); *CG 4* (Keeps toys/materials in designated location)

10 MINUTES   CIRCLE: HELLO SONG/ACTIVITY

Practice different ways to greet each other, sometimes including rolling a ball to each other or passing an object.

Potential Target Skills: *JA 4* (Uses eye gaze to maintain social interaction); *SL 3* (Initiates greetings/partings); *NV 1* (Reciprocates nonverbal interactions)

5 MINUTES   CIRCLE: REVIEW SCHEDULE

Have a visual schedule of the group activities and choose one of the children to help review it.

Potential Target Skills: *JA 6* (Follows eye gaze to objects); *SR 3* (Raises hand and waits to be called before speaking); *CG 10* (Remains in place in a group until called by teacher); *CG 20* (Attends to small-group, teacher-led listening activity for at least ten minutes)

10 MINUTES   CONVERSATION CHAIN (ACTIVITY #48)

Pick a topic—choose easy topics when the group first starts and move on to more complicated ones as the group progresses. As the children get better at this, try to have them talk about their peers' likes and interests. Topics can include: what our friends like to do on the playground, our friends' favorite colors, and our friends' favorite games.

Potential Target Skills: *SP 23* (Appropriately accepts that others' likes and interests may be different from their own); *SR 17* (Avoids perseveration on a topic or question); *SL 12* (Shares information about self, family, and major events); *SL 19* (Directs body and eyes toward social partner when listening)

2 MINUTES   MYSTERY ACTIVITY

Introduce a mystery time. This can involve making a change to the schedule or playing an unplanned game that a child has brought in. Tell the children that you do not know what it is because, "It's a mystery, but that's okay."

Potential Target Skills: *SR 7* (Demonstrates flexibility when things are different than planned); *SR 15* (Asks for help during novel or challenging activities); *CG 5* (Responds to teacher by looking or coming when directly or indirectly cued)

5 MINUTES	BATHROOM

Going to the bathroom presents opportunities to work on transition and waiting skills. The line leader is given reference points where he should stop (e.g., a "landmark" every ten to twenty feet) and told that at those points, it is his job to make sure his friends are following him. Upon reaching those locations, the line leader knows to stop, turn around, and say, "Come on friends!" We always use the same stopping points on our way to the bathroom and playground so the children are eventually able to stop at a well-known point without prompting. For us, those points include the end of one hallway, the preschool office door, and just before arriving at our destination. Children who are not the line leader get into the habit of keeping an appropriate distance behind the children in front of them.

Potential Target Skills: *CG 14* (Stays in place when walking in line and maintains pace with group); *SR 9* (Responds to feedback/correction without exhibiting challenging behaviors); *SR 16* (Waits for help, for a requested item, or when directed for up to one minute without exhibiting challenging behaviors)

10 MINUTES	SHOW

Have the children pretend to tune their TVs to a channel. Tell them it is the [make up a name] show. Group leaders act out a problem currently happening in the classroom. For example, one teacher might build a block tower and another teacher will carelessly knock it down. Both teachers will role-play how children with social-skills deficits might respond to one another in that situation. Next, ask the children to pretend to use their "remotes" to pause the show and ask them what the two "characters" could have done differently. Once the group has come up with a few ideas, ask the children to rewind the show and press play to see what happens when the show is "re-scripted" according to their ideas. Repeat the show, demonstrating a better social interaction. As the children get more skilled at solving these social situations, have a child from the group be part of the show with the teacher.

Potential Target Skills: *SE 3* (Shows empathy toward others); *SE 6* (Anticipates how a peer might respond to his behavior and responds accordingly); *SL 7* (Asks concrete questions about an item or information shared by others)

10 MINUTES	SHOW AND TELL (ACTIVITY #39)

This is a great opportunity to work on Joint Attending and perspective-taking skills. Have the child hide the box behind her back and ask the other children in the group, "What do you think Ellie brought in today? What do we know about Ellie?" The group already may know a lot about Ellie, either from Friendship Books or the Conversation Chain (Activity #48). Based on that knowledge, they can ask Ellie if she brought in something pink, a picture of her sister, or a Madeline doll. As the children learn more about each other, their guesses get better, and they become more comfortable with being wrong. Children sometimes bring in games from home that we learn to play in the group. This can help children expand their own interests. During this exercise, they also learn to wait and attend while the other children comment or ask questions about the shared items.

Potential Target Skills: *JA 8* (Points to objects and makes eye contact to share interest); *SE 5* (Expresses appropriate level of enthusiasm about actions or belonging of others); *SL 14* (Makes reciprocal comments); *CG 23* (Passes items to peers)

10 MINUTES   MOVEMENT ACTIVITY

At this point, children have been sitting a long time and it's time to move around. We often have the children vote (one vote per person!) on the movement activity. Musical Chairs is a favorite, where children learn to claim a chair. Freeze Dance is also popular. To help children keep their own space, we use masking tape to create squares on the ground. Each child needs to dance within her own square. Simon Says is another great way to have the children move around in the group environment.

Potential Target Skills: *SP 7* (Takes turns as part of a structured game and sustains attention until completion of the game); *SP 16* (Accepts losing games or getting called "out"); *SR 2* (Appropriately handles denied requests); *SR 11* (Demonstrates awareness of own and other's space); *CG 6* (Imitates a peer who is leading songs/activities)

10 MINUTES   BOOK

We read a book related to the current theme (examples include recognizing and managing emotions, friendship, and calming strategies)

Potential Target Skills: *SE 2* (Gives a simple explanation of the emotional state of self and others when asked); *SL 7* (Asks concrete questions about an item or information shared by others); *SL 11* (Answers questions about ongoing activities); *CG 21* (Responds together with group to teacher or peer leading activity)

15 MINUTES   TABLE TOP ACTIVITY

At this time, we do a table top project related to the current theme of the group. If we are working on problem solving, the project might be sorting big problems from little problems and gluing them onto a piece of paper. If it is friendship, we might work on Friendship Books. These table top projects are meant to be shared with families at home. We have also created joke books and idiom books for high functioning children.

Potential Target Skills: *JA 9* (Comments on what self or others are doing); *SP 4* (Shares toys/materials); *SR 10* (Responds to mistakes made by self or others without exhibiting challenging behaviors); *SL 8* (Requests attention); *CG 12* (Follows directions during novel activities)

15 MINUTES   PLAYGROUND GAMES

We often incorporate playground games into the schedule to provide another movement time and to work on skills in that setting. Possible games include tag, Duck-Duck-Goose, and Red Light/Green Light. When it is not possible to go outside, we find a large enough space to play similar playground games. Although these "kids" games seem simple, it can be challenging for children to attend and follow the rules, and these games help develop skills of following rules, attending (e.g., knowing who is "It"), and taking turns.

Potential Target Skills: *SP 16* (Accepts losing games or getting called "out"); *SP 19* (Appropriately plays games involving a person being "It"); *CG 8* (Uses playground equipment appropriately); *NV 5* (Follows basic gestures and nonverbal cues)

Or

INDOOR GAMES

When it is not possible to go outside, there is not space for movement activities, or the children do not need another movement time, indoor games can be a fun alternative. Examples include board games or verbal games like "Who Am I?" (Activity #5) or "Guess What's Different" (Activity #2).

Potential Target Skills: *SP 7* (Takes turns as part of a structured game and sustains attention until completion of the game); *SR 15* (Asks for help during novel or challenging activities); *SL 4* (Addresses peers by name); *SL 9* (Gains listener attention appropriately)

5 MINUTES   GOODBYE

During Goodbye, we review our activities during the group. Children may share their favorite parts of the group, or we might summarize the work we did together. As with many transitions, leaving group can be a challenge for many children. Saying "goodbye," collecting things, and waiting for parents should occur in a routine way.

Potential Target Skills: *SE 5* (Expresses appropriate level of enthusiasm about the actions or belongings of others); *SL 3* (Initiates greetings/partings); *SL 15* (Shares information about immediate past or future events); *CG 10* (Remains in place in a group until called by a teacher)

Groups offer a focused and strategic way to target social skills, but it is important to remember that nearly every moment can be a teachable moment. When a child goes to get the Show and Tell box, play a quick eye contact game that requires no material. When walking to the bathroom or playground, find ways to help children know where their bodies are in relation to other children. Even when you are not collecting data, you can turn waiting or transition time into social time.

JOINT ATTENDING

	Item	General Intervention Ideas
JA 1	Orients (e.g., looks or makes a related response) when an object is presented	This skill can be worked on incidentally through a variety of interactive activities. For example, throughout interactions with the child, present him with various objects and use minimal prompting to be sure he looks at the object. Start with highly preferred items known to get the child's attention. Many activities address this skill because they require the child to look at various objects or materials presented by the teacher or another child. Activities: 8, 16, 21, 25, 33
JA 2	Repeats own behavior to maintain social interaction	This skill can easily be addressed by enthusiastically responding to a child's naturally occurring behaviors or by facilitating the occurrence of certain behaviors and enthusiastically responding when the child exhibits them. For example, physically prompt the child to clap her hands and then quickly provide excited praise. Initially, it may be necessary to pair a tangible or edible reinforcer with praise.
JA 3	Repeats action with toy to maintain social interaction	Similar to *JA 2*, this skill can easily be addressed by enthusiastically responding to a child's naturally occurring play behaviors or by facilitating the occurrence of certain play actions and enthusiastically responding when the child exhibits them. Various cause-effect toys (e.g., marble run, pop-up toys, musical toy with buttons) can be used to target this skill. Initially, it may be necessary to pair a tangible or edible reinforcer with praise.
JA 4	Uses eye gaze to maintain social interaction (i.e., looks directly at the other person's face for at least one second multiple times throughout the interaction)	To work on this skill, simply stop or interrupt ongoing activities that the child is enjoying and wait for her to make eye contact. It may be necessary to use a prompting procedure that involves gesturing for the child to make eye contact. The continuation of the activity should serve as the reinforcer. Therefore, it is important to attempt this during an activity that the child enjoys. Otherwise, it may be necessary to pair a tangible or edible reinforce with praise. Activities: 8, 11, 12, 14, 18, 21, 23 Lesson Plan: Uses Eye Gaze to Maintain a Social Interaction

Joint Attending continued on next page

JA 5	Follows point or gesture to objects	This skill can incidentally be addressed throughout the day by setting up opportunities in which a person points out pictures or objects in the environment and expects the child to look toward that object/picture. Initially, it may be necessary to work on this in a more controlled environment or to provide some additional prompting (e.g., gesture from child's eyes to the object). Initially, it may be helpful to use highly preferred reference items. Activities: 10, 31, 38–40 Lesson Plan: Follows Gesture/Eye Gaze
JA 6	Follows eye gaze to objects	Different activities can be set up in which the child has to look at and track an adult's eyes. It is probably best to start by setting up situations in which the child is taught to follow your eye gaze to find a treat or favorite toy (e.g., that is hidden under a container). It will also likely be helpful to start with items in close proximity (e.g., on table near the child) and gradually increase the distance. Activities: 8, 10, 38, 39 Lesson Plan: Follows Gesture/Eye Gaze
JA 7	Shows others objects and makes eye contact to share interest	Because the child may not inherently enjoy sharing, it may be necessary to set up situations in which the child is specifically required to bring objects to another person, and the natural social consequence is paired with an edible or tangible reinforcer. This skill can be targeted during small-group Circle Times or during structured sharing activities (e.g., have children take turns sharing objects they bring from home). One way to address this skill initially is to teach the child to complete close-ended toys (e.g., puzzles, file folder games) and then bring the completed activity to another person to share (e.g., "Look, I did the puzzle."). Activities: 30, 37, 39
JA 8	Points to objects and makes eye contact to share interest	As with JA 7, some children may not inherently enjoy sharing. Thus, it may be necessary to set up situations in which children are specifically required to point to and label objects in the environment, perhaps in a turn-taking format. For example, put a variety of objects on the table and take turns pointing to and labeling them while making eye contact. Another format would be to go for a walk and take turns pointing to and labeling things along the way. It may also be necessary initially to pair an edible or tangible reinforcer with the natural social consequence. Activities: 31, 39, 40 Lesson Plan: Joint Attending with Books

Joint Attending continued on next page

JA 9	Comments on what self or others are doing (e.g., "I am (action).")	Initially, it might be easier for the child to learn the expectation if this skill is targeted during predetermined activities (e.g., during specific Free-Play activities, such as blocks or house area). It may be helpful to use a visual support to target this skill (e.g., have a visual with a number of different actions and/or topic boards related specific activities). It may also be necessary initially to pair an edible or tangible reinforcer with the natural social consequence. Activities: 4, 31, 41, 47

SOCIAL PLAY

	Item	General Intervention Ideas
SP 1	Engages in social interactive games (e.g., Peek-a-Boo, tickling game)	For a child who exhibits little Social Play with adults, it might be necessary to start by trying to engage the child in some simple interactive play. This might include covering your face with a blanket and uncovering it excitedly, tickling a child's arms, or shaking a child's arms and then stopping. Signs that indicate that the child is engaged in the activity and wants to continue might include him making an expectant look or grabbing at the adult's hands.
SP 2	Plays parallel for five to ten minutes, close to peers with close-ended toys (e.g., puzzles, shape sorters)	Blocks of times can be set up in which children must transition within various centers that involve different close-ended activities. Another option is to teach a child to follow a picture activity schedule with a peer so that the two children are transitioning from activity to activity together. It is important that the child has the skills to play with these close-ended activities independently. Initially, individualized instruction with these close-ended toys might be required.
SP 3	Plays parallel for five to ten minutes, close to peers with open-ended toys (e.g., blocks, trucks, LEGOs)	Similar to *SP 2*, blocks of times can be set up in which children must transition within various centers that involve different open-ended activities. Another option is to teach a child to follow a picture activity schedule with a peer so that the two children are transitioning from activity to activity together. It is important that the child has the skills to play with these open-ended activities independently. Initially, individualized instruction with these open-ended activities might be required.
SP 4	Shares toys/materials (e.g., allows others to play with materials, gives materials when asked)	This skill can be targeted incidentally many times throughout the school day, especially in Free-Play situations. One easy way to work on this skill in a small-group format is to provide the children with access to some preferred toys, but have fewer toys than children so that some children will have to wait while others are playing with the toys. Initially, the children will likely need prompting to wait, ask for a turn, and to share. It might be easier to first practice waiting and sharing with an adult. For some children, it may be necessary to systematically increase the time that they share toys. Activities: 39, 41, 47 Lesson Plan: Sharing

Social Play continued on next page

SP 5	Plays cooperatively (gives and takes directions from peer) for five to ten minutes with close-ended toys (e.g., puzzles, shape sorters)	Cooperative play activities can be set up that require two children to take turns giving and following directions to complete close-ended activities. For example, two children can be given a puzzle or Mr. Potato Head and instructed to take turns telling the other person which piece to put in. For some cooperative activities, it might be helpful to have a visual of the completed product. Initially, the children will likely need assistance to provide simple directions and to follow the direction from a peer in a timely manner. Visual scripts or topic boards might be helpful (e.g., visual with all the Mr. Potato Head body parts). Lesson Plan: Cooperative Play
SP 6	Plays cooperatively (gives and takes directions from peer) for five to ten minutes with open-ended toys (e.g., blocks, trucks, LEGOs)	As with *SP 5*, cooperative play activities can be set up that require two children to take turns giving and following directions, but with more open-ended activities and manipulatives. Two children can be given a set of blocks and instructed to take turns telling the other person which block to use and where to put it. The children will likely need assistance initially to provide simple directions and to follow the direction from a peer in a timely manner. Lesson Plan: Cooperative Play
SP 7	Takes turns as part of a structured game and sustains attention until completion of the game	Simple board games are often the easiest format to use to work on this skill. It is best to start with games that do not involve a lot of pieces and that only require simple actions (e.g., Don't Break the Ice, Don't Spill the Beans). It is also often helpful when part of the game has to be passed between players to indicate whose turn it is. It is important to remember that the skill of turn taking is not to say, "My turn/Your turn," but rather to follow the game, take a turn at the appropriate time, pass the pieces, and wait when a turn is completed. Once a child is able to play a game with one other child, the number of children playing a game can be slowly increased. Also, once a child is able to play more basic turn-taking games, games that involve a verbal component (e.g., Go Fish) can be taught. Activities: 2–8, 10–12, 15–17, 28, 36, 47
SP 8	Plays outdoor games with a group until the completion of the activity (e.g., Duck-Duck-Goose, Red Rover)	Initially, it is important to teach children the rules of targeted games. The use of visual supports or modeling, including video modeling, can be helpful. To help children be successful, it is important to start with simple games that only involve two or three rules and slowly expand to more complex games. Activities: 1, 9, 10, 18, 20, 27

Social Play continued on next page

SP 9	Stops action when requested by a peer	This is a skill that must be individually targeted based on the behavior peers are asking a child to stop. Most often, this skill will need to be addressed incidentally as opportunities arise. However, if activities are identified in which a child often engages in a particular behavior that is bothersome to peers, these activities can be targeted more frequently and systematically. Use of specific visual rules, prompting procedures, and reinforcement systems will likely be helpful. Activities: 18, 27, 29, 41
SP 10	Ends structured play/game with peer appropriately	Based on the way in which other children end activities, specific targets can be identified that the child can be taught to say/do when ending an activity (e.g., "Let's play a different game." "I'm going to the block area now."). This skill can be addressed during a Choice Time or as part of a structured picture activity schedule. Staff should be sure to always model appropriately ending activities and ensure that other children also end activities appropriately. During teacher-led lessons, it may be helpful to role-play different ways to end activities.
SP 11	Takes a role in an imaginative play theme and sustains for up to three to five actions, both verbally or nonverbally (e.g., restaurant, doctor, firefighter)	This skill can be targeted when thematic play areas are available during Free-Play or as a part of a picture activity schedule. For some children, it is helpful to use visual supports to work on this skill (e.g., a topic board or scripts of different play actions within a targeted theme). It may also be helpful to teach the child to engage in this type of imaginative play with an adult first, so that the play can be more easily facilitated. Lesson Plan: Reciprocal Symbolic Play
SP 12	Trades toys/materials (e.g., participates in negotiation to swap materials during an art project)	This skill can be targeted incidentally many times throughout the day, especially in Free-Play situations. One easy way to work on this skill in a small-group format is to provide the children with access to a set of preferred toys. Have each child select a toy and give her a minute or two to play with the toy. Then have the child stop and negotiate switching toys with another child. Another option is for each child to have his own set of toys and have the children take turns swapping with each other. Initially, the children will likely need prompting to ask to trade and to actually trade toys. It might be easier to first practice this skill with an adult. Activities: 47

Social Play continued on next page

SP 13	Invites peer to play in a preferred activity	This skill can be targeted as part of transition routines (e.g., teach children that it is their responsibility at start of Free-Play to find a play partner). This skill can also be targeted as part of a picture activity schedule. One of the steps on the schedule could be for the child to take part in a particular activity with a peer (e.g., picture of peer and of blocks). The child can be taught that this requires them to approach another child and ask the child to join her in play. For some children, this may initially require much adult facilitation. Activities: 41 Lesson Plan: Inviting a Peer to Play and Joining an Ongoing Activity
SP 14	Approaches peers and appropriately joins in the ongoing activity	This skill can be worked on incidentally during any Free-Play situation. When the child enters an activity where other children are playing, he can be taught to ask to join. To structure this more, the child could follow a picture schedule to ensure that he goes to activities where other children are playing. The specific ways of joining an activity should be based on observation of how other children approach and join in activities. Lesson Plan: Inviting a Peer to Play and Joining an Ongoing Activity
SP 15	Accepts invitation to play in an activity of peer's choice	This skill can be targeted incidentally or by having peers invite a child to play. One way to structure the environment is to have two children take turns choosing an activity using a picture activity schedule. Another option is for the children to take turns being the leader. The child who is the leader is called on, picks a play area, and then asks one of his friends to join him. Activities: 41
SP 16	Accepts losing games or getting called "out"	Any games that involve winning and losing or getting called "out" can serve as contexts to work on this skill. A favorite game for most children, and thus an engaging way to work on winning and losing, is Musical Chairs. With a small group of children, this activity goes fairly fast, and all of the children have opportunities to sit out. It may be helpful to identify a variety of phrases children can say when they get called out (e.g., "Bummer!" "Oh, well.") and model and prompt these at appropriate times. Social stories about winning and losing can be helpful for some children. Activities: 9, 11, 18, 25, 27, 36, 41

Social Play continued on next page

SP 17	Remains appropriately engaged during unstructured times (e.g., moves to new activity once completes first; engages in age-appropriate play)	This skill can be worked on incidentally during Free-Play. Many children also benefit from the use of a visual schedule, at least initially, to help them structure their time. Many preschool classrooms have a system in which the children have to sign in and out of activities (e.g., put their name or picture next to the activity where they are going to play). This can also help children to learn that they have to make a choice and participate in an activity. Lesson Plan: Leisure Activity Schedule
SP 18	Follows changes in play ideas of others and ssustains the changes during open-ended play (e.g., changes in play scheme/scenario)	For many children, this can be a difficult skill to work on incidentally, so structured activities should be set up. During Free-Play that involves symbolic or dramatic play, have the children pick a card to guide them how they are going to play (e.g., pet store, doctor, restaurant). Periodically, the children are directed to pick another card that specifies either a different play scheme (e.g., shift from building a road to building a castle) or introduces a change in the ongoing play scheme (e.g., doll gets sick and has to go to the doctor). Another way to work on this skill is to introduce new materials into those currently being used (e.g., dinosaurs are added to the blocks and cars are added to the LEGOs). The child needs to effectively incorporate these materials into the ongoing play. It might be easier to first practice this skill with an adult. Activity: 28 Lesson Plan: Shifting Play Ideas
SP 19	Appropriately plays games involving a person being "It"	Any type of tag game can be an appropriate context for working on this skill. The use of visual supports or modeling, including video modeling, and social stories previewed before the start of games can be helpful. Activities: 1, 9, 18, 20, 27
SP 20	Demonstrates flexibility in following changes in the rules of a game or in accepting novel ideas from peers	This skill can be targeted by playing a familiar game but changing some rule or aspect of the game. For example, in a game of tag, keep changing the person who is "It" or change where the base is. Some children may benefit from a social story related to dealing with changes in activities. Activities: 1, 4, 5, 8–10, 16–18, 22, 28, 35, 41, 47
SP 21	Plans a play scheme with a peer and follows it through (e.g., decides to build a house out of blocks and then builds it)	This skill can be targeted during naturally occurring Free-Play times or during structured pretend play activities. It may be helpful to have a visual depicting different play themes posted in target areas. For example, in the block area, you could have a visual of things children could build (e.g., castle, city, fort, highway). You want to make it clear that the children playing in this area must jointly choose a play scheme and work on this together. Initially, a lot of adult facilitation will likely be necessary. Lesson Plan: Cooperative Pretend Play

Social Play continued on next page

SP 22	Identifies children who are their friends and can give a simple explanation why	This skill can be targeted using discussions during small-group times about how to be a good friend (e.g., share toys, play together, take turns) and what other children do to make us want to be friends with them. Initially, children might identify friends as the children sitting near them, but as they begin to better understand friendship, they will name children that are not present and explain that they are a friend because they are "nice" or because they play together. During naturally occurring opportunities, it is important to point out when a child is being a "good friend" (e.g., "Johnny, you are being such a good friend by ...."). A social story about being a "good friend" might also be helpful. Activities: 42
SP 23	Appropriately accepts that others' likes and interests may be different from their own	This skill might best be addressed through reading stories about differences and doing some simple art projects or activities that highlight children's different likes and interests. For example, have the children draw pictures of their favorite foods, toys, etc. The artwork can then be used to facilitate discussion about which children share interests and which children like different things. Have the children try red, green, and yellow apples and then share with the group which kind each child likes the most. A social story about differences can also be helpful. Activities: 13, 24, 34, 45, 48, 49
SP 24	Wins without making bragging comments/gestures	This skill can be targeted during any activity that involves winning and losing. It may be helpful to develop a social story and review it with children prior to the games. It may also be helpful to role-play ways to be a "good winner" and include visuals showing things a person can say or do when they win or lose a game. As with handling losing, Musical Chairs is an engaging way to practice being a good winner. Activities: 1, 11, 25, 41, 45

Social Play continued on next page

SELF-REGULATION

	Item	General Intervention Ideas
SR 1	Demonstrates flexibility with new tasks/activities	This skill can be addressed incidentally but will likely require more practice by setting up situations in which new tasks or activities are introduced and/or significant changes are made to familiar activities. It may be helpful to provide the child with a social story about how to handle new and unexpected situations and to then help the child refer to the social story when she encounters these situations. Similarly, it may be helpful to role-play ways to tolerate new activities or tasks. Activities: 1, 16, 28
SR 2	Appropriately handles denied requests	This can be addressed like any other coping skill by teaching the child different ways to handle being told "No." Additionally, the use of a social story and role-playing may be helpful. A visual to refer to during naturally occurring situations may also be useful (e.g., visual of how a child could respond when frustrated).

Self-Regulation continued on next page

SR 3	Raises hand and waits to be called before speaking	This can best be addressed by making "waiting to be called on" a group rule and consistently requiring that children raise their hands and wait to be called on during various turn-taking activities. It is important to reinforce when children are following this rule (e.g., by calling on them or by acknowledging and reinforcing their behavior) and to not reinforce the child when she is not raising her hand and not waiting (i.e., do not attend to the child if she is calling out). You may also need to have a plan for how to respond to a child who repeatedly has difficulty waiting and not calling out. Sometimes an individualized plan is required for a specific child (e.g., present a "quiet voice" visual, have the child take a short break from the group). This skill can be addressed during any group activity that requires taking turns or waiting to be called. Activities: 2–5, 13, 26, 30, 31, 34, 37, 39, 46
SR 4	Responds to calming strategies prompted by an adult	Calming strategies can be introduced to the entire group or class and can be practiced during group lesson times. Visual supports should also be available to remind children of strategies that they can use. It is likely that calming strategies will also need to be developed based on the specific needs of the child. Additionally, the use of a social story and role-playing may be helpful.
SR 5	Identifies when upset/frustrated and appropriately asks for a break or a calming item/activity	This extension of *SR 4* will likely require that individualized calming strategies be developed for the child. The first step is to teach the child to recognize when he is upset. The use of a social story identifying situations that are difficult for the child can be helpful. The social story should also include coping strategies that the child can use when upset. Visual supports should also be available to remind the child of strategies that he can use, and role-playing a range of coping strategies will also likely be helpful. Activities: 50
SR 6	Follows classroom expectations and demonstrates flexibility during transitions	This skill can be worked on incidentally throughout the school day. As much as possible, it is important that transitions happen in a planned/consistent manner. The use of a visual schedule is often helpful to make transitions more predictable for the child. For some children, it may also be helpful initially to build in reinforcement for making transitions successfully. Activities: 41

Self-Regulation continued on next page

SR 7	Demonstrates flexibility when things are different than planned	This can be addressed both incidentally and through contrived changes in activities or schedule, which provide more opportunities to practice being flexible. For many children, social stories about dealing with changes, along with practicing these situations, can be helpful. Visual supports should also be available to remind children of strategies to use when things are different than planned. The first step is often teaching the child to identify changes or interruptions that are hard for her, to identify how "big" of a problem it is, and then to use a strategy that helps her be flexible. It is also important to remember to provide reinforcement to the child for demonstrating flexibility. Activities: 1, 16, 21, 28, 29, 34, 41, 50
SR 8	Demonstrates flexibility when preferred activities are interrupted	This skill can be addressed incidentally as natural interruptions occur, but can also be addressed through contrived interruptions that require the child to stop the ongoing activity for brief periods or to leave the activity earlier than anticipated. For many children, social stories about dealing with interruptions, along with practicing these situations, can be helpful. The first step is often teaching the child to identify changes or interruptions that are hard for him, to identify how "big" of a problem it is, and then to use a strategy that helps him be flexible. It is also important to remember to provide reinforcement to the child for demonstrating flexibility. Activities: 41, 50
SR 9	Responds to feedback/correction without exhibiting challenging behaviors	This skill can be addressed during different group lessons in which children are asked to respond to questions for which they might provide incorrect responses or as part of games that involve making guesses. It can also be addressed during art projects or Table Top activities in which children might receive corrective feedback. It is important to always provide children with far more positive feedback for appropriate behavior rather than attention for challenging behaviors. This is also a skill for which many children benefit from the use of social stories and role-play practice. Activities: 2–5, 7, 26, 31, 49
SR 10	Responds to mistakes made by self or others without exhibiting challenging behaviors	This skill can be addressed in activities and situations similar to those described for *SR 9*, or in any activity in which the child might make mistakes (e.g., art projects, answering questions). This is also a skill in which many children benefit from the use of social stories and role-play practice. Visual supports should also be available to remind children of strategies to use when they, or others, make mistakes. In providing reinforcement, it is important to remember to reinforce the child for appropriately responding when mistakes are made, but to limit attention provided to redirect challenging behaviors. Activities: 2–5, 7, 26, 31

Self-Regulation continued on next page

SR 11	Demonstrates awareness of own and other's space (e.g., not stepping on other's feet when walking in line, not crowding a person during Circle Time, keeping an arm's distance when interacting with others)	This skill can be practiced by walking in a line or by exercises that require navigating a busy environment without bumping into other people (e.g., Obstacle Course). During these lessons, you can periodically remind the children to freeze and reinforce those children who show that they are respecting other people's space. This skill should also be worked on incidentally so that children can be given feedback when they do or do not respect other people's space. Activities: 1, 8, 9, 20, 29, 32
SR 12	Modifies behavior in response to feedback	This skill can be targeted incidentally by providing children with feedback, modeling for them how to fix their behavior, and reinforcing them when they are able to modify their behavior. For situations that are consistently challenging for a child (e.g., sitting correctly in a group activity), it may be helpful to use social stories or role-playing. In some situations, it may also be necessary to establish specific behavior guidelines. It is important that the teaching staff do not get into the habit of over-cueing a child to fix her behavior and remember to provide positive reinforcement when a child responds appropriately to feedback. Activities: 48–50
SR 13	Uses appropriate words and voice tone to turn down requests from others	Setting up situations in which peers make requests of the child, such as during Free-Play, can target this skill. Initially, much facilitation will likely be required for the child to appropriately accept or refuse these requests, including modeling appropriate words and voice tone. It may be helpful to role-play a variety of ways to appropriately refuse requests. Although you want the child to learn to appropriately turn down requests from others, it is important that the child's responses are monitored closely so that the child is not always refusing requests. It is even more important that the child learns to accept and expand on requests from others.
SR 14	Advocates for oneself (e.g., "I didn't get one." "I can't see." "Please move." "Stop.") without exhibiting challenging behaviors (e.g., bullying, teasing, aggression)	This skill can be addressed incidentally, but you will probably need to set up situations so that children have sufficient practice. For example, an adult can invade a child's space, block his view, etc. Teaching children how to respond to situations involving bullying, teasing, or aggression will likely require role-playing, and many children with social-skills deficits have a difficult time recognizing when they are being bullied or teased. Social stories or visual supports that clearly depict situations in which children may need to advocate for themselves, as well as appropriate ways in which they can do so, are very helpful for many children. Lesson Plan: Advocating for Oneself

Self-Regulation continued on next page

SR 15	Asks for help during novel or challenging activities	This skill can be addressed incidentally as situations arise. Situations can also be set up in which the child is given tasks for which she will need help or for which routines are changed in some way. More complex games and activities, such as games that require memorization of information or involve guessing, are also opportunities to practice asking for assistance from peers. For example, children can ask for more information or a clue. Activities: 2, 4, 5, 9, 17, 31
SR 16	Waits for help, for a requested item, or when directed to do so for up to one minute without exhibiting challenging behaviors	For many children, you will need to systematically target this skill, beginning slowly and gradually increasing the amount of time they have to wait. It is also important to ensure that this skill generalizes across situations. You'll want to identify the specific situations in which children have difficulty, as well as how long a child can currently wait in these situations. These situations can then be contrived so that adults have control over how long a child has to wait. For example, if a child asks for a preferred toy, acknowledge them but let them know that they need to wait. Start by only having the child wait for five or ten seconds, but then systematically increase this as she shows that she can wait without exhibiting challenging behaviors. Activities: 44 Lesson Plan: Waiting
SR 17	Avoids perseveration on a topic or question	Some children need to have clear guidelines in terms of when certain topics are appropriate (e.g., specific times of day) or how often certain topics are appropriate (e.g., specific number of times per day). Interventions in this area will likely need to be very individualized and based on a thorough assessment of the function of the perseverative behavior. Visual supports can be very useful to remind the child when it is ok or not ok to talk about certain topics. It is important to remember that children should first be able to respond to an adult redirecting preferred topics or questions before they can be expected to do this on their own. It may also be necessary to focus on teaching the child to talk about a wider variety of topics. Activities: 15, 30, 37, 39, 41, 48, 49
SR 18	Uses conversational voice level and tone when speaking	Some children need to learn to discriminate voice volume and tone by practicing talking in a quiet voice versus a loud voice or with different voice tones. Specific language related to the appropriate volume and tone should be taught (e.g., "Use an inside voice." "Use a number one voice.") and then used in more natural situations when voice level is an issue. In addition, practice using different voice levels can be built into a variety of activities (e.g., sing the same song at different volumes or with different tones). Activities: 8, 48–50

Self-Regulation continued on next page

SOCIAL/EMOTIONAL

	Item	General Intervention Ideas
SE 1	Recognizes emotions in others and self (e.g., happy, sad)	This skill should be worked on incidentally as situations arise by labeling emotions exhibited by others and teaching children to label these emotions as well. Pictures depicting emotions can also be used to teach this skill. Through role-playing or as part of a game, children can also demonstrate what different emotions look like and identify emotions when others demonstrate them. Activities: 4, 5, 34, 43 Lesson Plan: Identifying Emotions
SE 2	Gives a simple explanation for the emotional state of self and others (e.g., happy, sad) when asked	This skill can be worked on incidentally by labeling emotions exhibited by others, explaining why people are showing these emotions, and teaching children to label and identify the causes of emotions. However, teachers might also provide verbal descriptions of scenarios in which a person is demonstrating a particular emotion. Through role-playing or as part of games, children can practice identifying both the emotions expressed and the reasons why (e.g., "Mary is sad because she wanted to go to the playground but it is raining outside."). Activities: 4, 5, 34, 43 Lesson Plan: Identifying of Causes of Emotions
SE 3	Shows empathy toward others (e.g., says, "Are you Ok?" to peer who falls on playground, hugs a peer who is crying)	This skill will also likely need to be addressed by providing verbal descriptions of situations, possibly with visual supports. Next, the child can practice identifying the emotion, the cause, and the appropriate response-and then practice performing that response. Another way to teach this skill is to give a child the responsibility of being a caretaker. For example, at home, the child can be given some responsibility for caring for a pet (e.g., giving the pet food or water). If the child has a younger sibling, they can help a parent feed his younger brother or sister. In the school setting, older children can help the younger children get ready to go outside, open lunch boxes, and retrieve items. It is important to remember to reinforce when children demonstrate empathy and to point out when other people respond empathically (e.g., use the "Bucket Filling" analogy and have the children add objects to their buckets when they make empathetic responses). Activities: 4, 34, 43, 48, 49

Social/Emotional continued on next page

SE 4	Expresses negative emotions without exhibiting challenging behaviors	This skill can be addressed incidentally as situations arise, but most children will require extra practice in contrived situations. The first step is to teach the child to recognize when he is upset. The use of a social story that talks about situations known to trigger negative emotions and corresponding challenging behaviors can be helpful. The social story should also include alternate and appropriate ways for the child to express his feelings. Visual supports should also be available to remind the child of strategies that he can use. Role-playing appropriate ways to express negative emotions will also likely be helpful. For some children, it may be necessary to complete a more comprehensive assessment and develop an individualized intervention plan.
SE 5	Expresses appropriate level of enthusiasm about the actions or belongings of others	During naturally occurring situations, children can be provided with prompts and modeling to help them respond appropriately to the positive behaviors or good fortune of other children (e.g., congratulating a peer for winning a game, thanking a peer for sharing with them). In a more structured way, children can take turns showing their artwork or sharing a toy during small-group activities. Each child should have the opportunity to make a comment about another child's artwork or shared toy (e.g., "I like that you colored the dog brown." "That is a cool toy."). The child sharing should also be taught to say, "Thank you," to each compliment. This skill can also be practiced through role-playing scenarios in which it is appropriate for a child to respond to the positive actions of others. Many children will also benefit from having a visual of a variety of comments that they can make. It is important to focus on not only the words provided to express enthusiasm, but the level of affect paired with the words. Activities: 14, 39
SE 6	Anticipates how a peer might respond to his behavior (e.g., knocking down a tower might make a peer mad, helping a peer might make her happy) and responds accordingly	During naturally occurring situations, children can be provided with prompts and modeling to help them anticipate responses to their actions and responding accordingly. However, for most children, it will be necessary to identify those situations in which they have difficulty with this skill. These situations can then be contrived so that children have more practice. For example, if a child frequently has difficulty refraining from grabbing materials being used by peers, activities can be set up in which the child can practice asking first. Role-playing situations known to be challenging for a child can also provide additional practice. Use of a visual support that identifies scenarios (e.g., peer dropping a box of crayons on the floor), possible responses by the child (e.g., help peer pick up crayons, walk away from the peer), and how these different responses may make the peer respond (e.g., peer will smile and be happy if child helps, peer may be sad and not want to play with the child later if the child walks away). This visual can then be used during role-play situations, as well as during naturally occurring situations. Activities: 43

Social/Emotional continued on next page

SOCIAL LANGUAGE

	Item	General Intervention Ideas
SL 1	Responds to greetings/ partings	This skill can be addressed incidentally many times throughout the day, ensuring that the child always responds to initiations from others. For some children, this may also require a systematic prompting hierarchy and/or providing external reinforcement. This skill can also be worked on in a more structured way during Circle Time songs and activities that require the children to greet one another. Activities: 8, 21, 41 Lesson Plan: Respond to Greetings
SL 2	Follows directions involving named adults or peers	This skill can be addressed incidentally throughout the day (e.g., provide directions to pass or deliver materials to specific peers), but activities can also be set up that require the child to follow a direction to engage in an interaction with a specific child (e.g., sit in a circle and have children roll a ball to one another following the teacher's directions, such as "Pass the ball to Timmy."). Activities: 8, 47 Lesson Plan: Receptive Identification of Familiar People
SL 3	Initiates greetings/partings	This skill can be addressed throughout the day as children enter and leave activities or settings. To ensure that children have multiple opportunities during Free-Play times, this skill can also be addressed by having a child follow an activity schedule that involves her transitioning to various activities in the room. Each time she enters or leaves an activity, the child can be required to initiate an appropriate greeting/parting. For more practice, during group times, you can also have the child who is the group leader initiate a greeting with each of the other children. A visual to remind the child to initiate greetings/partings when joining and leaving activities, as well as a formal reinforcement system (e.g., earning tokens for greeting friends), can also be helpful for some children. For children to become independent with this skill, it is important that the expectation be that a child always initiates greetings when joining and leaving activities. Activities: 8, 21, 41
SL 4	Addresses peers by name	This skill can be addressed as an extension of initiating greetings by requiring that the child also use the other person's name. Practicing this skill can also be built into a variety of activities, such as having a child call on other children during a guessing game or call a peer's name to ask them to "unfreeze" them during Freeze Tag. Initially, many children will need verbal or visual models of how to respond during targeted activities. Activities: 2–5, 7–9, 18, 19, 23, 26, 27, 31, 32, 36, 39, 45–47

Social Language continued on next page

SL 5	Answers social questions (e.g., name, age, family names, pet names)	This is skill is often initially taught in a structured teaching format with an adult. However, you can also teach this skill in an activity-based setting from the start (e.g., during a greeting activity that involves rolling a ball to each child, also ask each child a social question) or after the child works on it in a one-on-one situation with an adult. Providing verbal or visual models of how to respond during targeted activities will likely be necessary initially for many children. Activities: 8, 13, 23, 30, 37, 39, 45, 48, 49 Lesson Plan: Social Questions
SL 6	Asks social questions (e.g., name, age, family names, pet names)	This is an extension of *SL 5* and requires that the child begin to initiate social questions. One of the easiest ways to work on this skill is through activities in which the child must take turns asking other children questions. Providing verbal or visual models of how to respond during targeted activities will likely be necessary initially for many children. For example, the children can take turns picking cards from a deck, with each card specifying a social question to ask. Early on, the cards can be more detailed in what to ask (e.g., "What is your favorite food?"), and shift to general topics as children become familiar with the exercise (e.g., "Food"). Activities: 8, 13, 23, 30, 37, 39, 45, 48, 49 Lesson Plan: Reciprocal Social Questions
SL 7	Asks concrete questions about an item or information shared by others (e.g., name of object, location of object, who has something)	Many activities offer children the opportunity to share things or information (e.g., favorite toy, artwork, what they did on vacation or during a holiday) and for other children to take turns asking questions about what is being shared. For some children, this skill may need to be taught systematically first with an adult by setting up specific practice situations in which the child has to ask for information. Visual supports, such as a pictorial list of different questions, can be very helpful. Activities: 2, 4, 5, 13, 15, 26, 30, 31, 37, 39, 41, 46, 48, 49
SL 8	Requests attention (e.g., "Look at what I made." "Watch how far I can jump.")	Initially, this skill is best introduced by teaching the child to ask for attention after completing specific concrete, close-ended tasks (e.g., completing a puzzle). The completion of the activity is the cue for the child to ask for attention. Gradually, instruction needs to shift to more intermittent or natural situations. Prompts to request attention may need to be built into picture activity schedules or token systems (e.g., when child requests attention five times and get five tokens, they can earn a favorite toy or activity). Visual supports can also help provide different examples of what a child can say to request attention. Lesson Plan: Requesting Attention

Social Language continued on next page

SL 9	Gains listener attention appropriately (e.g., calls name, taps shoulder)	This skill can initially be addressed by making this a part of the behavioral expectation for making requests (i.e., require child to tap listener or call the listener's name before making a request). This skill can also be taught through a variety of activities in which a child must get a peer's attention to initiate an interaction (e.g., call on person to make a guess during Charades or 20 Questions). As with many skills where the natural consequence may be social attention, it may initially be necessary to provide additional reinforcement. Activities: 2–5, 9, 13, 23, 26, 31, 32, 37, 39, 45, 47, 48
SL 10	Responds to initiations from others	Initially, it is easiest to focus on the child providing nonverbal responses (e.g., passing materials, taking an item from peer) and then work toward verbal responses (e.g., answering a question or reply to a comment). There are many simple interactions that can be set up with peers throughout the day that require the child to respond to initiations (e.g., passing materials during art activities, responding to social questions). Activities: 5, 7–9, 18, 23, 24, 26, 29–32, 35, 37, 39, 41, 45, 46, 48, 49
SL 11	Answers questions about ongoing activities	This skill can be addressed during any daily activity by briefly stopping the activity and asking the child concrete questions about what is going on around him. For example, during a board game, the adult can stop and ask the child something such as, "What color is your game piece?" or "Who is ahead right now?" Some children will need to have this skill systematically taught with specific prompting and reinforcement procedures. Activities: 24, 30, 37, 39 Lesson Plan: Answers Questions about Present, Past, and Future
SL 12	Shares information about self, family, and major events (e.g., school day, holidays, family events)	In general, it is best to start with more specific questions (e.g., "Who did you play with at recess?") and then move toward more general questions (e.g., "What did you do over the weekend?"). It is also helpful to identify a list of questions and/or a variety of topics related to the child, his family, and family events. You can then systematically teach these questions/topics, with specific prompting and reinforcement procedures as needed. The use of visual supports can also be helpful, including photos of the activities sent in by parents and topic boards related to holidays, special events, or general family information (e.g., siblings, pets). Activities: 13, 15, 19, 30, 37, 45, 48, 49 Lesson Plan: Answers Questions about Self, Family, and Major Events

Social Language continued on next page

SL 13	Answers more than five questions on a preferred topic	For most children, it is helpful to identify a variety of preferred topics and to target a list of questions relevant to each. Visuals can help facilitate language on a preferred topic. A topic board or photographs of a preferred subject are often enough to prompt a meaningful exchange. Activities: 26, 30, 37, 39, 45, 48
SL 14	Makes reciprocal comments (e.g., child responds to peer: "I like that movie too!" "I don't have (that), I have (this).")	In teaching this skill, the typical progression is from a child answering a question to a child responding to a comment. Additionally, once a child can respond to a question with a comment, the expectation is to next ask them to respond with a follow-up question (e.g., "I like that movie too. Did you like the part where they went to the circus?"). Most children need to have this skill systematically taught with specific prompting and reinforcement procedures. Activities: 13, 15, 30, 37, 39, 41, 45, 48, 49
SL 15	Shares information about immediate past or future events	As a prerequisite, the child must be able to talk about events in the immediate environment and answer basic "wh" questions. In general, it is best to start with specific questions (e.g., "Who did you play with at recess?") and then move toward more general, open-ended questions (e.g., "What did you do over the weekend?"). Ideally, you should start by asking questions about activities that have just occurred and then systematically increase the length of time between the end of the event or activity and the time when you ask the child questions about it. After a child has mastered sharing information about past events, you can target questions about future events. Again, it is best to start with events that are about to happen immediately and then systematically increase the length of time between when you ask the questions and when the event will occur. The use of visual supports can also be helpful, including photos of the activities sent in by parents, visual representations of types of activities or aspects of activities, and topic boards. Activities: 23, 30, 37, 48 Lesson Plan: Answering Questions about Present, Past, and Future

Social Language continued on next page

SL 16	Answers questions, asks questions, or makes comments to maintain conversation for three to four exchanges	Before being able to maintain conversations, the child must demonstrate a number of prerequisite skills, including being able to answer basic "wh" questions, make reciprocal comments, and answer a variety of questions on a topic. Most children will need to have this skill systematically taught with specific prompting and reinforcement procedures, as well as with the use of visuals (e.g., topic boards, scripts). Starting with conversational exchanges in a very structured, game-like format can be very helpful. For example, you might have children pick a topic card and talk about that topic for a certain number of exchanges. Activities: 13, 15, 41, 48, 49 Lesson Plan: Answers Questions about Self, Family, and Major Events
SL 17	Responds appropriately when a peer changes topic	Because some children may not be aware when there is a change in topic, it is best to have children first practice this skill with an adult who provides corrective feedback and reinforcement. It also may be helpful to have children read a social story, especially if part of the difficulty is that the child only wants to talk about one or two specific topics. Activities: 13, 15, 48, 49
SL 18	Directs body and eyes toward social partner when speaking	This skill will often be addressed simultaneously with other skills, such as responding to initiations or requesting attention. You can target this skill along with the verbal component or after the verbal component is mastered. A social story can be helpful for some children. It is also important to remember that, although a child may require some corrective feedback, she will also need reinforcement for appropriately orienting toward the listener when she is speaking. Activities: 2–5, 8, 13, 15, 23, 26, 30, 31, 34, 37, 41, 45, 47–49
SL 19	Directs body and eyes toward social partner when listening	Initially, it will be easier to practice this skill when children are listening to an adult, because the adult can pause and wait for children to listen during an interaction. It is best to start by talking about topics that are of high interest to the children. It is also important to remember that, although children may require some corrective feedback, they will also need reinforcement for appropriately orienting toward the speaker. Outlining the expectations for "good listening" in a social story or through visual rules can be helpful. Generally speaking, adults should always ensure that a child's body and eyes are oriented toward them when they speak to the child. Activities: 2, 4, 5, 8, 11, 13, 15, 23, 26, 30, 31, 34, 37, 41, 45, 47–49

Social Language continued on next page

SL 20	Speaks using polite phrases (e.g., "Please," "Thank you," "Sorry," "Excuse me," "You're welcome")	Teaching children to use polite phrases generally happens through modeling and ensuring that children use these phrases during naturally occurring situations. However, many children will need to be taught precisely when they should use each phrase (e.g., to say, "Thank you," when someone gives them something or when someone gives a compliment). For this reason, it may be necessary to target specific polite phrases and set up opportunities for the child to need to use them.
SL 21	Accepts people who are different (e.g., does not make negative comments)	Accepting differences is something that can most easily be addressed through small-group activities in which children identify things that are the same and different about people. Commercial books that talk about differences are often helpful (e.g., Todd Parr's *The Family Book* or *It's Okay to Be Different*). It may also be helpful to discuss and role-play ways that a child can be welcoming to a person who is different (e.g., asking the person to play with them, giving the person a compliment). In terms of determining whether this skill is actually generalized to real situations, adults should closely monitor and provide either corrective feedback or reinforcement when naturally occurring opportunities arise. For the adult, providing corrective feedback can be tricky because you want to provide constructive feedback that acknowledges differences without implying that difference itself is "bad." For example, it can leave a child with the impression that a child in a wheelchair is "bad" when an adult says something like "Don't ever say that!"
SL 22	Seeks to repair or clarify breakdowns in social interactions	For some children, it is necessary to identify examples of breakdowns in social interactions and teach them specific ways to repair them (e.g., ask, "Can you say that again?" when they did not understand or hear what the other person said; "I don't like that. Please stop." when the other person is invading their personal space). Opportunities to practice this can be built into a variety of activities that involve giving and taking directions from one another (e.g., Scavenger Hunt, 20 Questions, I Spy). Activities: 2, 5, 15, 30, 34, 37, 39, 45, 48 Lesson Plan: Advocating for Oneself
SL 23	Converses on age-appropriate topics (i.e., talks about topics similar and of interest to peers)	For many children, it will be necessary to identify topics commonly of interest to other children their age and to provide more information on these topics to the target children. Start by identifying a list of topics and corresponding facts for each. Children can first be taught to answer a variety of questions related to a given topic and then to stay on that topic for up to four exchanges. Many children will also need to have this skill systematically taught with specific prompting and reinforcement procedures, as well as with the use of visuals (e.g., topic boards, scripts). It may also be helpful to start by working on conversational exchanges in a very structured, game-like format, such as having children pick a topic card and talk about that topic for a certain number of exchanges. Activities: 13, 23, 30, 48, 49

Social Language continued on next page

SL 24	Uses contextually appropriate language/introduces topic	Once a child is able to maintain at least several conversational exchanges on a topic, he may need to be taught to appropriately introduce topics, to stay on topic, and to introduce when a topic is being changed. Discussion and role-play are good for this. Many children find it helpful to be given specific lead-in phrases to introduce or transition a topic of conversation (e.g., "I want to tell you about …"). A social story or visual support with set transition phrases can be useful in teaching this skill. Activities: 13, 30, 37, 39, 41, 45, 48, 49

CLASSROOM/GROUP BEHAVIOR

	Item	General Intervention Ideas
CG 1	Follows schedule and classroom rules (including playground rules)	This skill should be worked on incidentally in a classroom or group setting by regularly reviewing the classroom rules and ensuring that the children follow them. Rules should be simple and concrete. It can be helpful to have the children practice showing how to follow the rules. In some group situations, it may be necessary to build in formal reinforcement systems (e.g., periodically providing a token when the child follows a rule). When children are not following the rules, clear procedures should be in place for how teachers should respond (e.g., reinforce children who are following the rules or remind the children what they need to do to earn tokens).
CG 2	Follows verbal directions as part of classroom routines or activities (e.g., get materials, put away lunch)	This skill can be addressed through any routine activities, including lunch, Circle Time, or art projects. For many children, it is helpful to start by targeting specific directions that occur during one or two routine activities. Additionally, it can be helpful to begin with simple one-step directions (e.g., "Get the scissors.") and then systematically expand to complex or multi-step directions (e.g., "Get your blue folder and a pencil and go to the round table."). It is important to remember that some children will initially require external reinforcement when an activity itself is not inherently reinforcing. Lesson Plan: Follow Classroom Instructions
CG 3	Recognizes belongings of own, others, and group	This skill can be addressed by verbally labeling who "owns" what (e.g., things that go into child's cubby belong to her, things that are on the teacher's desk belong to the teacher, books in the library area belong to the group). This skill can also be addressed during activities that require sharing. For example, children can bring in items to share. The children sit together at a table, with each child having control over their items. The children can take turns requesting a turn with different peers' toys. You can also use classroom items, and the teacher can have control over these. Activities: 46
CG 4	Keeps toys/materials in designated locations	This skill can be addressed as part of any activity that requires the use of materials (e.g., Free-Play time, art projects). It is important that the adults are clear and consistent in their expectation that children put away supplies and toys in designated areas for children to learn this skill. The more organized the classroom is, the easier it is for children to learn this skill. Initially, some children may require external reinforcement or the use of a first-then visual (e.g., "first" clean up, "then" snack).

Classroom/Group Behavior continued on next page

CG 5	Responds to teacher by looking or coming when directly or indirectly cued	This skill can be addressed many times throughout the day by calling the child's name while she is engaged in various activities. Some children may need to systematically be taught to respond to their names, either by increasing the distance of the child from the adult or by decreasing the amount of prompting. Because some children may not be motivated to respond to the teacher, planned reinforcement may also need to be used to increase responding. It is important that adults do not to overuse a child's name or do not call a child's name and then not follow-through with the expectation to attend. Lesson Plan: Respond to Name
CG 6	Imitates a peer who is leading songs/activities (e.g., Simon Says)	This skill can be addressed during group times when one of the children, rather than an adult, is leading an activity. Some children will need to have this skill systematically taught with specific prompting and reinforcement procedures. Other children will also need to first be taught with an adult and then in a one-on-one situation with a peer before it can be generalized to a group situation. Activities: 11, 22 Lesson Plan: Gross-Motor Imitation from a Peer
CG 7	Responds to indirect cueing (e.g., "Where are your friends?" when child needs to line up)	Throughout a variety of activities and routines, opportunities can be set up to teach children to respond to indirect cues. Most indirect cues require a child to observe and imitate what other children are doing or to attend to particular aspects of the environment. Thus, as a prerequisite, children must be able to imitate other children and to respond to a variety of specific and concrete directions. For many children, it will be necessary to target specific indirect cues and teach children to respond to these (e.g., "Where are you friends?" "What is missing?" "What do you need to finish?"). Similarly, it might also be helpful to target specific activities or routines (e.g., transitions, art projects). For this approach to be effective, children must be motivated to complete the targeted activity or additional reinforcement must be provided. Initially, it may be helpful to provide a visual specifying the necessary materials or a model of the completed activity.
CG 8	Uses playground equipment appropriately	Some children need to be provided with systematic guidance in how to use different playground equipment. For these children, other specialists should be involved to provide input around any motor or sensory issues that might be impacting the children's ability to use playground equipment successfully. Others might know how to use playground equipment but instead spend their time engaged in repetitive or solitary activities. For many of these children, the use of visual schedules to help them access different areas of the playground can be very helpful. For example, a picture schedule of different equipment can be provided, with the final activity being one that is highly preferred by the child.

Classroom/Group Behavior continued on next page

CG 9	Helps others, both spontaneously and when asked	This skill can be addressed incidentally or by setting up situations in which other children ask the target child for help. Many cooperative activities in which children have to work together (e.g., building a structure together with blocks) can occur naturally or may be set up. It can be helpful to work with the children to identify specific situations where a friend might need help (e.g., when someone falls down, when someone cannot open a container, when someone is crying). These situations can then be addressed during small group lessons with the use of role-playing. Some children may also benefit initially from the use of a reinforcement system. Activities: 2, 4, 5, 9, 17, 31, 40, 45, 46
CG 10	Remains in place in a group until called by teacher (e.g., staying in seat until called to line up)	Remaining in place in a group until called can be worked on many times throughout the day as part of transitions within or from different group activities. Children can be called to line up or to make a choice by name, by some attribute (e.g., gender, color of clothing), or by whether they are showing "ready" behavior. It is important to reinforce when children are waiting to be called by the teacher and to not unintentionally reinforce the child when he transitions or leaves his place in the group without adult permission. For example, if a child gets in line before he is called, be sure that he is required to go back to the group, show that he is ready, and then transition when called. Having a visual of the rules for children to refer to can also be helpful. For some children, it may be necessary initially to use some additional external reinforcement. Activities: 10, 14, 18, 19, 27, 29, 32, 35
CG 11	Prepares for activity by locating area/materials (e.g., chair, coat)	This skill can be addressed through a variety of naturally occurring activities throughout the day, such as art projects or Center Time lessons. However, for some children, it may be necessary initially to target specific activities and use visual task analyses to help them know what materials they need for specific activities. For example, when told that it is time for snack, the child could be shown a visual task analysis to get lunch box, get placemat, and sit at the green table.
CG 12	Follows directions during novel activities	As a prerequisite, children should be taught to follow a variety of routine directions that are a part of daily or common activities. This skill can then be generalized by introducing new activities or by modifying activities with novel directions. For some children, it may be helpful to target specific novel activities and to systematically introduce new directions within these activities. Initially, some children may also require systematic prompting and/or external reinforcement.

Classroom/Group Behavior continued on next page

CG 13	Gives directions during novel activities	As a prerequisite, children should be taught to give directions during more familiar or routine activities. This skill can then be addressed during new activities that require children to give directions to one another or as part of familiar activities that are modified to include novel directions. It will likely be helpful to target specific activities that involve very specific directions. Some children may initially require systematic prompting and/or external reinforcement.
CG 14	Stays in place when walking in line and maintains pace with group	This skill can be worked on incidentally by ensuring that children always walk at the same pace as the other children in line and maintain a set distance. It can also be helpful to practice this skill by going for walks and periodically stopping and reinforcing those children who are walking in pace with others. Activities: 29, 40
CG 15	Repeats words/actions from a song, book, or play activity	For children who are not actively participating in songs or activities, it will be necessary to either pre-teach some of these words or actions and/or to provide reinforcement for active participation. The use of visuals can also be helpful. For example, for Five Little Monkeys Jumping on the Bed, have laminated pictures of monkeys Velcro-ed on a bed that the child can take off as the group sings. Activities: 1, 6, 8, 11, 17, 22, 25, 32, 33
CG 16	Accepts that some peers may follow different rules or schedules	Different children require different rules. Some may need more breaks, while some may receive different types of reinforcement and so on. As much as possible, the teaching staff should work to minimize the appearance of these differences. It may be helpful to incorporate this into a lesson on differences. A variety of commercially available books about differences can be used, modified, or serve as a starting point for activities about differences. In-class exercises might include an art project where all children have the same assignment, but some children must use markers, some must use crayons, and others must use paint. It can also be helpful if all members of the teaching staff have a consistent and set response for a child who asks why another child has different materials, rules, or schedule.
CG 17	Asks permission to use another's possessions	This skill can be addressed incidentally as opportunities arise. However, this skill can also be addressed by setting up activities in which children bring in items to share. A specific time can be set aside for children to play with their toys at a table or area together. The children can then take turns asking permission to use other children's toys. Similarly, during art activities, Play-Doh center, or any activity that involves different materials, each child can be put in charge of a specific supply, and the other children have to ask before using any of that material. For example, during an art activity, one child could be in charge of markers, another could be in charge of scissors, and a third could be in charge of glue.

Classroom/Group Behavior continued on next page

CG 18	Attends to small-group, teacher-led, hands-on activity for at least ten minutes	This skill can be worked on incidentally during a variety of hands-on activities (e.g., art projects, simple worksheets). For some children, it is necessary to systematically increase the amount of time that they are expected to attend during teacher-directed activities. Children need to be successful, so it is better to start by having a child participate in teacher-directed activities for only as long as she can do so appropriately, and then slowly increase the amount of time. It is important that a child does not end a teacher-directed activity by exhibiting off-task behavior, but rather by exhibiting a positive behavior (e.g., asking to leave, successfully completing an activity). Use of a systematic reinforcement plan for attending and participating during teacher-led activities can also be helpful for many children. Activities: 33, 42–44
CG 19	Sits quietly in circle for at least ten minutes	This skill can be worked on incidentally during the daily Circle Time that is common in most preschool classrooms. For some children, it will be necessary to systematically increase the amount of time that children are expected to attend during Circle Time. Children need to be successful, so it is better to start by having a child participate in these activities for only as long as he can do so appropriately, and then slowly increase the amount of time. It is important that a child does not end a Circle Time by exhibiting off-task behavior, but rather by exhibiting a positive behavior (e.g., asking to leave, successfully completing an activity). Use of a systematic reinforcement plan for sitting quietly can also be helpful for many children.
CG 20	Attends to small-group, teacher-led listening activity for at least ten minutes	This skill can be worked on incidentally during any small-group listening activity. For some children, it will be necessary to systematically increase the amount of time that children are expected to attend during listening activities. Children need to be successful, so it is better to start by having a child participate in these activities for only as long as she can do so appropriately, and then slowly increase the amount of time. It is important that a child does not end a listening activity by exhibiting off-task behavior, but rather by exhibiting a positive behavior (e.g., answering a question correctly). Use of a systematic reinforcement plan for attending and participating during teacher-led activities can also be helpful for many children. Activities: 13, 15, 24, 26, 30, 33, 34, 37, 39, 44
CG 21	Responds together with group to teacher or peer leading activity	This skill can be taught during activities in which children are instructed to call out the response to a question together or "fill in the blank." For example, the teacher could read a familiar story or recite a poem and stop at certain parts to have the children fill in the next word or phrase. For some children, it may be necessary to first practice responding to specific questions, directions, or pauses one-on-one with the teacher and then generalize to a group environment. Use of a systematic reinforcement plan for responding along with peers can also be helpful for some children. Activities: 4, 11, 16, 22, 25, 32–34, 46

Classroom/Group Behavior continued on next page

CG 22	Follows basic two- to three-step verbal directions in a group	Many activities require children to follow multiple-step directions. This skill can be targeted many times throughout the day. Some children need to start in a direct instruction format and then generalize into naturally occurring situations. Even within more natural situations, it might be necessary to systematically increase the complexity of directions, starting with one-step directions, then two-step directions, and finally targeting three-step directions. For some children, it might also be necessary to target a few specific activities and a set of directions within each activity. Systematic prompting and/or external reinforcement procedures may also be helpful for some children. Activities: 11, 47 Lesson Plan: Follow Classroom Instructions
CG 23	Passes items to peers (e.g., passing out materials, taking turns looking at a shared object and passing to next person)	This skill can be addressed by giving a child the assignment to pass out materials to peers (e.g., paper and crayons during art projects, napkins during snack) Passing materials can also occur during a group activity in which the children take turns looking at something and then pass it to the child next to him. It is important that children be expected to make eye contact with other children when passing materials and to use other children's names or catch their attention in appropriate ways. Systematic prompting and reinforcement procedures may also be helpful for some children. Some children may also benefit from a visual of what is expected (e.g., get crayons, ask each peer what color they want, give them the color they request). Activities: 8, 25, 39, 47

Classroom/Group Behavior continued on next page

NONVERBAL SOCIAL LANGUAGE

	Item	General Intervention Ideas
NV 1	Reciprocates nonverbal interactions (e.g., high five, wave, thumbs-up, fist bump, smile)	This skill can be built into a variety of interactive games in which the child is required to respond to a nonverbal direction from another person. It is important that the child is always expected to respond to social initiations from others. Initially, some children may require systematic prompting and/or external reinforcement. Additionally, some children may need to have only one or two nonverbal interactions targeted at a time. Activities: 22, 35
NV 2	Initiates nonverbal interactions (e.g., high five, wave, thumbs-up, fist bump, smile) with appropriate adults and peers	As with NV 2, this skill can be built into a variety of interactive games. For example, children can take turns picking a card that shows a specific nonverbal interaction, asks them to approach a peer, and instructs them to engage in this action. Initially, some children may require systematic prompting and/or external reinforcement. Additionally, some children may need to have only one or two nonverbal interactions targeted at a time. Activities: 22, 29, 35

Nonverbal Social Language continued on next page

NV 3	Identifies basic actions without words (e.g., Charades)	This skill can be addressed during a variety of Charades-like games that require children to take turns acting out something while the other children take turns guessing what that person is doing. As children learn to identify more basic targets (e.g., animals, simple actions), you can begin to introduce more complex or abstract targets (e.g., emotions, social interactions). Visual supports can be useful for the child who is acting things out, as well as the children trying to guess what that child is acting. Activities: 4
NV 4	Demonstrates an appropriate level of affection based on history, relationship, and familiarity with the person (e.g., hugs parent, gives high five to friend, does not initiate with unfamiliar person)	This skill can be addressed incidentally when opportunities arise, but children often require more direct instruction. Commercially available books and materials can help guide discussions about appropriate ways to express affection across a range of relationships. This skill can also be built into a variety of interactive games. For example, children can take turns picking a card that shows a specific affectionate interaction and asks them to approach a peer and engage in this interaction. As an alternative, children can role-play being different people (e.g., friend, parent, teacher, community helper), and the other children can identify the most appropriate expressions of affection.
NV 5	Follows basic gestures and nonverbal cues (e.g., stops when person holds up hand, comes when person motions with hand)	This skill can be incorporated into a variety of activities in which children give and follow directions with one another, or can be incorporated into Charades-like games. However, instead of providing verbal directions to one another, the children are instructed to give directions without using words. Additionally, teachers can also intersperse nonverbal directions into their verbal directions. For some children, it may be necessary to target only one or two gestures or nonverbal cues at a time. Activities: 4, 10, 18, 27, 29, 32, 38, 47
NV 6	Modifies own behavior based on the body language, actions, or eye gaze of others	As a prerequisite to this skill, children should first be able to modify their behavior when provided with verbal feedback. This skill can be built into any teacher-led activity by having the teacher use targeted body language or actions instead of verbal directions. Children who are leading an activity can also be taught to look to a teacher for a signal before the start of an activity. For some children, it may be necessary to target only one or two types of body language at a time. Additionally, it may also be necessary to use systematic prompting and/or external reinforcement for some children. Activities: 8, 18, 21, 29

Nonverbal Social Language continued on next page

CHAPTER 5:
Activities for Teaching Social Skills

Young children learn most efficiently, effectively, and joyfully through play. This is particularly true when it comes to social skills. Children who struggle to develop these skills through organic play make progress through organized and strategic games and activities. Our experience shows that children love to play these games, group leaders love to teach them, and, most importantly, they are effective.

This chapter includes fifty activities to teach a variety of social skills in activity-based groups, in dyads, or individually as needed. These activities include many familiar group games, created or modified during our work with children, and ones created by other teachers and colleagues. Because these activities are easy to do, parents can use them to work on these skills at home in a format that is fun and familiar to their children.

To choose the most appropriate activities for your social-skills group, first complete a Socially Savvy Checklist for each child. Common areas of need within the group often emerge. For example, you may find that half of the children in the group need to work on *SL 16* (Answers questions, asks questions, or makes comments to maintain conversation for three to four exchanges), whereas half might need help with *SR 10* (Responds to mistakes made by self or others without exhibiting challenging behaviors).

Once you identify a set of common objectives, choose the games that target those goals and are a good fit for your group. Games like It's All about You (Activity #13) or Conversation Chain (Activity #48) can be fun activities to work on conversational skills, while Guess What's Different? (Activity #2) or Head Honcho Directions (Activity #7) work on handling mistakes. If you find that the children in the group have very different needs, or that one or two children exhibit skill deficits that the other children do not, select games and activities that address multiple social skills. For example, if you find that all of the children need to work on *CG 10* (Remains in place in a group until called by teacher), but one child needs to work on *SP 9* (Stops action when requested by a peer), you could select games like Category Game (Activity #27) or Obstacle Course (Activity #29), which provide an opportunity to work on both skills.

The description of each activity includes a list of targeted social skills for that activity, directions for play, and variations to make the activity more or less challenging. We include a list of materials required for each game and recommendations on when and where the games can be played. Most require few supplies and can be played almost anywhere. We also provide teaching tips because some of the games require special consideration with some children at times. Although our list is extensive, it isn't exhaustive. Other games and activities can also work well and over time, you may find ways to modify the games we offer here.

ACTIVITY 1: DUCK-DUCK-ANIMAL

Social Skills:

Social Play

SP 8 (Plays outdoor games with a group until the completion of the activity); SP 19 (Appropriately plays games involving a person being "It"); SP 20 (Demonstrates flexibility in following changes in the rules of a game or in accepting novel ideas from peers); SP 24 (Wins without making bragging comments/gestures)

Self-Regulation

SR 1 (Demonstrates flexibility with new tasks/activities); SR 7 (Demonstrates flexibility when things are different than planned); SR 11 (Demonstrates awareness of own and other's space)

Classroom/Group Behavior

CG 15 (Repeats words/actions from a song, book, or play activity)

Materials:

Cards with pictures of different animals that children might choose

When/Where to Play:

Playground; Gym; Movement Time

Directions:

- This game follows the same general format as Duck-Duck-Goose.
- The teacher should first model how to play the game, playing the role of "ducker."
- The "ducker" repeats "Duck" as normal, but instead of saying "Goose," the child chooses a different animal when tapping a peer on the head.
- The child who is tapped then has to act like the animal while attempting to catch the "ducker," who is running around the circle. For example, if the "ducker" said, "Duck, Duck, Rabbit," the tagged child would hop around the circle.
- If the child does not catch the "ducker" before the "ducker" reaches the other child's seat, then that person becomes the "ducker."
- If the "ducker" is caught, the same "ducker" gets another turn.

Variations:

- Play using categories of animals (e.g., animals that fly, zoo animals, ocean animals).

Helpful Hints for Teaching:

Children may sometimes have difficulty thinking of an animal. Keep a box of "Mystery Animals" nearby and let a child who might have a hard time choosing an animal pick one from the box before his turn.

ACTIVITY 2: GUESS WHAT'S DIFFERENT?

Social Skills:

Social Play

SP 7 (Takes turns as part of a structured game and sustains attention until completion of the game)

Self-Regulation

SR 3 (Raises hand and waits to be called before speaking); SR 9 (Responds to feedback/correction without exhibiting challenging behaviors); SR 10 (Responds to mistakes made by self or others without exhibiting challenging behaviors); SR 15 (Asks for help during novel or challenging activities)

Social Language

SL 4 (Addresses peers by name); SL 7 (Asks concrete questions about an item or information shared by others); SL 9 (Gains listener attention appropriately); SL 18 (Directs body and eyes toward social partner when speaking); SL 19 (Directs body and eyes toward social partner when listening); SL 22 (Seeks to repair or clarify breakdowns in social interactions)

Classroom/Group Behavior

CG 9 (Helps others, both spontaneously and when asked)

Materials:

None

When/Where to Play:

Circle Time; Transitions; Waiting Time

Directions:

- One child leaves the classroom and changes something about his or her appearance (e.g., rolls up a pant leg or turns shirt inside out).
- The child then comes back into the room and goes into the middle of the group.
- The other children raise their hands to be called on to guess.
- The child in the middle of the group calls on children to make a guess.
- The child who guesses correctly gets a turn to leave the room and change something about his or her appearance.
- Adults should first model the game.

Helpful Hints for Teaching:

Ensure that the children look at the child closely before he leaves the room. Point out what that child is wearing. If the child leaving the room has the verbal skills, have him describe his outfit before he leaves the room (e.g., "I am wearing a long-sleeved shirt with a monkey on it, long pants, ankle socks, and sneakers on the correct feet. I am not wearing anything on my hands or in my hair."). When first playing this game, the child leaving the classroom should make an obvious change (e.g., take off shoes). Once children are familiar with the game, the child leaving the classroom can make more subtle changes (e.g., change part in his hair).

ACTIVITY 3: MONKEY UNDER THE BLANKET

Social Skills:

Social Play

SP 7 (Takes turns as part of a structured game and sustains attention until completion of the game)

Self-Regulation

SR 3 (Raises hand and waits to be called before speaking); *SR 9* (Responds to feedback/correction without exhibiting challenging behaviors); *SR 10* (Responds to mistakes made by self or others without exhibiting challenging behaviors)

Social Language

SL 4 (Addresses peers by name); *SL 18* (Directs body and eyes toward social partner when speaking)

Materials:

Blanket or sheet

When/Where to Play:

Circle Time; Movement Time; Rainy Day

Directions:

- Divide the children into two groups.
- Send one group out of the room.
- The other group chooses a person to go under the blanket.
- Ask the other group to come back into the room and try to guess who is under the blanket.
- One of the children who stayed in the room should be given the role of calling on children to make a guess.
- The children who are guessing should raise their hands to be called on to make a guess.
- Once one of the children from the group that left guesses correctly, the groups switch places.

Helpful Hints for Teaching:

Keep group size in mind when playing this activity. This game is more fun when there is a large group. However, with children who are not aware of their peers, this game can be challenging even in a small group. Before children leave the room, have one of them name all the children in the group. When the children re-enter the room, have one of them name all the children that they see as a strategy for figuring out which children are accounted for and which children might be under the blanket.

ACTIVITY 4: CHARADES

Social Skills:

Joint Attending

JA 9 (Comments on what self or others are doing)

Social Play

SP 7 (Takes turns as part of a structured game and sustains attention until completion of the game); *SP 20* (Demonstrates flexibility in following changes in the rules of a game or in accepting novel ideas from peers)

Self-Regulation

SR 3 (Raises hand and waits to be called before speaking); *SR 9* (Responds to feedback/correction without exhibiting challenging behaviors); *SR 10* (Responds to mistakes made by self or others without exhibiting challenging behaviors); *SR 15* (Asks for help during novel or challenging activities)

Social/Emotional

SE 1 (Recognizes emotions in others and self); *SE 2* (Gives a simple explanation for the emotional state of self and others when asked); *SE 3* (Shows empathy toward others)

Social Language

SL 4 (Addresses peers by name); *SL 7* (Asks concrete questions about an item or information shared by others); *SL 9* (Gains listener attention appropriately); *SL 18* (Directs body and eyes toward social partner when speaking)

Classroom/Group Behavior

CG 9 (Helps others, both spontaneously and when asked); *CG 21* (Responds together with group to teacher or peer leading activity)

Nonverbal Social Language

NV 3 (Identifies basic actions without words); *NV 5* (Follows basic gestures and nonverbal cues)

Materials:

Cards with pictures of different concepts, actions, animals, etc.

When/Where to Play:

Circle Time; Choice Time if an adult is present to facilitate

Directions:

- Each child takes turns picking a card and acting out what is on the card without using words.
- The other children guess what the child is acting out by raising their hands and waiting to be called on by the actor.
- The teacher and assistant should first model how to act out what is on a card and how to guess.

Activity 4 continued on next page

Variations:

- Have children call out in unison rather than raising their hands and waiting to be called.
- Have the teacher call on the children making guesses.
- Rather than providing verbal feedback about guesses, have the actor use gestures.
- Have the actor act out emotions and/or situations that might cause particular emotions. The teacher can also have children act out how to respond to emotions exhibited by the actor.

Helpful Hints for Teaching:

This game is easier to teach if the children are given cards in a certain order. For example, the game could be taught with animals first (and the children are allowed to use animal noises). Then actions only (no verbal cues), and then the children guess more difficult things, such as concepts and occupations. From there, children may come up with their own ideas, but generally, they understand the concept better if they can go gradually into more complex actions (and rely less on verbal cues).

ACTIVITY 5: WHO AM I?

Social Skills:

Social Play

SP 7 (Takes turns as part of a structured game and sustains attention until completion of the game); *SP 20* (Demonstrates flexibility in following changes in the rules of a game or in accepting novel ideas from peers)

Self-Regulation

SR 3 (Raises hand and waits to be called before speaking); *SR 9* (Responds to feedback/correction without exhibiting challenging behaviors); *SR 10* (Responds to mistakes made by self or others without exhibiting challenging behaviors); *SR 15* (Asks for help during novel or challenging activities)

Social/Emotional

SE 1 (Recognizes emotions in others and self); *SE 2* (Gives a simple explanation for the emotional state of self and others when asked)

Social Language

SL 4 (Addresses peers by name); *SL 7* (Asks concrete questions about an item or information shared by others); *SL 10* (Responds to initiations from others); *SL 18* (Directs body and eyes toward social partner when speaking); *SL 19* (Directs body and eyes toward social partner when listening); *SL 22* (Seeks to repair or clarify breakdowns in social interactions)

Classroom/Group Behavior

CG 9 (Helps others, both spontaneously and when asked)

Materials:

Pictures of animals, visual to give children clues for questions to ask (e.g., "Does my animal have wings?" "Does my animal live on a farm?)

When/Where to Play:

Circle Time; Choice Time if an adult is present to facilitate

Directions:

- Tape a picture of an animal on the back of one child.
- Have the child ask his friends yes/no questions in order to figure out what animal is on his back (e.g., "Does my animal make a 'moo' sound?").
- The children who are asked questions can only answer with a yes/no response.

Variations:

- Use pictures of community helpers, different concepts, etc.
- Use pictures of different emotions, and have the child ask questions such as, "Would I feel this way if _____?"
- Place a picture on all the children's backs and have them walk around and ask questions to one another.

Helpful Hints for Teaching:

Figuring out what questions to ask can be the most difficult part of this game for many children. Visuals can facilitate this part of the game. For example, visuals can include where the animal lives (e.g., farm, ocean, jungle), sounds the animal makes, the color of the animal, or what the animal looks like (e.g., spots, stripes, long neck).

ACTIVITY 6: OPERATOR

Social Skills:

Social Play

SP 7 (Takes turns as part of a structured game and sustains attention until completion of the game)

Self-Regulation

SR 14 (Advocates for oneself without exhibiting challenging behaviors)

Classroom/Group Behavior

CG 15 (Repeats words/actions from a song, book, or play activity)

Materials:

None

When/Where to Play:

Circle Time; Transitions; Waiting Time

Directions:

- Have the children sit in a circle or row.
- Choose one child to start the game.
- That child whispers a word into the ear of the peer next to him.
- The second child then whispers the word she heard into the ear of the child on her other side and so on until it gets to the last child.
- The last child to hear the word in the operator chain says the word aloud.
- The child who started the game says the word aloud.
- The children decide if the words are a match or if the operator chain broke down.

Variations:

- Have the child who starts the chain say a letter or number, and the other children must say the next number or letter.
- Have the child who starts the chain name an item in a category, and the other children must say another item in that category. For example, if the children are talking about transportation, all operator words picked should be in the transportation category.

Helpful Hints for Teaching:

Although this game can be played anywhere, initially, it is played best in an environment free from noise and distraction.

ACTIVITY 7: HEAD HONCHO DIRECTIONS

Social Skills:

Social Play

SP 7 (Takes turns as part of a structured game and sustains attention until completion of the game)

Self-Regulation

SR 9 (Responds to feedback/correction without exhibiting challenging behaviors); *SR 10* (Responds to mistakes made by self or others without exhibiting challenging behaviors)

Social Language

SL 4 (Addresses peers by name); *SL 10* (Responds to initiations from others)

Materials:

Visual of possible actions, space where the guesser can go (hallway) while the other group members decide who the head honcho will be

When/Where to Play:

Circle Time; Break up a longer listening time

Directions:

- Have the children sit in a circle.
- Start with a warm-up activity with an adult as the leader. Have the adult make a body movement or pattern (e.g., taps legs, touches nose, claps hands) and have the children follow.
- Review directions/purpose of the game.
- Decide who the Guesser will be and have that person leave the room.
- Decide who the Head Honcho will be.
- Head Honcho starts a simple body movement or pattern and other group members follow.
- Invite the Guesser back into the room.
- Give the Guesser three chances to guess who the Head Honcho is.
- The Head Honcho should switch the body movement or pattern every 30 to 60 seconds, giving the Guesser a better chance to figure out who the Head Honcho is.
- Repeat so other children have a turn or have the child who guesses become the Head Honcho.

Helpful Hints for Teaching:

In teaching this game, the Head Honcho sometimes has difficulty knowing how and when to change movements. Visuals of possible movements (e.g., clapping hands, tapping legs, touching head) can help ensure that the Head Honcho models a variety of movements.

ACTIVITY 8: ROLL THE BALL

Social Skills:

Joint Attending

JA 1 (Orients when an object is presented); *JA 4* (Uses eye gaze to maintain social interaction); *JA 6* (Follows eye gaze to objects)

Social Play

SP 7 (Takes turns as part of a structured game and sustains attention until completion of the game); *SP 20* (Demonstrates flexibility in following changes in the rules of a game or in accepting novel ideas from peers)

Self-Regulation

SR 11 (Demonstrates awareness of own and other's space); *SR 18* (Uses conversational voice level and tone when speaking)

Social Language

SL 1 (Responds to greetings/partings); *SL 2* (Follows directions involving named adults or peers); *SL 3* (Initiates greetings/partings); *SL 4* (Addresses peers by name); *SL 5* (Answers social questions); *SL 6* (Asks social questions); *SL 10* (Responds to initiations from others); *SL 18* (Directs body and eyes toward social partner when speaking); *SL 19* (Directs body and eyes toward social partner when listening)

Classroom/Group Behavior

CG 15 (Repeats words/actions from a song, book, or play activity); *CG 22* (Follows basic two- to three-step verbal directions in a group)

Nonverbal Social Language

NV 6 (Modifies own behavior based on the body language, actions, or eye gaze of others)

Materials:

Ball

When/Where to Play:

Circle Time; Beginning of an activity to get the children focused

Directions:

- Have all of the children sit in a circle.
- Have each child roll the ball to another child in the group.
- Each child should look at the child to whom he is going to roll the ball. Then he should wait until that child returns eye contact before rolling the ball.
- As a child receives the ball, she should say the name of the child who rolled the ball to her.
- Go around the circle several times, or have each person stand up or lie down once they have received and rolled the ball to indicate that they have had a turn.

Activity 8 continued on next page

ACTIVITY 8: ROLL THE BALL (continued)

Variations:

- Have the children shout or whisper their names.
- Use a timer and have the children quickly pass the ball around and say their names, trying to "beat the timer."
- Have the child who has the ball say another child's name, wait for the other child to make eye contact, and then roll the ball to that child.
- Have the child who has the ball say another child's name, ask a social question (e.g., "What's your favorite color?"), and wait for the other child to respond before rolling the ball.

ACTIVITY 9: FREEZE TAG

Social Skills:

Social Play

SP 8 (Plays outdoor games with a group until the completion of the activity); *SP 16* (Accepts losing games or getting called "out"); *SP 19* (Appropriately plays games involving a person being "It"); *SP 20* (Demonstrates flexibility in following changes in the rules of a game or in accepting novel ideas from peers)

Self-Regulation

SR 11 (Demonstrates awareness of own and other's space); *SR 15* (Asks for help during novel or challenging activities)

Social Language

SL 4 (Addresses peers by name); *SL 9* (Gains listener attention appropriately); *SL 10* (Responds to initiations from others)

Classroom/Group Behavior

CG 9 (Helps others, both spontaneously and when asked)

Materials:

None

When/Where to Play:

Playground; Gym

Directions:

- One child is chosen to be "It."
- The child who is "It" tries to tag others.
- When tagged, a child must freeze.
- Others may touch the frozen child to free her or one child can be identified as the one who unfreezes the other children.
- The person who is "It" should be changed every few minutes until each child has had a turn.
- Depending on the space, the boundaries of the play area should be clearly specified.

Variations:

- Children stay frozen until they call out a word that falls within a category identified by the teacher (e.g., color, animal, song).
- Children stay frozen until they call a non-frozen child by name and ask for help (e.g., "Mary, unfreeze me.").
- Change the boundaries and or the number of children who are "It."

Helpful Hints for Teaching:

When first teaching the concept of "It," it is helpful to designate the person who is "It" with a visual (e.g., a large laminated colored card on a yarn necklace).

ACTIVITY 10: BUBBLE GUM RIVER

Social Skills:

Joint Attending

JA 5 (Follows point or gesture to objects); *JA 6* (Follows eye gaze to objects)

Social Play

SP 7 (Takes turns as part of a structured game and sustains attention until completion of the game); *SP 8* (Plays outdoor games with a group until the completion of the activity); *SP 20* (Demonstrates flexibility in following changes in the rules of a game or in accepting novel ideas from peers)

Classroom/Group Behavior

CG 10 (Remains in place in a group until called by teacher)

Nonverbal Social Language

NV 5 (Follows basic gestures and nonverbal cues)

Materials:

Chalk or tape, colored mats, various toys

When/Where to Play:

Playground; Gym; Movement Time; Rainy Day

Directions:

- Use chalk or tape to make two lines that represent the borders of a river.
- Place colored mats and different stuffed animals or toys between the lines.
- Tell children that this is a bubble gum river and they have to cross it without stepping in the river.
- One child (or initially an adult) should be given the role of providing nonverbal guidance to show the other children how to cross the river.
- Each child should take turns crossing the river by looking at the leader to follow her eye gaze or gesture to know where it is safe to step (e.g., if the leader looks at a blue mat, the child crossing the stream should step on the blue mat). This should continue until the child safely crosses the river.
- If a child steps on the wrong mat or steps into the river, the leader should shake her head and point for the child to start over or wait in line for another turn.

Variations:

- Have the leader provide verbal directions involving prepositions (e.g., "Go on the mat next to the red truck." "Step over the blue mat." "Go between the orange mat and the blue block.").

Helpful Hints for Teaching:

Because there can be many elements to the game, it works best if you start with a small group to reduce waiting time. If you are playing the game with a large group, have multiple river crossings facilitated by different children or teachers as leaders, or play this as a station in a facilitated Choice Time. As children get better at following directions and taking less time per "river crossing," it becomes easier to increase the number of children playing at one time.

ACTIVITY 11: SIMON SAYS

Social Skills:

Joint Attending

JA 4 (Uses eye gaze to maintain social interaction)

Social Play

SP 7 (Takes turns as part of a structured game and sustains attention until completion of the game); *SP 16* (Accepts losing games or getting called "out"); *SP 24* (Wins without making bragging comments/gestures)

Social Language

SL 19 (Directs body and eyes toward social partner when listening)

Classroom/Group Behavior

CG 6 (Imitates a peer who is leading songs/activities); *CG 15* (Repeats words/actions from a song or book); *CG 21* (Responds together with group to teacher or peer leading activity); *CG 22* (Follows basic two- to three-step verbal directions in a group)

Materials:

None

When/Where to Play:

Circle Time; Transitions; Waiting Time

Directions:

- The leader performs various movements, which the children imitate only when given the command, "Simon says ___."
- If a child imitates a movement when the leader does not say, "Simon says ___," the child is out and must sit and wait for the other children to finish the game.
- The last child that has not been called "out" is the winner.

Variations:

- Have the leader model different pretend actions, animals, etc.
- Have the leader verbally model parts of songs, nursery rhymes, or common phrases.
- Have the leader provide verbal directions without imitating actions, progressively moving toward multi-step directions.

Helpful Tips for Teaching:

To help ensure that children understand the expectations of the game, it is best to start with an adult as the leader. When children do well imitating an adult, progress to a child as the leader.

ACTIVITY 12: BUBBLES

Social Skills:

Joint Attending

JA 4 (Uses eye gaze to maintain a social interaction)

Self-Regulation

SR 11 (Demonstrates awareness of own and other's space)

Classroom/Group Behavior

CG 12 (Follows directions during novel activities); *CG 13* (Gives directions during novel activities)

Nonverbal Social Language

NV 5 (Follows basic gestures and nonverbal cues)

Materials:

None

When/Where to Play:

Movement Time; Rainy Day

Directions:

- Tell the children that they are each a bubble and they have to float around the room and try not to bump into other bubbles (i.e., children).
- Tell the children that if they bump into another child, they have to then hold hands and become a bigger bubble.
- Each child starts by taking off "floating" around the room.
- An adult, or a child, chosen to be a leader should periodically provide verbal directions to the groups (e.g., close your eyes, spin in a circle, hop).
- Once all of the bubbles are combined into one group, the giant bubble should fall to the floor with a loud "Pop!!"

Variations:

- When working with a large group, start by having the children in groups of two or three children/bubbles.
- Have the last child who is a lone bubble be the winner.
- Provide nonverbal directions (e.g., close your eyes and point to them, spin finger to indicate that the children should spin).
- Have children say "Pop!!" and fall to the floor when they bump into other children. The last child standing is the winner.

Helpful Hints for Teaching:

This game also teaches children about personal space. At times when not playing "Bubbles," children are reminded to not "pop" one another's bubbles by invading personal space without permission. Peers can use this reminder (e.g., "Don't pop my bubble!") all day long.

ACTIVITY 13: IT'S ALL ABOUT YOU!

Social Skills:

Self-Regulation

SR 3 (Raises hand and waits to be called before speaking)

Social Language

SL 5 (Answers social questions); *SL 6* (Asks social questions); *SL 7* (Asks concrete questions about an item or information shared by others); *SL 9* (Gains listener attention appropriately); *SL 12* (Shares information about self, family, and major events); *SL 14* (Makes reciprocal comments); *SL 16* (Answers questions, asks questions, or makes comments to maintain conversation); *SL 18* (Directs body and eyes toward social partner when speaking); *SL 19* (Directs body and eyes toward social partner when listening)

Classroom/Group Behavior

CG 20 (Attends to small-group, teacher-led listening activity for at least ten minutes)

Materials:

Paper, individual pictures representing different questions the Interviewer can ask (e.g., favorite color, favorite place to go, favorite thing on the playground), individual pictures representing a variety of different answers the Interviewee can provide (e.g., for favorite thing on playground—slide, swing, climber)

When/Where to Play:

Circle Time; Table Top Activity

Directions:

- Ask the children in a small group what a target child's favorite animal is, but do not let target child answer.
- Let the children guess. Talk about how knowing your friends' favorite things can make playing together more fun. Give an example of how knowing your friend's favorite color while painting can help your friend, especially if you have his favorite color and he does not.
- Have the children divide into pairs, and explain that each child will interview her partner on three of his favorite things and then she will be interviewed by her partner.
- Provide three pictures representing different questions the Interviewer can ask her friend. Also, provide a variety of pictures representing different answers the Interviewee can provide.
- Have the Interviewer ask the first question (e.g., "What's your favorite color?")
- Have the Interviewee pick from the colors on the table.
- The Interviewer should take the answer and glue it onto her paper next to the question, so that it can be read as a question and then the answer.
- At the end of the project, the children can "present" the friends they interviewed.
- You can add more questions and/or have the children interview more friends to make a book of their friends' favorite things.

Activity 13 continued on next page

ACTIVITY 13: IT'S ALL ABOUT YOU! (continued)

Helpful Tips for Teaching:

While learning about each other, teach the children the physical sign to show that there is a connection (i.e., thumb and pinky out, shake fist side to side). As children start to notice that they share common likes, have them sign and say, "Connection." In the beginning, helping the children make connections will need to be facilitated, but once children catch on, they will generally enjoy finding out what they have in common with their friends. This can also be tied into The Good Friend Book (Activity #42). Try to generalize this when you see the children playing. For example, remind a child, "What is Jarod's favorite animal? A pig? Do you think that maybe he would like to see this toy pig? Why don't you go ask him?"

ACTIVITY 14: SILLY FACE

Social Skills:

Joint Attending

JA 4 (Uses eye gaze to maintain social interaction)

Social/Emotional

SE 5 (Expresses appropriate level of enthusiasm about the actions or belongings of others)

Classroom/Group Behavior

CG 10 (Remains in place in a group until called by teacher)

Materials:

None

When to Play:

Circle Time; Transitions; Waiting Time

Directions:

- Have the children sit in a circle or row.
- The teacher explains that the purpose of the game is to try to make another child laugh by making silly faces.
- The teacher should also model how to play the game by trying to make one of the children laugh.
- Select one child to go first.
- The child picked to go first should approach one of the children and try to make him laugh by making silly faces.
- If after several attempts, the child does not laugh, the child who was picked can go to another child.
- Whenever one of the children in the circle laughs, that person then gets a turn to try and make another child in the group laugh.

Variations:

- Try making silly faces without making silly sounds and then try a version of the game where silly sounds are allowed.

Helpful Hints for Teaching:

For some children, it is helpful to have a mirror available to "try out" the silly face they plan on making.

ACTIVITY 15: MYSTERY STORY

Social Skills:

Social Language

SL 7 (Asks concrete questions about an item or information shared by others); *SL 12* (Shares information about self, family, and major events); *SL 14* (Makes reciprocal comments); *SL 16* (Answers questions, asks questions, or makes comments to maintain conversation); *SL 18* (Directs body and eyes toward social partner when speaking); *SL 19* (Directs body and eyes toward social partner when listening); *SL 22* (Seeks to repair or clarify breakdowns in social interactions)

Materials:

Commercially available children's book, picture board, pre-made visuals

When to Play:

Circle Time; Table Top Activity

Directions:

- Use a well-known commercially available book, like *Brown Bear, Brown Bear*; *Today is Monday*; or *There Was an Old Lady*.
- The teacher should read the story, stop after one or two pages, and offer three choices to change the story. The choices should be presented visually.
- Have the children take turns making choices about how to change the story.
- The choices should be put up on a felt board.
- The teacher should provide the opportunity to change the story every page or two by giving the children visual choices.
- Make the changes silly and fun.
- At the end of the story, "read" the revised story using the pictures.

Variations:

- Instead of using commercially available books, make up a story using different visual choices.
- Tell stories that have characters showing different emotions. Choices to change the story should include a variety of emotions and a range of ways to respond to specific emotions. For example, have children choose between feelings (happy, sad, scared) and causes of feelings (got an ice cream, fell in the mud, saw a spider) to fill in, "The cow was _____ when she _____." Then, have the children choose ways that cow's friend Donkey might respond by choosing different responses, appropriate to the cause of the feeling (a big smile, a towel to dry off, a stick to scare the spider) to fill in, "Donkey gave cow _____."

Helpful Hints for Teaching:

It can be helpful to show the children a physical sign to let them know that you don't know how the story will continue either (e.g., shrug shoulders dramatically and say, "I don't know! It's a mystery!"). Prompt the children to shrug their shoulders and say, "It's a mystery!" to show that the ending to the book is unknown, but it's okay. At other times during the day, when children show signs of inflexibility, try to generalize and say, for example, "I don't know when your bus is coming. It's a mystery! But that's okay!"

ACTIVITY 16: ALPHABET NAME GAME

Social Skills:

Joint Attending

JA 1 (Orients when an object is presented)

Social Play

SP 7 (Takes turns as part of a structured game and sustains attention until completion of the game); *SP 20* (Demonstrates flexibility in following changes in the rules of a game or in accepting novel ideas from peers)

Self-Regulation

SR 1 (Demonstrates flexibility with new tasks/activities); *SR 7* (Demonstrates flexibility when things are different than planned)

Classroom/Group Behavior

CG 10 (Remains in place in a group until called by teacher); *CG 21* (Responds together with group)

Materials:

White index cards, chalkboard, or small whiteboard

When to Play:

Circle Time; Transitions; Waiting Time

Directions:

- Hold up letter on a card or write a letter on the chalkboard or whiteboard.
- Ask the children whose name begins with that letter.
- Teach the children the following song using that letter to the tune of "Mary Had a Little Lamb":
- "If your name begins with ___, begins with ___, begins with ___. If your name begins with ____, stand up please."

Variations:

- Change the song so that you have the children whose name begins with that letter perform a specific action (e.g., jump, clap your hands, give friend a high five).
- Instead of using the alphabet, use different characteristics (e.g., gender, hair color, eye color) or clothing features (e.g., stripes, long-sleeved shirt, sneakers).

Helpful Hints for Teaching:

Pre-teaching can be helpful for children who may not know their letters or the specific characteristics being targeted in the game.

ACTIVITY 17: GOING TO THE MOON

Social Skills:

Social Play

SP 7 (Takes turns as part of a structured game and sustains attention until completion of the game); *SP 20* (Demonstrates flexibility in following changes in the rules of a game or in accepting novel ideas from peers)

Self-Regulation

SR 15 (Asks for help during novel or challenging activities)

Classroom/Group Behavior

CG 9 (Helps others, both spontaneously and when asked); *CG 15* (Repeats words/actions from song or book)

Materials:

Visuals of category items

When/Where to Play:

Circle Time; Transitions; Waiting Time; Beginning of an activity to get the children focused

Directions:

- Have the children sit in a circle or row.
- The teacher, as the leader, provides a destination (e.g., store, moon, picnic) and category (e.g., fruit, toy, color, clothing) using a phrase such as, "I am going to the store to get some fruit. I am going to buy some oranges."
- The next child adds on to the chain but also has to repeat what the previous people have said. For example, "I'm going to the store to get some fruit. I'm going to buy some oranges and apples."
- The game continues until all children have had a turn or someone is unable to remember the completed chain.
- Visuals can be used to make this game easier or until the children can memorize long chains.
- Once the children understand the game well enough, one of them can be the leader.

Helpful Hints for Teaching:

When beginning to play this game, skip the part about listing what other children brought and just have each child list something new to the growing list of items (e.g., fruits). As the children get better at this game, increase the challenge and have them recount everything that was listed before their turn.

ACTIVITY 18: RED ROVER

Social Skills:

Joint Attending

JA 4 (Uses eye gaze to maintain social interaction)

Social Play

SP 8 (Plays outdoor games with a group until the completion of the activity); *SP 9* (Stops action when requested by a peer); *SP 16* (Accepts losing games or getting called "out"); *SP 19* (Appropriately plays games involving a person being "It"); *SP 20* (Demonstrates flexibility in following changes in the rules of a game or in accepting novel ideas from peers)

Social Language

SL 4 (Addresses peers by name); *SL 10* (Responds to initiations from others)

Classroom/Group Behavior

CG 10 (Remains in place in a group until called by teacher)

Nonverbal Social Language

NV 5 (Follows basic gestures and nonverbal cues); *NV 6* (Modifies own behavior based on the body language, actions, or eye gaze of others)

Materials:

None

When/Where to Play:

Playground; Gym; Hallway; Rainy Day

Directions:

- This is a variation of the traditional Red Rover game.
- Have the children line up on one side of the room (or playground).
- One teacher should be with the children and another teacher should be on the other side of the room. One child is "It" in the middle.
- The teacher on the opposite side of the room from the children calls out, "Red Rover, Red Rover, let (child's name) come over." As the child tries to run to the other side, the child that is "It" tries to tag them.
- Once the child makes it to the other side of the room, they are safe. If they are caught, they are also "It" and help catch children being called over.
- This continues until all the children have been tagged.

Activity 18 continued on next page

ACTIVITY 18: RED ROVER (continued)

Variations:

- Call children over based on a clothing item, clothing color, first letter of name, etc. For example, call out "Red Rover, Red Rover, let all children wearing red come over." This allows more children to be active at one time.
- With younger children, you can play without anyone being "It" and have the children run from one side of the room to the other by following the directions.
- Instead of using words, call children over using gestures or eye gaze.
- Have the child who is "It" use different ways to tell the child running over to stop (e.g., verbal, hand gesture).

Helpful Hints for Teaching:

It can be helpful, when first teaching the concept of "It" to put a laminated large colored card on a yarn necklace, or something similar, on the person who is "It."

ACTIVITY 19: HELLO MY FRIEND

Social Skills:

Social Language

SL 4 (Addresses peer by name); SL 12 (Shares information about self, family, and major events)

Classroom/Group Behavior

CG 10 (Remains in place in a group until called by teacher)

Materials:

Chair, bandana

When/Where to Play:

Circle Time; Break up a longer listening time

Directions:

- Have one child sit in a chair in the middle of a circle.
- Use a bandana to cover his eyes.
- Pick one child to go up to the child in the middle and say, "Hello my friend, can you guess who I am?" The child in the middle gets three guesses, but the speaker can say, "Hello" again if the child has difficulty guessing.
- After guessing, the child who spoke sits in the middle and the child that was in the middle may pick another speaker.

Variations:

- The children can use their normal voices, but if they are very familiar with the person in the chair, silly voices can be more fun.
- Instead of having the child say, "Hello," have him give clues about himself, starting with physical characteristics (e.g., "I am a boy. I have blonde hair. I wear glasses.") and then move to likes, dislikes, and personal information (e.g., "My favorite color is blue. I like to play with Thomas the Tank Engine. I have a little sister named Rosie.").
- Instead of having the child give clues, have one of the other children provide clues about the target child.

Helpful Hints for Teaching:

Start out with a small group, but as the children get better at the game, try bringing in "guests" from other groups or classrooms.

ACTIVITY 20: BLOB TAG

Social Skills:

Social Play

SP 8 (Plays outdoor games with a group until the completion of the activity); *SP 19* (Appropriately plays games involving a person being "It")

Self-Regulation

SR 11 (Demonstrates awareness of own and other's space)

Materials:

None

When/Where to Play:

Playground; Gym

Directions:

- This is a variation of traditional Tag.
- The teacher picks a child to be "It" to form the blob.
- As children are tagged, they join hands with the person who is "It."
- This continues until the blob becomes larger and no one is left to tag.

Variations:

- Instead of tagging just any child, the teacher calls out some characteristic and has the person who is "It" tag people showing that characteristic (e.g., color of clothing, gender, wearing a certain type of shoes). The teacher keeps calling out different characteristics, so that the person who is "It" has to change who they are tagging.
- The teacher tapes pictures to the front of children's shirts, and has person who is "It" tag children based on the teacher calling out different categories or features (e.g., "Tag people who are wearing an animal." "Tag people who are wearing an animal that can fly.").

Helpful Hints for Teaching:

This game can get wild very quickly. Make sure to go through a list of rules ahead of time.

ACTIVITY 21: PASS THE WINK

Social Skills:

Joint Attending
JA 1 (Orients when an object is presented); *JA 4* (Uses eye gaze to maintain social interaction)

Self-Regulation
SR 7 (Demonstrates flexibility when things are different than planned)

Social Language
SL 1 (Responds to greetings/partings); *SL 3* (Initiates greetings/partings)

Nonverbal Social Language
NV 6 (Modifies own behavior based on the body language, actions, or eye gaze of others)

Materials:
Object to pass (e.g., ball)

When/Where to Play:
Circle Time; Beginning of an activity to get the children focused

Directions:
- Have the children sit in a circle.
- If this is a new activity, an adult should model how to play.
- One child should be selected to start and should be given the object to pass.
- The child who has the object should look to the child next to them, wink, and pass the object.
- The child should not wink or pass the object until the child next to him has made eye contact.
- One adult should monitor eye contact.

Variations:
- Once the children are consistent at winking at each other before passing the ball, you can have them speed up the passing. Use a timer/stop watch to challenge them to beat their time.
- Instead of passing the object to the person next to her, have the child make eye contact and wink at any person in the group before passing the object.
- Instead of passing an object, the children can pass words, such as different ways to say hello (e.g., "What's up?" "How was your weekend?").

Helpful Hints for Teaching:
This can be a hard game to teach. It can be easier for children to learn that a wink has happened if the "winker" passes the "winkee" an item.

ACTIVITY 22: PARTNER HOKEY POKEY

Social Skills:

Social Play

SP 20 (Demonstrates flexibility in following changes in the rules of a game or in accepting novel ideas from peers)

Classroom/Group Behavior

CG 6 (Imitates a peer who is leading songs/activities); *CG 12* (Follows directions during novel activities); *CG 15* (Repeats words/actions from a song, book, or play activity); *CG 21* (Responds together with group to teacher or peer leading activity)

Nonverbal Social Language

NV 1 (Reciprocates nonverbal interactions); *NV 2* (Initiates nonverbal interactions with appropriate adults and peers)

Materials:

Visual of possible actions

When/Where to Play:

Movement Time; Break up a longer listening time

Directions:

- Have the children stand in a circle.
- Divide children into pairs, with their partner standing next to them.
- Review the traditional Hokey Pokey activity with children and explain that the actions will be different during the game and will have to be something they can do with their partner (e.g., high five, thumbs-up, shake hands).
- Choose a pair of children to discuss and decide what the first action will be and have the pair lead the class in singing and acting out the Hokey Pokey, including the new direction. For example:

  You give a high five in
  You give a high five out
  You give a high five in
  And you shake it all about
  You do the Hokey Pokey and you turn yourself around
  That's what it's all about!

- Continue until all pairs have given an action direction or the activity time is completed.

Variations:

- Put pictures of actions on cards and put them into a box. When it is a child's turn to play, have the child pull a card from the box to see what action he will model for the group.

Helpful Hints for Teaching:

Some children may have a hard time coming up with an action. Keep a visual of possible actions to which children can refer if they need ideas.

ACTIVITY 23: SPIDER WEB QUESTIONS

Social Skills:

Joint Attending

JA 4 (Uses eye gaze to maintain social interaction)

Social Language

SL 4 (Addresses peers by name); *SL 5* (Answers social questions); *SL 6* (Asks social questions); *SL 9* (Gains listener attention appropriately); *SL 10* (Responds to initiations from others); *SL 15* (Shares information about immediate past or future events); *SL 18* (Directs body and eyes toward social partner when speaking); *SL 19* (Directs body and eyes toward social partner when listening); *SL 23* (Converses on age-appropriate topics)

Materials:

Ball of string/yarn, visual of social questions

When/Where to Play:

Circle Time

Directions:

- Have children sit on the floor in a circle.
- Explain that the group will make a spider web with the yarn by rolling it to peers across the circle from them.
- Explain that the child whose name is called will need to make eye contact with the teacher so the teacher knows he is ready for her to roll the ball of yarn to him.
- Model the activity first by gaining a child's attention by using his first name.
- After eye gaze is established, continue to hold the loose piece of yarn and roll the ball to the child. Have the child hold the ball while you ask him a personal social question (e.g., "How old are you?" "Do you have any pets?" "What is your favorite food?").
- After the child answers, it is his turn to call a friend's name, hold onto the string of yarn as well, roll the rest of the ball to the friend, and ask a question.
- Repeat the pattern until all children are holding onto the string of yarn, forming a "spider web."

Variations:

- Have children ask and answer questions about events that have or are about to happen (e.g., "What song did you like the most during singing time?" "What are you doing after school?").
- Identify a specific topic and have the children ask and answer questions about that topic.

Helpful Hints for Teaching:

It may be helpful to pre-teach conversational questions to reduce wait time for children both asking and answering the questions. It may also be helpful to have visuals of personal questions peers can ask one another.

ACTIVITY 24: WHAT DO YOU THINK?

Social Skills:

Social Play

SP 23 (Appropriately accepts that others' likes and interests may be different from their own)

Social Language

SL 10 (Responds to initiations from others); SL 11 (Answers questions about ongoing activities)

Classroom/Group Behavior

CG 20 (Attends to small-group teacher-led listening activity)

Materials:

Large piece of paper, markers, stickers

When/Where to Play:

Circle Time, especially at the beginning

Directions:

- Create a simple chart with questions related to the current or upcoming activity and three to four choices.
- Explain that the choice that the most children select will be what the entire class does.
- Call children to the chart one at a time and have each place a sticker or write her name under her preferred option.
- When everyone has had a turn, have the class count in unison to determine how many children voted for each choice, and then ask the children which choice got the most votes.

Variations:

- This activity can also be combined with It's All About You! (Activity #13), in which children learn about each other. Questions can include, "How many siblings do you have?" or "What's your favorite color?" It can be interesting to see if children can answer these questions about each other as they get to know each other better.
- This activity can also focus on having the children make predictions about an upcoming activity. For example, before going on a walk, the children can take turns making a guess about if it will be windy. Or, before reading a story, the children could be asked to predict whether the boy in the story will make a new friend.

Helpful Hints for Teaching:

It can be helpful to provide parents with a list of potential questions ahead of time to help children become familiar with the topics and think about their answers in advance.

ACTIVITY 25: WONDERBALL

Social Skills:

Joint Attending

JA 1 (Orients when an object is presented)

Social Play

SP 16 (Accepts losing games or getting called "out"); *SP 24* (Wins without making bragging comments/gestures)

Classroom/Group Behavior

CG 15 (Repeats words/actions from a song, book, or play activity); *CG 21* (Respond together with group); *CG 23* (Passes items to peers)

Materials:

Small ball

When/Where to Play:

Circle Time; Transitions; Waiting Time; Break up a longer listening time

Directions:

- Have children sit in a circle in close proximity to each other and pass a ball around the circle while singing/saying the words:

  > The wonderball
  > Goes round and round
  > To pass it quickly you are bound
  > If you're the one
  > To hold it last
  > The game for you
  > Has surely passed

- Whichever child is holding the ball when the singing stops is "out" of the game and moves to a designated area in the classroom.
- The game continues until only one child remains.

Variations:

- Play a type of "Hot Potato" game in which the child who gets the potato needs to name an item in a category. For example, if the category is fruit, then when the ball or potato lands with a child, the child needs to name a fruit.

Helpful Hints for Teaching:

This activity works best in small groups to reduce waiting time and to allow multiple times to play. However, this activity can also work well in a larger group because children get "out" fairly quickly, but there may only be a chance to play one round. If playing a variation where children need to name items in a category, visuals can be helpful.

ACTIVITY 26: 20 QUESTIONS

Social Skills:

Self-Regulation

SR 3 (Raises hand and waits to be called before speaking); SR 9 (Responds to feedback/correction without exhibiting challenging behaviors); SR 10 (Responds to mistakes made by self or others without exhibiting challenging behaviors)

Social Language

SL 4 (Addresses peers by name); SL 7 (Asks concrete questions about an item or information shared by others); SL 9 (Gains listener attention appropriately); SL 10 (Responds to initiations from others); SL 13 (Answers more than five questions on a preferred topic); SL 18 (Directs body and eyes toward partner when speaking); SL 19 (Directs body and eyes toward partner when listening)

Classroom/ Group Behavior

CG 20 (Attends to small-group, teacher-led listening activity for at least ten minutes)

Materials:

Visual of topics/categories and of the possible choices within those areas, visual of possible questions

When/Where to Play:

Circle Time; Transitions; Waiting Time

Directions:

- Select a topic/category (e.g., animals, fruits, pretend characters).
- Select a child to be the leader.
- Have the leader come up to the front of the group and select a picture or object that represents something from that topic/category (e.g., penguin for category of animals), but do not let them show or tell the other children.
- The other children should take turns asking yes/no questions to try to guess what the item/object is. For example, they may ask, "Does it have wings?" "Does it live on land?" "Does it eat grass?" "Is it blue?"

Variations:

- Once children are familiar with this game, visuals do not have to be used and you can have broader topics (e.g., person, place, thing).

Helpful Hints for Teaching:

As children are learning this game, it works well to have the leader pick an object/picture from a bin and use it to reference when children ask questions. For example, the child can look behind them and see if the object has a specific attribute (e.g., four legs). In addition, you can make a visual to show what questions can be asked, as well as what questions have already been asked. Once a question about a specific feature has been asked, put a blank piece of paper over that feature so it will not be asked again.

ACTIVITY 27: CATEGORY GAME

Social Skills:

Social Play

SP 8 (Plays outdoor games with a group until the completion of the activity); SP 9 (Stops action when requested by a peer); SP 16 (Accepts losing games or getting called "out"); SP 19 (Appropriately plays games involving a person being "It")

Social Language

SL 4 (Addresses peers by name)

Classroom/Group Behavior

CG 10 (Remains in place in a group until called by teacher)

Nonverbal Social Language

NV 5 (Follows basic gestures and nonverbal cues)

Materials:

Visuals of different categories (e.g., animals, colors) and different items or examples from the categories

When/Where to Play:

Playground; Gym; Open indoor space; Rainy Day

Directions:

- Have the children line up against one end of the room or play area.
- Choose one child to be "It," and have her stand on the opposite side of the room or play area from the other children.
- Have one teacher stand with the child who is "It," and another teacher stand with the other children.
- The child who is "It" chooses a category and tells the other children.
- Each of the other children picks one of the examples without letting the person who is "It" know. The teacher with the group will need to help with this.
- The child who is "It" then turns her back away from the other children and slowly begins to name examples from the category. The child can use a visual of examples from the category as a reference.
- Whenever the child who is "It" calls the example that another child has selected, that child tries to run quickly or sneak quietly up to the child who is "It."
- If the child who is "It" thinks she hears someone moving, she can quickly turn around and try to call the child's name before the child reaches her. If the child is caught, that child is also "It" and helps to call out examples and catch the other children.
- If the child from the group whose example is called reaches the child who is "It" before she turns and calls that child's name, that child is safe and can watch and cheer on the other players.
- This continues until all of the children have either made it safely to the child who is "It" or have been called out.

Activity 27 continued on next page

ACTIVITY 27: CATEGORY GAME (continued)

Variations:

- Have the child who is "It" use a gesture (e.g., hand up to stop) instead of calling the child's name who is trying to sneak up.

Helpful Hints for Teaching:

Once children are familiar with this game, you do not have to use the visual; however, it is important to do so at first to ensure that children can come up with an example from a category and that they follow the rules of the game by moving toward the child who is "It" when their example is called.

ACTIVITY 28: MYSTERY RULES

Social Skills:

Social Play

SP 7 (Takes turns as part of a structured game and sustains attention until completion of the game); *SP 18* (Follows changes in play ideas of others and sustains the changes during open-ended play); *SP 20* (Demonstrates flexibility in following changes in the rules of a game or in accepting novel ideas from peers)

Self-Regulation

SR 1 (Demonstrates flexibility with new tasks/activities); *SR 7* (Demonstrates flexibility when things are different than when planned)

Materials:

Board game if needed, timer, cards to choose new rules

When/Where to Play:

Within context of a well-known game or activity

Directions:

- Select a game familiar to the group with standard rules (e.g., Hi Ho Cherry-O).
- Explain that you are going to begin playing the game but that you will set a timer. When the timer goes off, you will change one of the rules of the game.
- Make a variety of cards to represent "new" (changed) rules. For example, "When the spinner lands on the bird, take three cherries off of your tree," or "When the spinner lands on the bucket, take all of the cherries off your tree and then take an extra turn."
- Begin to play the game normally and set the timer for several minutes. When the timer rings, have one child choose a card and help him read the new rule to the children.
- Continue to play until several rules have been changed or until the game is completed.

Variations:

- Start with an open-ended activity (e.g., blocks). When the bell rings, have a child turn a card that signals a change in the play scenario (e.g., the blocks become people going to the beach). The bell should ring several times during the activity to change the play scenario.

Helpful Hints for Teaching:

Make sure the rules that are changed are only for well-known games or this activity can become confusing for children. A fun way to implement this game is to declare that "Every Friday is Mystery Rule Day" or "Rainy Days are Mystery Rule Days!"

ACTIVITY 29: OBSTACLE COURSE

Social Skills:

Social Play

SP 9 (Stops action when requested by a peer)

Self-Regulation

SR 7 (Demonstrates flexibility when things are different than planned); *SR 11* (Demonstrates awareness of own and other's space)

Social Language

SL 10 (Responds to initiations from others)

Classroom/Group Behavior

CG 10 (Remains in place in a group until called by teacher); *CG 14* (Stays in place when walking in line and maintains pace with group)

Nonverbal Social Language

NV 2 (Initiates nonverbal interactions with appropriate adults and peers); *NV 5* (Follows basic gestures and nonverbal cues); *NV 6* (Modifies own behavior based on the body language, actions, or eye gaze of others)

Materials:

Various gross-motor materials, such as a mat, tunnel, cones, trampoline, etc.

When/Where to Play:

Playground; Gym; Hallway; Movement Time; Rainy Day

Directions:

- Set up an obstacle course with a variety of materials.
- Explain that children waiting for a particular part of the course (e.g., crawling through the tunnel) must wait for a nonverbal signal from the child in front of them (e.g., thumbs-up) before they can begin that part of the course.
- Choose two children to model how to complete the course, reminding the children in front to use thumbs-up or an equivalent signal to let the next child know that they can proceed.
- If a child does not wait for the signal to begin, the child in front should nonverbally signal and tell him to "stop" and wait for the signal.

Helpful Hints for Teaching:

It is important to keep the obstacle course simple. Gym equipment, although great, is not necessary. You can simply cut out construction paper footprints and laminate them to indicate where to hop, take a step, or crawl. Pails are great for tossing beanbags into before moving on to a masking tape line on the floor where the children attempt to stay on the line while walking. With a little creativity, you can create an engaging obstacle course from miscellaneous items in the classroom.

ACTIVITY 30: SHARING NEWS

Social Skills:

Self-Regulation

SR 3 (Raises hand and waits to be called before speaking); SR 7 (Shows others objects and makes eye contact to share interest); SR 17 (Avoids perseveration on a topic or question)

Social Language

SL 5 (Answers social questions); SL 6 (Asks social questions); SL 7 (Asks concrete questions about an item or information shared by others); SL 9 (Gains listener attention appropriately); SL 10 (Responds to initiations from others); SL 11 (Answers questions about ongoing activities); SL 12 (Shares information about self, family, and major events); SL 13 (Answers more than five questions on a preferred topic); SL 14 (Makes reciprocal comments); SL 15 (Shares information about immediate past or future events); SL 18 (Directs body and eyes toward social partner when speaking); SL 19 (Directs body and eyes toward social partner when listening); SL 22 (Seeks to repair or clarify breakdowns in social interactions); SL 23 (Converses on age-appropriate topics); SL 24 (Uses contextually appropriate language/introduces topic)

Classroom/Group Behavior

CG 20 (Attends to small-group, teacher-led listening activity)

Materials:

Sharing News book for each child with blank pages, visual of questions to ask about news

When/Where to Play:

Circle Time

Directions:

- Make Sharing News books containing blank pages for each child. A simple report binder with some lined notebook pages will do.
- Send Sharing News books home with each child. Ask parents to help their children write news about something happening in their lives that they would like to share with the class. The news should be no longer than a few sentences (e.g., "I went to the park with my friend Alex. We went on the swings and had a snack."). It is also helpful if parents can add photographs.
- Assign each child a specific day of the week for sharing. On their designated day, children bring their Sharing News book with them to the group.
- The child sharing sits in a special chair in front of the class and reads his news to his friends, with as much help as needed from an adult.
- The child can answer questions from other children in the group. Remind the children in the group that their questions must be about that child's news.
- Instruct the children in the group to raise their hands quietly so that the sharing child can choose who will ask a question.
- Encourage children to ask questions about parts of the sharing news they did not understand.

Helpful Hints for Teaching:

Having visual supports available with suggested questions is helpful, in addition to providing reminders to stay on topic.

ACTIVITY 31: I SPY

Social Skills:

Joint Attending

JA 5 (Follows point or gesture to objects); *JA 8* (Points to objects and makes eye contact to share interest)

Self-Regulation

SR 3 (Raises hand and waits to be called before speaking); *SR 9* (Responds to feedback/correction without exhibiting challenging behaviors); *SR 10* (Responds to mistakes made by self or others without exhibiting challenging behaviors); *SR 15* (Asks for help during novel or challenging activities)

Social Language

SL 4 (Addresses peers by name); *SL 7* (Asks concrete questions about an item or information shared by others); *SL 9* (Gains listener attention appropriately); *SL 10* (Responds to initiations from others); *SL 18* (Directs body and eyes toward social partner when speaking); *SL 19* (Directs body and eyes toward social partner when listening)

Classroom/Group Behavior

CG 9 (Helps others, both spontaneously and when asked); *CG 10* (Remains in place in a group until called by teacher)

Materials:

Objects already present in the classroom environment

When/Where to Play:

Circle Time; Transitions; Waiting Times; Almost anywhere

Directions:

- Have the children sit in a specific area of the classroom and choose a child to be the clue-giver.
- Ask the clue-giver to choose a classroom object visible in the area where the children are sitting but not to tell anyone what she has chosen.
- Set specific criteria that children must use to describe the object to peers (e.g., give three clues about the object, tell the color, tell what you use it for).
- After the clue-giver has given the clues to the group, ask the children to raise their hands quietly and wait to be called if they think they know the object.
- Have the clue-giver call on children until the object has been guessed.
- Children can guess by labeling an object in the room and/or pointing to the object that they are guessing (e.g., point to clock on the wall and ask, "Is it the clock?"; point to the clock on the wall and say, "The clock.")
- The child that guesses correctly can then become the clue-giver.
- Continue until everyone has had a turn or the activity time is completed.

Variations:

- Instead of having the leader give a color clue, have them give a positional clue (e.g., "I spy something next to the big book shelf." I spy something near the door.").
- Have the leader give feedback to the children guessing by telling them something such as, "You are getting warmer," or "You are getting colder."

ACTIVITY 32: ONE ELEPHANT

Social Skills:

Self-Regulation

SR 11 (Demonstrates awareness of own and other's space)

Social Language

SL 4 (Addresses peers by name); SL 9 (Gains listener attention appropriately); SL 10 (Responds to initiations from others)

Classroom/Group Behavior

CG 10 (Remains in place in a group until called by teacher); CG 15 (Repeats words/actions from a song, book, or play activity); CG 21 (Responds together with group to teacher or peer leading activity)

Nonverbal Social Language

NV 5 (Follows basic gestures and nonverbal cues)

Materials:

Long piece of string or yarn

When/Where to Play:

Circle Time; Movement Time

Directions:

- Place the string on the floor, stretched out into a long line or shaped into a large circle.
- Explain that the children are going to pretend they are elephants trying to balance on a very thin tightrope and talk about making sure the elephants have enough space between their bodies so that they do not fall off of the tightrope.
- Call one child to stand on the string and sing the following song to the tune of "Three Little Ducks" while she is on the string:

    One elephant went out to play
    On a tightrope string one day
    She/he had such enormous fun
    That s/he called for another elephant to come

- Have the child call a friend by name to come to the string and tell the friend where to stand by giving a direction including a spatial concept (e.g., "Katherine, come stand behind me/in front of me/at the end of the line/near the bookcase.").
- Sing the elephant song as each child joins the group, changing the number of elephants accordingly.
- Continue until all children have had a turn.
- When the last child has been called to the string, sing the following as the last line:

    But there were no more elephants left to come

Activity 32 continued on next page

Variations:

- Have the child give nonverbal cues by looking or gesturing toward the person being picked to join the tightrope and by looking or pointing to the spot on the tightrope that the joining child should stand.

- Have the child call children over using clues, rather than names (e.g., "Come to the line if you are wearing white shoes.").

ACTIVITY 33: CHILDREN, CHILDREN, WHO DO YOU SEE?

Social Skills:

Joint Attending

JA 1 (Orients when an object is presented)

Classroom/Group Behavior

CG 15 (Repeats words/actions from a song, book, or play activity); *CG 18* (Attends to small-group, teacher-led, hands-on activity for at least ten minutes); *CG 20* (Attends to small-group, teacher-led listening activity for at least ten minutes); *CG 21* (Responds together with group)

Materials:

Construction paper, crayons, markers, stickers, digital camera, laminator—ideally, you'll want to take a photo of each child in the class and have it printed out before you begin this activity

When/Where to Play:

Circle Time; Table Top Activity

Directions:

- Read the children the book *Brown Bear, Brown Bear, What Do You See?* by Eric Carle.
- Explain that the children are going to make a similar classroom book but that, instead of animal characters, the book's characters will be all of the children.
- Have each child either decorate a picture of a bear or create a unique picture on construction paper using crayons, markers, and/or stickers.
- Print the digital pictures of the children and glue each onto a piece of construction paper.
- Compile the pages so that each child's picture page and decorated page are next to each other. Add text to each page under the child's picture, including "Name, name, who do you see?"
- End the book with, "I see lots of friends looking at me. That's who I see."
- Laminate the pages and bind together.
- Read to the class and then place in the book corner for children to read during Choice Time. Encourage children to look at the book in pairs, with partners taking turns reading each page.

Helpful Hints for Teaching:

It can be helpful to veer from the text of the book to include personal information about each child. This will help the children to remember personal things about each of their peers.

ACTIVITY 34: FILL IN THE STORY

Social Skills:

Self-Regulation

SR 3 (Raises hand and waits to be called before speaking); SR 7 (Demonstrates flexibility when things are different than planned)

Social Language

SL 18 (Directs body and eyes toward social partner when speaking); SL 19 (Directs body and eyes toward social partner when listening); SL 22 (Seeks to repair or clarify breakdowns in social interactions)

Classroom/Group Behavior

CG 21 (Responds together with group to teacher or peer leading activity)

Materials:

Large piece of paper, numerous small (2x2 inches) pictures of people, animals, things, and places that can help to fill in a story

When/Where to Play:

Circle Time; Table Top Activity

Directions:

- Write on a large piece of paper the start of a story, leaving blanks where the children can add information. For example, "There once was a _____ that lived in a _____ and that liked _____."
- Have the children take turns filling in the blanks in the story.
- Each child is given pictures to choose from to fill in the blanks.
- Children may also come up with their own ideas to fill in the blanks.
- As the children get familiar with this activity, they can also continue the story with additional sentences and information.
- Once the story is complete, have the children read it together.

Variations:

- As children get better at telling a story, have them predict where the story will go. Having them say "Why" the character liked the moon, for example, can be a great detail to add to a story.
- Children may also enjoy taking a known story like "The Three Little Pigs" and changing the plot line. For example, "There once were three little pigs. They took a _____ to build a _____. "

Helpful Hints for Teaching:

Try to keep it simple (limit additions to only a few details) in the beginning. It can also be easier to use words or pictures to write out the frame of a story, laminate this, and leave blank space with a piece of Velcro as the spots where information is added.

ACTIVITY 35: PARTNER TWISTER

Social Skills:

Social Play

SP 20 (Demonstrates flexibility in following changes in the rules of a game or in accepting novel ideas from peers)

Social Language

SL 10 (Responds to initiations from others)

Classroom/Group Behavior

CG 10 (Remains in place in a group until called by teacher); *CG 22* (Follows basic two-to three-step verbal directions in a group)

Nonverbal Social Language

NV 1 (Reciprocates nonverbal interactions); *NV 2* (Initiates nonverbal interactions with appropriate adults and peers)

Materials:

Twister mat and spinner

When/Where to Play:

Circle Time; Movement Time

Directions:

- Divide children into pairs.
- Designate one pair of children at a time to be in charge of the spinner. Have that pair spin and tell the other pairs of children on which color they should place their hand/foot.
- Have each pair of children complete the instruction from the spinner. Tell children that both partners must put their hand/foot on the same spot and share that space without falling.
- You can play that the partners are out if they fall or, for younger children, you can play that initially no one gets out.
- Encourage partners to provide feedback to each other and/or advocate for themselves when needed (e.g., "I don't have enough space") to correctly complete the instructions.
- Continue until all pairs have had turns with the spinner and following directions.

Variations:

- The game can be modified so that pairs have to interact (e.g., give your partner a high five, say hello to your partner, wink at your partner) while standing on a certain color.
- Increase the complexity by having children follow two- to three-step directions (e.g., put your hand on red, your foot on red, and give the leader a thumbs-up).

Helpful Hints for Teaching:

Choose to include or omit the "right" and "left" portion of the directions according to the children's understanding of these concepts. Putting visuals on top of the twister spinner (e.g., high five on red, wink on green, and so on) can be helpful.

ACTIVITY 36: PEEK-A-WHO

Social Skills:

Social Play

SP 7 (Takes turns as part of a structured game and sustains attention until completion of the game); *SP 16* (Accepts losing games or getting called "out")

Social Language

SL 4 (Addresses peers by name)

Materials:

Blanket or sheet

When/Where to Play:

Circle Time; Movement Time; Break up a longer listening time

Directions:

- Divide children into two teams.
- Have two adults hold a blanket in the space between the two teams.
- Have each team choose a player to crouch in front of the blanket without seeing who is on the other side.
- When the children are ready, have the adults drop the blanket, and have the players look at each other and attempt to be the first to say the other person's name.
- Whoever says the other person's name first wins and stays on that team. The loser joins the winner's team.
- Continue play until all children are on the same team or have had a turn to be a player.

Helpful Hints for Teaching:

Make sure that children know each other's names. This game works better with larger groups.

ACTIVITY 37: ANIMAL PLAYDATE

Social Skills:

Joint Attending

JA 7 (Shows others objects and makes eye contact to share interest)

Self-Regulation

SR 3 (Raises hand and waits to be called before speaking); *SR 17* (Avoids perseveration on a topic or question)

Social Language

SL 5 (Answers social questions); *SL 7* (Asks concrete questions about an item or information shared by others); *SL 9* (Gains listener attention appropriately); *SL 10* (Responds to initiations from others); *SL 11* (Answers questions about ongoing activities); *SL 12* (Shares information about self, family, and major events); *SL 13* (Answers more than five questions on a preferred topic); *SL 14* (Makes reciprocal comments); *SL 18* (Directs body and eyes toward social partner when speaking); *SL 19* (Directs body and eyes toward social partner when listening); *SL 20* (Speaks using polite phrases); *SL 22* (Seeks to repair or clarify breakdowns in social interactions); *SL 24* (Uses contextually appropriate language/introduces topic)

Classroom/Group Behavior

CG 20 (Attends to small-group, teacher-led listening activity for at least ten minutes)

Materials:

Stuffed animal, basket, construction paper, crayons

When/Where to Play:

Circle Time

Directions:

- Give each child an opportunity to take a class stuffed animal or puppet home in a basket, along with a rolled up piece of construction paper tied with a string.
- Included in the basket should be directions for the parent to read aloud to the child. Something such as, "Thanks for taking me home with you today! I love to go on playdates! Together, we can have a lot of fun. When the playdate is over, you can color what we did on our playdate on this piece of paper in the basket. The basket, paper, and I all come back to school tomorrow so we can tell the rest of the class what we did! I can't wait! Love, Monkey."
- The child should come back the next day with the basket, Monkey, and the paper that she drew on.
- Have the child come to the front of the group and share what she did on her playdate with Monkey, using her picture as visual support.
- Have the other children raise their hand, wait to be called, and ask questions about the playdate or ask for clarification.
- The pictures can all be hung on the wall or made into a book about "You, Me, and Monkey Makes Three."

Activity 37 continued on next page

Variations:

- Have the child share a picture drawn about a playdate with a classmate or other child.
- Have the child walk around and share the picture with each child in the group. Each child in the group should make a compliment. The child sharing should then respond with polite phrases to acknowledge the compliments.

ACTIVITY 38: FOLLOW MY EYE!

Social Skills:

Joint Attending

JA 5 (Follows point or gesture to objects); *JA 6* (Follows eye gaze to objects)

Social Play

SP 7 (Takes turns as part of a structured game and sustains attention until completion of the game)

Nonverbal Social Language

NV 5 (Follows basic gestures and nonverbal cues)

Materials:

Blocks or other building materials (e.g., puzzles, Kid K'NEX)

When/Where to Play:

Structured Play Time

Directions:

- Tell the children that they are going to build a structure. Sometimes it is helpful to have a picture of the finished product in front of the children. For example, a picture of a house made from blocks or a picture of a duck made from Kid K'NEX.
- Tell the children that they will take turns showing their friends which piece to put in next by using their eyes. They should look at the piece they want to be placed next and then look to the place that it should go. The children should look at each piece very deliberately.
- Teachers should model this a few times, first with each other and then with the children.
- It may be easiest to start with two children.
- Place the blocks or building materials in front of the children and have one child go first and use her eyes to show the other child the piece to pick up and then where to place it.
- Once the child has correctly placed the object, it is that child's turn to use his eyes to give directions to the first child.

Helpful Tips for Teaching:

In the beginning, it may be easier to have children point to the blocks and location, rather than using their eyes.

ACTIVITY 39: SHOW AND TELL

Social Skills:

Joint Attending

JA 5 (Follows point or gesture to objects); *JA 6* (Follows eye gaze to objects); *JA 7* (Shows others objects and makes eye contact to share interest); *JA 8* (Points to objects and makes eye contact to share interest)

Social Play

SP 4 (Shares toys/materials)

Self-Regulation

SR 3 (Raises hand and waits to be called before speaking); *SR 17* (Avoids perseveration on a topic or question)

Social/Emotional

SE 5 (Expresses appropriate level of enthusiasm about the actions or belongings of others)

Social Language

SL 4 (Addresses peers by name); *SL 5* (Answers social questions); *SL 6* (Asks social questions); *SL 7* (Asks concrete questions about an item or information shared by others); *SL 9* (Gains listener attention appropriately); *SL 10* (Responds to initiations from others); *SL 11* (Answers questions about ongoing activities); *SL 13* (Answers more than five questions on a preferred topic); *SL 14* (Makes reciprocal comments); *SL 24* (Uses contextually appropriate language/introduces topic)

Classroom/Group Behavior

CG 20 (Attends to small-group, teacher-led listening activity for at least ten minutes); *CG 23* (Passes items to peers)

Materials:

Objects of interest that children bring from home

When/Where to Play:

Circle Time

Directions:

- Assign children turns to bring something from home to share with the group.
- Have the child stand in front of the group and show what he brought in.
- Have the child describe the object to the group (e.g., "This is my new toy." "This is a picture of my favorite park.").
- Have the child explain why he brought in this particular item (e.g., "I wanted to show this toy because I just got it for my birthday." "I wanted to show a picture of this park because I like to go here for playdates.").

Activity 39 continued on next page

- Have the children in the group raise their hands and wait for the child to call on them so that they can ask questions or make comments.
- Visual supports may need to be used to help the child describe the item and to help the children in the group to ask a variety of questions or make a variety of comments.

Helpful Tips for Teaching:

A guideline should be sent home for what is appropriate to send for Show and Tell. For example, it is best to avoid objects on which a child will perseverate. It can be helpful to have children bring in objects related to a unit, such as some things that are their favorite color if the group is learning new information about their friends. Children can also bring in games to share and play with the group, which can help that child be better able to play the game at home.

ACTIVITY 40: LIST WALK

Social Skills:

Joint Attending

JA 5 (Follows point or gesture to objects); *JA 8* (Points to objects and makes eye contact to share interest)

Classroom/Group Behavior

CG 9 (Helps others, both spontaneously and when asked); *CG 14* (Stays in place when walking in line and maintains pace with group)

Materials:

A visual/picture list of items that children will find on the walk

When/Where to Play:

Playground; Around the building; Rainy Day

Directions:

- Each child should be given a list of items that he or she will find on a walk. Each child's list should be different. This list can be of items that they will see in the hallway or outdoors (e.g., letter "A," chair, yellow paper, fence, woodchips, swing).
- Tell the children that they are going on a hunt to find all the things on their list.
- As soon as a child finds something on her list, she should point to the item and say, "I found it!" The child should then cross the item off the list.
- The walk continues until all of the children have crossed all of the items off their list.

Variations:

- To make the walk more fun, place items related to themes or holidays along the route of the walk. For example, during St. Patrick's Day, place decorations of leprechauns or pots of gold on the walk; during Thanksgiving, turkeys; during Valentine's Day, hearts.
- Have children find the items on their list with a partner or as a group.
- For children who are working on Joint Attending or where moving out of the room may be more challenging, pick items in the room that will be reinforcing. For example, if Jason likes Thomas the Tank Engine, have him find Thomas in the room.

Helpful Hints for Teaching:

This game works well if the list is completely visual. It also works well if you are careful to go over the list with the children ahead of time. If you are working in a school environment, make sure to send out an email to let other classrooms and staff know not to move things around that you may have deliberately left out for the children to find. It can also be fun to involve other classrooms and teachers!

ACTIVITY 41: SELF-MONITORING CHECKLIST

Social Skills:

Joint Attending

JA 9 (Comments on what self or others are doing)

Social Play

SP 4 (Shares toys/materials); *SP 9* (Stops action when requested by a peer); *SP 13* (Invites peer to play in a preferred activity); *SP 15* (Accepts invitation to play in an activity of a peer's choice)

Self-Regulation

SR 6 (Follows classroom expectations and demonstrates flexibility during transitions); *SR 7* (Demonstrates flexibility when things are different than planned); *SR 8* (Demonstrates flexibility when preferred activities are interrupted); *SR 17* (Avoids perseveration on a topic or question)

Social/Emotional

SE 6 (Anticipates how a peer might respond to his his behavior and responds accordingly)

Social Language

SL 1 (Responds to greetings/partings); *SL 3* (Initiates greetings/partings); *SL 7* (Asks concrete questions about an item or information shared by others); *SL 10* (Responds to initiations of others); *SL 14* (Makes reciprocal comments); *SL 16* (Answers questions, asks questions, or makes comments to maintain conversation); *SL 18* (Directs body and eyes toward social partner when speaking); *SL 24* (Uses contextually appropriate language/introduces topic)

Materials:

Self-monitoring checklist, marker

When/Where to Play:

Circle Time; Cooperative Play Activity; Anytime, depending on target skills

Directions:

- Give each child a checklist of targeted social skills or behaviors, as well as a marker, at the beginning of an activity or the beginning of the group.
- Review the skills with the children in a group format.
- The checklist can include skills/behaviors such as: Say "hi" to three friends; Ask a friend to play with you; Ask before taking toys that other are using.
- At predetermined intervals (e.g., transitions between activities, when a timer goes off every five minutes), have each child check off "Yes/No" whether they used the skill.
- As the child utilizes each skill, he can check it off his list with a marker.
- Initially, children will need help in using the checklist and accurately monitoring their use of skills/behaviors.

Activity 41 continued on next page

ACTIVITY 41: SELF-MONITORING CHECKLIST (continued)

Helpful Hints for Teaching:

Using pictures to depict the skills/behaviors on the checklist increases children's ability to be independent. Start by focusing on only one or two skills and build up to no more than three or four skills. For some children, the checklist can be as simple as a picture of one to three children with whom the child will initiate a greeting or respond to a greeting. For other children, they can keep track of how many social initiations they make in a morning. Some children will also benefit from receiving a reinforcer for completing their checklist.

ACTIVITY 42: THE GOOD FRIEND BOOK

Social Skills:

Social Play
SP 22 (Identifies children who are their friends and can give a simple explanation why)

Social/Emotional
SE 6 (Anticipates how a peer might respond to his behavior and responds accordingly)

Classroom/Group Behavior
CG 18 (Attends to small-group, teacher-led, hands-on activity for at least ten minutes)

Materials:
Pictures taken of the children working and playing together, glue, construction paper, laminating sheets, binding

When/Where to Play:
Circle Time; Table Top Activity

Directions:
- In a small-group format, lead a discussion about what qualities make a good friend (e.g., someone who plays nicely, shares, listens).
- In advance, take pictures of the children playing appropriately together in different situations.
- Give the children copies of the pictures of them playing and working together with one another.
- Have the children pick out which pictures best show them being good friends.
- Have the children glue these onto construction paper and label the pictures, with adult's help ("I'm a good friend here because I'm sharing a toy.").
- After each child has glued and labeled a number of different pictures, laminate and bind the pictures into a book for each child.
- Pair up the children to read the books to each other and talk about what makes them a good friend.

Helpful Hints for Teaching:
Children will initially need a lot of help identifying what makes a good friend. It is important to start with just simple things (e.g., "John is a good friend because he plays with me.").

ACTIVITY 43: THE EMOTION BOOK

Social Skills:

Social/Emotional

SE 1 (Recognizes emotions in others and self); *SE 2* (Gives simple explanation for the emotional state for self and others); *SE 6* (Anticipates how a peer might respond to his behavior and responds accordingly)

Classroom/Group Behavior

CG 18 (Attends to small-group, hands-on activity)

Materials:

Magazines, pictures of people experiencing different emotions downloaded from the Internet, glue, construction paper, laminating sheets, binding

When/Where to Play:

Circle Time; Table Top Activity

Directions:

- In a small-group format, lead a discussion about emotions.
- In advance, get pictures from magazines or the Internet of different people showing different emotions.
- Show the children several pictures of people experiencing different emotions (e.g., a girl crying because she dropped her ice cream cone) and ask how the person is feeling and why.
- Tell the children that they are going to make their own book of emotions from pictures that they find in magazines or from ones that the teacher has printed.
- Have the children cut out and glue pictures onto construction paper.
- With an adult's help, the children can label the pictures (e.g., "The boy is happy because he is jumping on the trampoline.").
- After each child has glued and labeled a number of different pictures, laminate and bind the pictures into a book for each child.
- Pair up the children to read the books to each other and talk about the different pictures and emotions.

Variations:

- Once children are able to identify emotions and why a person might be experiencing the emotions, focus on having the children identify how they could respond to people in these different situations.

Helpful Hints for Teaching:

Depending on the group, you can either focus on one emotion at a time (e.g., have the children find many different pictures of people who are happy) or you can work on the children discriminating a range of emotions.

ACTIVITY 44: THE WAITING BOOK

Social Skills:

Self-Regulation

SR 3 (Raises hand and waits to be called before speaking); *SR 16* (Waits for help, for a requested item, or when directed for up to one minute without exhibiting challenging behaviors)

Classroom/Group Behavior

CG 10 (Remains in place in a group until called by teacher); *CG 18* (Attends to a small-group, teacher-led, hands-on activity for at least ten minutes); *CG 20* (Attends to small-group, teacher-led, listening activity for at least ten minutes)

Materials:

Pictures downloaded from the Internet or photographs taken of the children showing situations in which they might need to wait and pictures or photographs of children as they are engaged in activities while waiting appropriately (e.g., coloring, completing mazes, chatting with each other, playing clapping games together, and so on), glue, construction paper, scissors, laminating sheets, binding

When/Where to Play:

Circle Time; Table Top Activity

Directions:

- In a small-group format, lead a discussion about times that the children have to wait. Have the children list all the times that they have to wait (e.g., wait to share a toy, wait in line, wait while parents are talking, wait while teacher is busy with someone else).
- Tell the children that they are going to make their own books about waiting.
- Have the children glue one picture of a situation in which they might need to wait on to the left side of a piece of construction paper.
- With an adult's help, have the children list all the things they can do while they wait (e.g., count to 10, say "Excuse me," go play, take a deep breath).
- Provide pictures of different activities or strategies children might use when they are waiting and have them glue one of these pictures onto the right of the construction paper.
- After the children have glued different pictures of waiting and of strategies that they can use when waiting, laminate and bind the pictures into a book.
- Pair up the children to read the books to each other and talk about the different pictures.
- During small-group, teacher-led lessons, read the book and have the children role-play different scenarios (e.g., one person pretends to be busy while another child points to the "teacher is busy" picture and then points to an appropriate coping strategy and acts it out).

Helpful Hints for Teaching:

Noting children's behavior when waiting during naturally occurring situations can help the children to learn to identify situations in which they need to wait and things that they can do when waiting. These books should be used to teach waiting skills before the skill is required, but after having a lesson in waiting, bring the books along the next time the children need to wait. Eventually, the books will not be needed and a "wait box" can be brought instead. Inside the box, put activities that can keep the children busy but that were also depicted in the Waiting Book. Children should be able to choose an activity to keep themselves busy while waiting for the next activity to begin.

ACTIVITY 45: ICE BREAKER

Social Skills:

Social Play

SP 23 (Appropriately accepts that others likes and interests may be different than their own); *SP 24* (Wins without making bragging comments/gestures)

Social Language

SL 4 (Addresses peers by name); *SL 5* (Answers social questions); *SL 6* (Asks social questions); *SL 9* (Gains listener attention appropriately); *SL 10* (Responds to initiations from others); *SL 12* (Shares information about self, family, and major events); *SL 13* (Answers more than five questions on a preferred topic); *SL 14* (Makes reciprocal comments); *SL 18* (Directs body and eyes toward social partner when speaking); *SL 19* (Directs body and eyes toward social partner when listening); *SL 24* (Uses contextually appropriate language/introduces topic)

Materials:

Pre-made bingo cards (Each card has four squares and each square contains an image. Each image represents information about one of the children.), marker or crayon

When/Where to Play:

Circle Time

Directions:

- Give each child an individualized bingo card with information in each square about another child (e.g., "I have a cat named Lizzie at home." "My favorite thing to do on the playground is play tag.").
- Use visuals to describe the information (e.g., picture of swing to represent one child's favorite thing on the playground; picture of Caribou to represent another child's favorite game) to minimize the amount of adult assistance needed.
- Review the information in each square with the children.
- Instruct the children to ask one another questions (e.g., "Do you have a brother named Max?") to find out which child goes with each piece of information.
- Either have the children go around the group and take turns asking questions, or have the children walk around the room and approach one another and ask questions.
- Tell the children to put an "X" on each square when they know who the information in that square describes.
- The first person to fill up their bingo card wins.

Variations:

Pick a theme (e.g., playground) and learn all about the children's preferences in one particular area.

Helpful Hints for Teaching:

It is helpful to play this after teaching It's All About You! (Activity #13) so that the children have already been introduced to the topic of their friends' preferences and characteristics. Initially, start with bingo cards with only three or four squares, but increase the number of squares as children are more familiar with this activity.

ACTIVITY 46: WHOSE IS THAT?

Social Skills:

Self-Regulation

SR 3 (Raises hand and waits to be called before speaking)

Social Language

SL 4 (Addresses peers by name); SL 7 (Asks concrete questions about an item or information shared by others); SL 10 (Responds to initiations from others)

Classroom/Group Behavior

CG 3 (Recognizes belongings of own, others, and group); CG 9 (Helps others, both spontaneously and when asked); CG 21 (Responds together with group to teacher or peer leading activity)

Materials:

Various objects that belong to the children

When/Where to Play:

Circle Time

Directions:

- Have the children sit in a circle with an object that belongs to them (e.g., a toy that they brought from home, a picture that they drew).
- Have one child leave the room. Put an object that belongs to one of the other children in the middle of the circle. Have the other children hide their objects behind them or under them.
- Have the child return to the room and go into the middle of the circle.
- Have the child pick up the item, and have the other children say:

    Round and round the circle
    Running here and there
    One step...Two step

- Have the child in the middle finish the poem by saying:

    (Name) is this your _____ here?

- The child in the middle should fill in the blank with the object that he is holding and should stand in front of the child to whom he thinks the object belongs.
- If the child is correct, the child who is the owner of the object becomes the guesser.
- If the child is wrong, the children say the poem again, and the child makes another guess.
- This continues until the child guesses correctly.

ACTIVITY 47: ANIMAL PASS

Social Skills:

Joint Attending

JA 9 (Comments on what self or others are doing)

Social Play

SP 4 (Shares toys/materials); *SP 7* (Takes turns as part of a structured game and sustains attention until completion); *SP 12* (Trades toys/materials); *SP 20* (Demonstrates flexibility in following changes in the rules of a game or in accepting novel ideas from peers)

Social/Emotional

SE 5 (Expresses appropriate level of enthusiasm about the actions or belongings of others)

Social Language

SL 2 (Follows directions involving named adults or peers); *SL 4* (Addresses peers by name); *SL 9* (Gains listener attention appropriately); *SL 18* (Directs body and eyes toward social partner when speaking); *SL 19* (Directs body and eyes toward social partner when listening)

Classroom/Group Behavior

CG 22 (Follows basic two-to three-step verbal directions in a group); *CG 23* (Passes items to peers)

Nonverbal Behavior

NV 5 (Follows basic gestures and nonverbal cues)

Materials:

Stuffed animals, balls, beanbags, or other small objects; set of cards with pictures describing different actions

When/Where to Play:

Circle Time; Movement Time

Directions:

- Have the children sit in a circle, and give each child a stuffed animal.
- Identify one child to start.
- Have the child select a card from a pile in the middle and do what is indicated (e.g., put the animal on your head, make the animal dance, trade with a person who has on green).
- Continue around the circle having each child pick a card and do what is indicated.

Variations:

- Have only one stuffed animal, and have the children pass it around as they take a turn.
- Have the children take turns describing what the peer who picked a card is doing (e.g., "Bobby, put the bird on his head.").

Helpful Hints for Teaching:

When introducing this game, start with simple actions and use more complex actions as the children become familiar with the game.

ACTIVITY 48: CONVERSATION CHAIN

Social Skills:

Social Play

SP 23 (Appropriately accepts that others' likes and interests may be different from their own)

Self-Regulation

SR 12 (Modifies behavior in response to feedback); SR 17 (Avoids perseveration on a topic or question); SR 18 (Uses conversational voice level and tone when speaking)

Social/Emotional

SE 3 (Shows empathy toward others)

Social Language

SL 5 (Answers social questions); SL 6 (Asks social questions); SL 7 (Asks concrete questions about an item or information shared by others); SL 9 (Gains listener attention appropriately); SL 10 (Responds to initiations from others); SL 12 (Shares information about self, family, and major events); SL 14 (Makes reciprocal comments); SL 16 (Maintains conversation); SL 17 (Responds appropriately when a peer changes topic); SL 18 (Directs body and eyes toward social partner when speaking); SL 19 (Directs body and eyes toward social partner when listening); SL 23 (Converses on age-appropriate topics); SL 24 (Uses contextually appropriate language/introduces topic)

Materials:

Strips of colored paper for making a chain, tape or stapler, visual of different conversational topics

When/Where to Play:

Circle Time; Snack/Lunch

Directions:

- Give each child a stack of colored paper strips (one color per child).
- Pick a conversation topic or have the children pick a topic from a topic board.
- Have the children take turns making a comment or asking a question related to the conversation topic. For example, if the topic is "playground," have each child make a comment or ask a question about the playground.
- If the comment or question is on topic, assist the child with making a circle with their colored paper and taping or stapling it into a loop, combining their loop into a chain with the other children's loops.
- If the child does not have a comment or question about the topic or is off topic, move to another child.
- At the end, let the children count how many "colors" or comments they were able to add to the conversation. They should be able to see their color added to all the other colors on the conversation chain.
- Hang the chain somewhere in the room or allow one of the children to take the chain home.

Variations:

- Instead of each child getting a color, each topic gets a color. When the topic is changed, the color should be changed. The children can talk about what they talked about the longest, what was most fun to talk about, and what types of things were conversation stoppers (things that ended the conversation).
- Instead of making a chain, make a Conversation Pizza. Every child gets different "slices" or pizza ingredients (e.g., pepperoni, pepper, mushroom). When a child adds to the conversation, they add a slice to the larger pizza.

ACTIVITY 49: IN THE WOODS

Social Skills:

Social Play

SP 23 (Appropriately accepts that others' likes and interests may be different from their own)

Self-Regulation

SR 9 (Responds to feedback/correction without exhibiting challenging behaviors); SR 12 (Modifies behavior in response to feedback); SR 17 (Avoids perseveration on a topic or question); SR 18 (Uses conversational voice level and tone when speaking)

Social/Emotional

SE 3 (Shows empathy toward others)

Social Language

SL 5 (Answers social questions); SL 6 (Asks social questions); SL 7 (Asks concrete questions about an item or information shared by others); SL 9 (Gains listener attention appropriately); SL 10 (Responds to initiations from others); SL 12 (Shares information about self, family, and major events); SL 14 (Makes reciprocal comments); SL 16 (Maintains conversation); SL 17 (Responds appropriately when a peer changes topic); SL 18 (Directs body and eyes toward social partner when speaking); SL 19 (Directs body and eyes toward social partner when listening); SL 23 (Converses on age-appropriate topics); SL 24 (Uses contextually appropriate language/introduces topic)

Materials:

A large piece of construction paper with trees on the left side and the right side, and space in the middle with squares, each representing a comment or question that a child will make in a conversation; game pieces (e.g., construction paper stars or circles in different colors)

When/Where to Play:

Circle Time; Snack/Lunch

Directions:

- Have the children pick a topic of conversation or choose one from a topic board.
- Have the children take turns making a comment or asking a question related to the conversation topic.
- For example, if the topic is "playground," have each child make a comment or ask a question about the playground.
- If the comment or question is on topic, assist the child with moving their game piece up one of the squares toward the top of the board.
- If the child does not have a comment or question about the topic or is off topic, move to another child.
- If a child makes a comment or asks a question that is off topic, put their game piece "In the Woods" and tell them, "Oh! You are in the woods! We are talking about ____."
- When a child who is "In the Woods" has another turn, have him move out of the woods when he makes a comment or asks a question on topic. The child can continue the game on the square he left off on before going "In the woods."
- The first child to the top of the board is the winner.

Activity 49 continued on next page

Variations:

- Have only one game piece, and have the children try to get to the top of the board together.

- This game can also be played as a Conversation Pizza with children adding conversational "toppings." If they make a relevant comment, they can pick a "topping" to add to the pizza, like pepperoni, mushrooms, cheese, and so on (made out of construction paper). At the end, the children will have collaboratively made a playground pizza, for example, that they can visually see how many comments or questions were added. If a non-contextual comment was made, the child should not be allowed to add a topping.

- This game can also be done as a Conversation Tree. Every time the topic shifts, a new branch is added to the tree. Comments and questions about a certain topic can be added as leaves. If someone says a "conversation stopper" (something non-contextual that no one can add a comment or question to), you can visually add a small piece of red construction paper to that branch to show that this branch can no longer be added to. The goal is to not have any conversation stoppers.

Helpful Hints for Teaching:

Instead of a piece of construction paper, use a game board with cardboard trees to each side.

ACTIVITY 50: HOW DOES THAT RATE?

Social Skills:

Self-Regulation

SR 4 (Responds to calming strategies prompted by an adult); *SR 5* (Identifies when upset/frustrated and appropriately asks for a break or calming item/activity); *SR 7* (Demonstrates flexibility when things are different than planned); *SR 8* (Demonstrates flexibility when preferred activities are interrupted); *SR 12* (Modifies behavior in response to feedback); *SR 18* (Uses conversational voice level and tone when speaking)

Materials:

Large piece of construction paper, markers, different pictures can either be colored by the children or be copied from the Internet

When to Play:

Circle Time; Table Top Activity

Directions:

- Pick the emotion (e.g., frustration, anxiety) or environmental condition (e.g., noise) that you want to target.
- Using construction paper and markers, have the children make a 5-4-3-2-1 scale related to the target.
- Have the children identify what word and picture should go with each number. For example, for Noise Volume a tornado could be paired with with 5, a party with 4, the playground with 3, playing inside with 2, and working at table top with 1.
- Have the children draw and color pictures to go with each number, or use pictures from the Internet. If you decide to use pictures from the Internet, it is helpful to have the children talk about what they think each number looks like (e.g., "What sound do you think of when you think of a 1?" and so on). This can be easier to do with sound, which is a fairly concrete idea for children. Often, it is helpful to start with a sound scale before moving to a less concrete scale, such as emotions.
- Have the children glue the pictures on to the 5-4-3-2-1 scale next to the corresponding number.
- Model different levels of the target or pick children to take turns role-playing different situations related to the target.
- Have the other children identify on the scale where the modeled target fits.
- Have the visual visible during the group or school day and periodically label the level of the target.
- For Noise Volume, tell the children something like, "I like how you are all at a number 2," when they are demonstrating an appropriate noise level during Free-Play, or tell them, "You are at a number 3, can you bring it down to a number 1 for table top?" if they are too noisy.
- Also, periodically ask children, "What number do you think you are at right now?"

Variations:

- Once children are able to accurately rate the target emotion/condition, work on having them identify calming or coping strategies they can use.

Helpful Hints for Teaching:

It is important to carry this over throughout the group or school day, using the language and ratings identified during structured lessons. It can also be helpful for some children to start with a 3-2-1 scale because it is smaller and children have to think of fewer emotions/conditions.

Socially Savvy: An Assessment and Curriculum Guide for Young Children

CHAPTER 6:
Data Collection

It can be cumbersome to collect data when facilitating an individual child's social interactions, and even more challenging when leading a social-skills group, but there are several important reasons to make the effort. With some children who are struggling to learn a skill, it can seem like there is no progress being made unless we are collecting data. If we rely only on our impressions, we might constantly feel frustrated and eventually give up trying to teach that skill. Data removes the emotion (and possible frustration) out of the equation. While we might be feeling frustrated, the data indicates that the child is actually making progress, albeit slowly, and that in and of itself can be incredibly powerful for a teacher to realize. Conversely, if a child has been working on a skill for a period of time and the data indicates that there is no change in the child's ability to perform the skill, we need to rethink how we teach the skill. Perhaps the child requires an additional or different form of prompting, or maybe we need to increase the reinforcement that we are providing. Without data, it would be much more difficult to obtain this information and make these decisions. Presumably, children are in a social group because they need to work on certain targeted skills. If we are not collecting data on targeted skills, we may not realize the progress that a child has made and continue targeting the same skill for longer than necessary. In these situations, a number of things could take place, including a child becoming bored and beginning to use a learned skill less consistently and/or a child not being allowed to work on more sophisticated or advanced skills.

For these reasons, it is important to make data collection procedures as simple and easy to use as possible. The good news is that it is possible to develop data collection procedures that can be used in a group and that accurately reflect the skill level of all the children within the group. The first step, and one of the most important, is determining what type of data to collect. The most common types of data that we collect for measuring social skills are:

Frequency

For behaviors that have a clear beginning and end (e.g., greeting, sharing, answering a question), the most common measurement system is to record the number of times that a behavior occurs.

Number of Prompts

Often, we want to reduce the amount of support that a child needs to demonstrate a skill or participate in an activity. In this case, we might choose to measure the number of times that a child is prompted to demonstrate a targeted skill. Sometimes it is also helpful to record the type of prompt, such as verbal model, gesture, or independent.

Interval

For skills or behaviors that do not have a clear beginning or end, or that occur at a high rate, we may use an interval measurement system. This typically involves taking a short time sample (e.g., five minutes) and dividing the time sample into very short intervals (e.g., ten or fifteen seconds). Depending on the skill or behavior that we are measuring, we may choose to use a partial interval system and record whether the skill or behavior occurs at any point during the interval. This might be good for skills such as imitating a peer or responding together with the group. Another interval option for measuring behaviors is to use a momentary time sample system. This involves recording whether a behavior is occurring at the end of the interval, hence "momentary." This measurement system is particularly useful for measuring a child's attending during an activity (e.g., sitting quietly in circle, attending to a small-group activity). Both interval measurement systems result in a percentage (i.e., the number of intervals that a skill or behavior occurred out of the total number of intervals—12 out of 20 intervals, or 60%.

Occurrence/Nonoccurrence

In some cases, we simply want to know whether a skill or behavior occurs. For example, you might record at the end of each group whether the child exhibited specific behaviors (e.g., if there were occurrences of calling out in a listening activity or demonstrating flexibility when preferred activities are interrupted).

Percent Correct or Percent of Occurrences

For skills that provide multiple opportunities to practice and demonstrate a skill within a session, we might record the number of times that the child responded correctly or independently with a skill out of the total number of opportunities. For example, for responding to social questions, a child might respond correctly for three out of five questions or 60%.

One of the most important steps in implementing a successful social-skills program, is to develop the best possible data sheet. There are several things to consider when creating a data sheet:

- What is enough data to be able to make decisions about the child's progress?
- What type of data is necessary or appropriate (e.g., frequency, number of prompts)?
- What information should be included on the data sheet?
- How many children will be recorded on the data sheet?
- In what contexts will the data sheet be used (e.g., structured teaching environment, Free-Play situation, structured games)?

The first question to ask is how often you need to collect data. It is not necessary to collect data every time a skill or behavior occurs, or even on a daily basis. Data on a skill just needs to be collected frequently enough to allow you to make decisions about whether a child is making progress or whether changes need to be made. In many cases, collecting data on each targeted skill once a week is a reasonable expectation and provides a snapshot of where each child is in their progress. This does not mean that data on targeted skills can be collected inconsistently (every now and then or when you remember to record it). If you don't have a specific plan for when data will be collected, then, despite all good intentions, data will not be accurately recorded. One of the best ways to ensure that data is collected consistently is to pick a day (e.g., "Data Mondays") or target certain children on certain days (e.g., "Tara Tuesdays").

The type of data you need to collect should be determined when you initially select target skills and develop objectives or benchmarks. The benchmarks should specify the type of data that should be collected, such as the number of prompts or frequency of a skill. In determining what type of data to collect, consider again what is the easiest type of data to collect that will give you the information you need. For example, while it could be beneficial to collect data on the type of prompt required for a child to share (e.g., expectant look, gesture, physical prompt), it might be more practical to simply record whether the child independently shares or needs a prompt. The question that you have to ask is what level of detail is needed. For some children, it is important to know what type of prompt was needed, because progress may be particularly slow or children may continue to rely on prompts rather than spontaneously demonstrating skills.

The data sheet can also serve multiple functions, not only providing a format for recording data on targeted skills, but also serving as a guide to (1) the specific targets within a skill, (2) the type of prompting that is needed for a child, (3) the specific situations in which a child should use a skill, and (4) the time or location to record data. In other words, the data sheet can be your guide during a social-skills group. For example, when targeting commenting on actions, you might specify the type of prompting needed (e.g., presence of a visual support), the situation in which the child should comment (e.g., when the child or others in an activity perform some action), and the specific activities during which to target the skill (e.g., art, Play-Doh, blocks).

If you are collecting data on the social skills of multiple children, it is helpful to think about how you can develop the data sheet so that you can collect data on more than one child by having all the children grouped together for the same skill. For example, if one of the targeted skills is "Taking Turns," have all the children's names together for this skill. This way, when you are recording data on the children taking turns, you only have one sheet of paper in front of you and do not have to flip through multiple pages to collect data on different children. The more you can organize data sheets to reflect skills being targeted with multiple children, the easier it will be to record data.

Knowing when you are going to collect data also helps you decide how best to develop and organize data sheets. If you are collecting data on an individual child during a structured teaching session, you can organize your data sheet by skill. As discussed, you can also organize your data sheet by skill if you are collecting data on multiple children who are working on the same skill during teacher-led activities. Another way to organize your data sheet is by activity. For example, if your social-skills group typically includes a turn-taking game, a small group lesson, and snack, you can organize your data sheet by activity, with the specific skills specified within each of those activities. This is also helpful if you are collecting data on multiple children during more naturally occurring social situations.

There are countless ways to set up the data sheets. A helpful hint is that if a teacher does not feel comfortable with the way that it is set up (if there is too much data to take or if the data collection is too unwieldy while working with a child or running a group), the data will be the first thing dropped from the teacher's plate. Make the data sheets manageable and be open to suggestions to making the data sheets more user friendly. It is better to get less data than get no data or inaccurate data. At the end of this chapter, there are some examples of data sheets that consider the different questions that you might ask when developing a data sheet.

 Interspersed Data Sheet for an Individual Child

For children who are working on more entry-level social skills (e.g., greetings, waiting, answering social questions), the one child is likely the focus of intervention, and thus the focus of data collection. Any other children in the environment are likely not receiving direct services for social skills but might be serving as models or as social partners. For children receiving this level of social-skills intervention, it is more likely that they are being taught using specific, detailed teaching plans that outline how to prompt and reinforce, as well as record data. An interspersed data sheet, which allows for data to be collected on skills that are targeted within a more natural or activity-based context, can be very helpful. Prior to the start of the school day or the social-skills time, the teacher must complete information on the current prompt and target levels, as well as the specific situations in which the child will need to respond. All of this information comes from the specific teaching plans.

2 Activity-Based Data Sheet for Dyad

In other situations, for different children, or as children progress, social-skills intervention may occur in a dyad or triad, with two or three children all receiving intervention. An interspersed type of data sheet might still be useful and appropriate, and it might also be easier to organize the data sheet by activity. It might also be necessary to specify the specific prompt and target levels.

3 Group Data Sheet by Skill

Children who can consistently use their skills within a dyad are ready to use their skills in a larger group. These children still require data to be collected, but perhaps their skills can be worked on in other ways or in different formats, such as through social stories, role-playing, games, and table top projects (art projects). The data sheet can be organized by targeted skill, with examples of the types of activities or format within which to target these skills. Also, it might be sufficient to record only whether the child responds independently or needs to be prompted for targeted skills.

4 Group Data Sheet by Activity

The alternative to organizing the data sheet by skill when collecting data on multiple children in a group is to organize by activity. Within each activity, you specify the skill being targeted for each child. Again, it is easier to collect data on multiple children when you record only whether the child responds independently or needs to be prompted for the targeted skills.

1

Interspersed Data Sheet for an Individual Child

NAME:_____   DATE:_____

PROGRAM	PROMPT LEVEL	WHEN CHILD SHOULD RESPOND	TARGET	1	2	3	4	5	6	7	8	9	10	TOTAL % ACCURACY	STAFF INITIALS
Initiate Greetings (SL 3)	Independent (Ind)	Enter room or activity	Three peers												
Follows Point (JA 5)	Gesture	"Look at ___" and point	Book												
Comments on Actions (JA 9)	Ind with visual support present	Ongoing action of self and others	Art, Play-Doh, blocks												
Requesting Attention (SL 8)	Full verbal model	Finishing close-ended activity	Puzzle, file folder, or other close-ended activity												

Activity Schedule (SL 17)

Prompt Level:_____   Target Level: _____

ACTIVITY	POINTS TO/ LOOKS AT PICTURE OF ACTIVITY	OBTAINS ACTIVITY	COMPLETES ACTIVITY	PUTS ACTIVITY AWAY	REMOVES PICTURES OF ACTIVITY

Turn Taking (SP 7)

Game:_____   Target Level: _____

TURNS	1	2	3	4	5
1. Waits for turn					
2. Takes and completes turn, including verbal response					
3. Responds to other player if necessary					
Total # of Prompts					

2

Activity-Based Data Sheet for Dyad

DATE: _____ STAFF: _____

Turn Taking (SP 7)

Game: _____

STEP	Child:_____ Prompt:_____					Child:_____ Prompt:_____				
1. Waits for turn										
2. Takes and completes turn										
3. Passes game piece										
Total Independent Steps										

Cooperative Play (SP 5 and SP 6)

Game/Activity: _____

CHILD	PROMPT	STEP	1	2	3	4	5	%
		Gives Direction						
		Follows Direction						
		Gives Direction						
		Follows Direction						

Circle Time

CHILD	RESPONDS TO GREETINGS (SL 1)		INITIATES GREETINGS (SL 3)		CHARADES (NV 3) # OF PROMPTS		RAISING HAND (SR 3)		ANSWERING QUESTIONS ON TOPIC (SL 13)	
	Prompt		Prompt		Prompt		Prompt		Prompt	
	Prompt		Prompt		Prompt		Prompt		Prompt	

Conversation During Snack/Lunch (SL 16)

	RESPOND WITH VERBAL RESPONSE USING APPROPRIATE VOICE VOLUME		INITIATE VERBAL INTERACTION USING APPROPRIATE VOICE VOLUME	
	Independent	Prompted	Independent	Prompted
Child:				
Child:				

3

Group Data Sheet by Skills

DATE: _____

Directions: Mark a + if Independent and a − if prompted or no response. Ensure there are at least five opportunities per child.

PROGRAMS	ACTIVITY	CHILD 1	CHILD 2	CHILD 3	CHILD 4	CHILD 5
Flexibility (SR 7 and SR 8)	Activities 1, 16, 21, 28, 29, 34					
Gains listener attention appropriately (SL 9)	Table Top, Puzzles, Activities 2–5, 9, 12, 23, 26, 31, 32, 37, 39, 45, 47					
Responds to initiations from others (SL 10)	Table Top, Puzzles, Activities 5–9, 18, 23, 24, 26, 29–32, 35, 37, 39, 45, 46, 48, 49					
Advocates for oneself without exhibiting challenging behaviors (SR 14)	Act out problem situation and ask child to offer solution					
Follows basic gestures (NV 5)	Substitute directions with gesture (e.g., stand up, go to table)					
Identifies actions without words (NV 3)	Charades (Activity 4)	Act Guess	Act Guess	Act Guess	Act Guess	Act Guess
Shares information about self, family, and major events (SL 12)	Conversation Chain (Activity 48) (Use cards with conversation topics)					
Imitates peer leading activity (CG 6)	Simon Says (Activity 11)					
Commenting about self or others (JA 9)	Activities 4, 31, 47					

Group Data Sheet by Activity

DATE: _____   STAFF: _____

Show and Tell

STEP	CHILD 1		CHILD 2		CHILD 3		CHILD 4		CHILD 5	
Independent vs. Prompted	I	P	I	P	I	P	I	P	I	P
1. Shows others objects and makes eye contact (JA 7)										
2. Points to objects and makes eye contact to share interest (JA 8)										
3. Raises hand and waits to be called before speaking (SR 3)										
4. Addresses peers by name (SL 4)										
5. Makes reciprocal comments (SL 14)										

Turn Taking

STEP	CHILD 1	CHILD 2	CHILD 3	CHILD 4	CHILD 5
1. Takes turns (SP 7)					
2. Passes game piece (CG 23)					
Total Independent Steps					

Conversation

CHILD	CHILD 1		CHILD 2		CHILD 3		CHILD 4		CHILD 5	
Independent vs. Prompted	I	P	I	P	I	P	I	P	I	P
1. Responds to initiations from others (SL 10)										
2. Makes reciprocal comments (SL 14)										
3. Answers questions, asks questions, or makes comments to maintain conversation (SL 16)										

Group Data Sheet by Activity continued on next page

Musical Chairs

CHILD	CHILD 1		CHILD 2		CHILD 3		CHILD 4		CHILD 5	
Independent vs. Prompted	I	P	I	P	I	P	I	P	I	P
1. Stays in place when walking in a line (CG 14)										
2. Wins without bragging (SP 24)										
3. Expresses enthusiasm for friends (SE 5)										

What Am I?

CHILD	CHILD 1		CHILD 2		CHILD 3		CHILD 4		CHILD 5	
Independent vs. Prompted	I	P	I	P	I	P	I	P	I	P
1. Raises hand (SR 3)										
2. Asks a question (SL 7)										
3. Answers a question (SL 16)										

Charades

CHILD	CHILD 1		CHILD 2		CHILD 3		CHILD 4		CHILD 5	
Independent vs. Prompted	I	P	I	P	I	P	I	P	I	P
1. Raises hand (SR 3)										
2. Guesses action/animal (NV 3)										

CHAPTER 7:
Case Studies

1

BACKGROUND INFORMATION

Ethan K., a 5-year-old boy, was entering kindergarten several months after this assessment. Ethan had been diagnosed with Autism Spectrum Disorder at 3 years and 3 months old (39 months) and had subsequently been enrolled in a preschool program, which had included intensive intervention using Applied Behavior Analysis (ABA). Prior to turning 3 years old and being diagnosed with Autism Spectrum Disorder, Ethan had received early intervention services because of his language delays. In preschool, Ethan had participated in social groups for two years to work on generalizing his skills beyond using them with adults in a one-on-one setting. The social-skills groups lasted two and a half hours and Ethan attended the group four afternoons a week.

When beginning preschool services, the Assessment of Basic Language and Learning Skills-Revised (ABLLS-R) was completed for Ethan to help guide his educational programming. Ethan presented as a bright boy who expressed himself clearly with adults, but showed little interest in his peers. It was difficult for him to participate in small groups. Ethan was easily able to use descriptive sentences of five to six words with adults to request, comment, and answer questions. Ethan even said things like, "I just want to work with you alone," rather than being with a peer. His eye contact was poor. Ethan's play skills were not at the same level as his language skills, mostly because he preferred to be alone and did not want to play with other children. Play that involved completing a close-ended activity, like a puzzle or shape sorter, was easy for Ethan. When play included other children, Ethan would lose interest and wander away.

Ethan responded well in the social-skills group he attended and made progress with taking turns, playing cooperatively, and being flexible with peers. The Socially Savvy Checklist was completed to determine what areas were still challenging for Ethan as a new IEP was being developed.

RESULTS OF SOCIALLY SAVVY CHECKLIST

The results of the Socially Savvy Checklist highlighted areas of continuing need for Ethan. In the area of Joint Attending, Ethan's eye contact was still variable, but when motivated, he showed good eye contact with adults and peers. Although it was agreed that everyone on his team should be mindful about eye contact, it was also agreed that eye contact could be addressed when working on other skills. The Socially Savvy Checklist assesses skills at a granularity that allows for setting specific goals, some of which can be targeted as secondary to other interventions. Because eye contact is part of almost all face-to-face social interactions, the team decided to address this issue incidentally as Ethan naturally interacted with peers throughout the day. Ethan still was not demonstrating the Joint Attending skills of sharing objects or interests with others (*JA 7* and *JA 8*), and these were identified as a target skill.

In the area of Social Play, Ethan had mastered the skills that had been specifically targeted over the past two years through systematic programming; however, he still needed to work on taking turns as part of a structured game (*SP 7*). In addition, Ethan needed to become proficient in additional skills that were not among the initial targets, such as ending a structured game appropriately, taking a role in imaginative play, winning without bragging (*SP 10, SP 11, and SP 24*). Skills in this area would be a significant focus of intervention.

Although many skills in the Social/Emotional area were marked Emerging, it was agreed that we could target these skills while working on more critical areas (e.g., Social Play). Ethan also had a number of emerging skills in the area of Self-Regulation. Because these skills would be especially important as Ethan entered kindergarten, we set Self-Regulation goals as a high priority—these targets included raising his hand and waiting to be called (*SR 3*) and showing awareness of other's space (*SR 11*).

Despite his fantastic language, Ethan had not mastered many Social Language skills. He could not access this language ability when interacting with peers. We determined that interventions should focus on teaching Ethan to use those strong language skills in one-on-one sessions with his peers. Using peers' names (*SL 4*) and making reciprocal comments with peers (*SL 14*) were specific targets.

Ethan did not show mastery of many of the skills in the area of Classroom/Group Behavior, even though he spent two years in an integrated preschool classroom and in a social-skills group. This was not a surprise to his team because Ethan did not seem to enjoy group activities and required extra incentives to participate. We decided that an effective strategy would depend in part on finding a way to motivate him in group settings. Our goal was to increase his participation and independence in teacher-led activities.

In the area of Nonverbal Social Language, Ethan's skills were inconsistent. When motivated and attentive, he could follow nonverbal language, but his lack of consistency kept him from showing Mastery for some skills. Targets for intervention in this area included teaching Ethan to identify common actions, emotions, etc. without words.

Ethan's social-skills group included four other children. We took the social-skills needs of the other children in the group into consideration when selecting the specific skills to target in that setting. In other words, we did our best to practice the skills that would benefit all children in the group.

IDENTIFICATION OF TARGET SOCIAL SKILLS AND IEP BENCHMARKS

Joint Attending

Skill: (*JA 7*) Shows others objects and makes eye contact to share interest
Benchmark: During a structured sharing activity (e.g., Show and Tell), Ethan will show objects to share interest to an adult or peer at a frequency at least 80% of a typical peer across two weeks.

Social Play

Skill: (*SP 7*) Takes turns as part of a structured game and sustains attention until completion of the game
Benchmark: During a simple game with another child, Ethan will independently take his turn, pass the game piece, and wait for the other child to take a turn until the completion of the game for four out of five consecutive games.

Skill: *(SP 10)* Ends structured play/game with peer appropriately

Benchmark: Ethan will end a structured play/game with peers appropriately (e.g., say, "Let's play something else!") in four out of five consecutive opportunities.

Skill: *(SP 11)* Takes a role in an imaginative play theme and sustains for three to five actions (verbal and nonverbal)

Benchmark: Ethan will take a role in an imaginative play theme (e.g., restaurant, doctor, firefighter) and sustain for up to three to five actions (both verbal and nonverbal) requiring no more prompts than a typical peer across play themes.

Skill: *(SP 24)* Wins without making bragging comments/gestures

Benchmark: During games that involve a person winning, Ethan will win gracefully (e.g., saying, "Good game!" or a similar statement instead of negative comments like, "Loser!") in four out of five consecutive opportunities.

Self-Regulation

Skill: *(SR 3)* Raises hand and waits to be called before speaking

Benchmark: During small-group interactive activities, Ethan will raise his hand and wait to be called for four out of five consecutive opportunities.

Skill: *(SR 11)* Demonstrates awareness of own and other's space

Benchmark: During a ten-minute activity that involves walking in line or moving through a busy environment (e.g., Musical Chairs, Follow the Leader), Ethan will require no prompts to maintain appropriate space (e.g., not stepping on other's feet, keeping an appropriate distance) for four out for five measured opportunities.

Social Language

Skill: *(SL 4)* Child will address peers by name

Benchmark: In game-like activities in which children have to engage in turn taking that requires verbal interactions, Ethan will address peers by name in 80% of measured opportunities across three consecutive opportunities.

Skill: *(SL 14)* Child will make reciprocal comments to a peer

Benchmark: When a peer shares an object and/or makes a comment, Ethan will make a reciprocal comment (e.g., child responds to peer: "I like that movie, too!" "I have that same toy at home.") in four out of five measured opportunities across.

Classroom/Group Behavior

Skill: *(CG 18)* Attends to small-group, teacher-led, hands-on activity for at least ten minutes

Benchmark: Ethan will attend to a small-group, teacher-led, hands-on activity for at least ten minutes, requiring no more than three prompts for three consecutive opportunities.

Nonverbal Social Language

Skill: *(NV 3)* Identifies common actions without words

Benchmark: During a Charades-like game, Ethan will identify common actions, animals, or emotions demonstrated without words in four out of five measured opportunities.

MEASUREMENT

Data collection for most skills involved recording whether Ethan independently demonstrated specific skills or required prompting. The data sheet was organized by activity so it was easy to collect data for Ethan as well as the four other children in the social-skills group.

TEACHING STRATEGIES AND RESPONSE

Ethan, although not highly motivated to participate in group activities with other children, did best when fun and novel activities served as the context for learning. With this in mind, we incorporated as many games as possible into Ethan's social-skills group. We tried to choose activities that would be engaging for all five children in the groups and that would enable us to target a range of social skills.

Ethan participated in the social-skills group for two hours four times a week. The general structure of the group was as follows:

PRETEND PLAY (15 minutes)

As the children entered the group, pretend play materials were available for the children to use. Pretend play materials varied but included a doctor's kit, a baby doll, toy animals, and a vet kit. When a pretend play theme was introduced (e.g., doctor's kit), least-to-most modeling was used to introduce ideas of what could be done with the materials. As the children were able to play with the materials, and, more importantly, play with each other, adult prompting was slowly decreased, and the children were encouraged to use the materials with each other (e.g., use doctor's kit together on a doll or on each other).

Target Skills: *(SP 11)* Takes a role in an imaginative play theme and sustains for three to five actions

CIRCLE TIME (15 minutes)

Circle Time would typically involve a greeting activity, such as rolling a ball to each other or passing an object, reviewing the schedule for the day, and an interactive activity. Common interactive activities included Conversation Chain (Activity #48), Guess What's Different (Activity #2), or Head Honcho Directions (Activity #7). This was also a good time to introduce the topic of the day/week/month. For example, if the teacher was leading a lesson on emotions, this would be a good time to read a story about a specific emotion.

Target Skills: *(SR 3)* Raises hand and waits to be called before speaking, *(CG 18)* Attends to small-group, teacher-led, hands-on activity for ten minutes

SHOW AND TELL (15 minutes)

Show and Tell (Activity #39) was a popular activity with all of the children. The children took turns taking the Show and Tell box home and bringing back a special object, toy, or game to share. The child sharing would hide the box behind her back and ask the other children in the group to guess what was in the box. The child sharing might give some hints to help the children guess. The child would then show the toy or object to each child individually by making a comment and looking at the child. Each child in the group would then make a reciprocal comment or ask a question. Initially, Ethan and many of the children required verbal models of what to say when sharing and of appropriate comments or questions. During this exercise, the children learned to wait and attend while the other children commented or asked questions about the shared items.

Target Skills: *(JA 7)* Shows others objects and makes eye contact to share interest, *(JA 7)* Makes a verbal comment to share, *(SR 3)* Raises hand and waits to be called before speaking, *(SL 4)* Addresses peers by name, *(SL 14)* Makes reciprocal comments

MOVEMENT ACTIVITY (15 minutes)

Movement activities might include Musical Chairs, Follow the Leader, Scavenger Hunt, Freeze Dance, Simon Says, or Obstacle Course. The activity selected would be one that helped children practice maintaining appropriate personal space and/or winning without bragging. We created a social story about being a good winner or loser that was read prior to the activity or during another group time.

Target Skills: *(SR 11)* Demonstrates awareness of own and other's space, *(SP 24)* Wins without making bragging comments/gestures

BOOK (15 minutes)

The book chosen was always related to an ongoing theme (e.g., friendship, calming strategies). After reading the book, the teacher would lead a discussion and might also have the children participate in an activity related to the book and theme. For example, when talking about friendship, the teacher might call out certain topics or interests (e.g., "I like trains." "My favorite color is green.") and ask children to stand with friends who share similar interests.

Target Skills: *(CG 20)* Attends to small-group, teacher-led listening activity for at least ten minutes, *(SR 3)* Raises hand and waits to be called before speaking

TABLE TOP ACTIVITY (15 minutes)

The group would also participate in a table-top project related to the current theme of the group. For example, when talking about friendship, the children worked on Friendship Books (It's All About You Activity #13).

Target Skills: *(CG 20)* Attends to small-group, teacher-led listening activity for at least ten minutes

BATHROOM (10 minutes)

Going to the bathroom presented natural opportunities to practice walking in line and maintaining personal space. Additionally, games such as I Spy or Simon Says might also be built into the transition to and from the bathroom or while children waited for their turn to use the bathroom.

Target Skills: *(SR 11)* Demonstrates awareness of own and other's space

TURN-TAKING GAME (15 minutes)

We taught the children a variety of commercially available board games (e.g., Caribou, Go Fish, and Pop-Up Pirate). Two children would play one game, while three children would play a different game. Ethan understood the expectation of taking turns in a game but required extra reinforcement to maintain his attention to complete the game. To end a game appropriately, Ethan was initially provided with a variety of scripts to pick from each time (e.g., "That was fun." "Next time let's play Caribou.").

Target Skills: (SP 7) Takes turns as part of a structured game and sustains attention until completion of the game, (SP 10) Ends structured play/game with peer appropriately

GOODBYE (5 minutes)

This was a time to wrap-up the day and review our activities during the group. Typically, each child would have to answer the "question of the day" before leaving group (e.g., "What was your favorite part of group?" "Name one thing that you learned.").

Target Skills: (SR 3) Raises hand and waits to be called before speaking

OUTCOME OF INTERVENTION

Ethan is now in kindergarten. This socially unmotivated preschooler now has friends and willingly shares experiences with them. Unprompted, he will talk excitedly at the snack/lunch table about his food and compare what he is eating to what other children are eating. From there, the conversation naturally flows to age-appropriate topics (bugs, superheroes, toys, etc.). Ethan can still struggle with Self-Regulation. For example, Ethan will get silly with other children but may not be able to calm down as quickly. He has a large repertoire of functional communication responses that he knows how to use and is working on a five-point scale to identify when he is getting too silly and how to calm down more quickly. The silliness is more an outcome of his disregulation. Many children can get silly but then calm down. For some children, it can be hard to calm down, and learning how to regulate themselves, including using functional communication, is an incredibly important life and social skill. Right now, Ethan is not the child to set the pace of play. As much as his parents would like him to be a leader, he tends to be more of a follower. He can get into a habit of imitating the challenging behaviors of others if he thinks that someone may laugh. Although Ethan may have a little more work to do than his fellow kindergarteners, the deficits he has to overcome are minor compared with those we saw in the unmotivated and withdrawn child that came into the preschool. Continuing to monitor his social skills will be important. To highlight how far he has come in the previous two years, Ethan is now telling jokes to his peers. This involves a complex back and forth interaction between Ethan and the person listening to the joke, including pausing for laughter or to finish telling the joke. It also requires understanding why the joke is funny, or at least understanding that the point of a joke is to try and make other people laugh. Sometimes the jokes Ethan tells are funny, sometimes they aren't (as is typical for most young kids), but either way, his team takes great joy and satisfaction in Ethan's humor.

SOCIALLY SAVVY CHECKLIST SUMMARY REPORT

Child: *Ethan K.*   Age: *5.0*

Date of Evaluation: *June 9, 2013*   Evaluator: *Christine Almeida,*
                                        M.S.Ed., Ed.S., BCBA

The Socially Savvy Checklist evaluates the social skills of preschool and early elementary school children. It provides a picture of a child's social skills in a variety of areas, including Joint Attending, Social Play, Self-Regulation, Social/Emotional, Social Language, Classroom/Group Behavior, and Nonverbal Social Language. Specific skills are identified within each of the seven areas, for a total of 127 separate social skills. Within each section, skills generally move from simpler to more complex and are in the order in which a typically developing child would master them. That is, within each section, the lower numbered skills are simpler or may be prerequisites for later skills.

Any person with firsthand experience or understanding of a child's overall social functioning can complete the Socially Savvy Checklist—including, but not limited to, teachers and parents. The evaluator should have observed the child in a social setting for at least a two-week period and ratings should be based on observations of the child in this environment. The Socially Savvy Checklist consists of a four-point rating system: 0 = rarely or never demonstrates this skill; 1 = has demonstrated this skill but only on a few occasions; 2 = can demonstrate this skill but does not do so consistently; 3 = consistently demonstrates this skill; and N/A = not applicable due to setting or because child compensates in other ways. For the purpose of completing the report, skills receiving a score of either 1 or 2 are combined within the category of Emerging Acquisition, a score of 3 is Mastered, and a score of 0 is Not Yet in Repertoire.

The Socially Savvy Checklist helps identify a child's specific strengths and challenges. By evaluating these general areas and specific social skills with fine granularity, teachers and parents can prioritize the specific skills most in need of intervention.

JOINT ATTENDING

SKILL	MASTERED	EMERGING ACQUISITION	NOT YET IN REPERTOIRE
JA 1 Orients (e.g., looks or makes a related response) when an object is presented	X		
JA 2 Repeats own behavior to maintain social interaction	X		
JA 3 Repeats action with toy to maintain social interaction	X		
JA 4 Uses eye gaze to maintain social interaction		X	
JA 5 Follows point or gesture to objects	X		
JA 6 Follows eye gaze to objects		X	
JA 7 Shows others objects and makes eye contact to share interest			X
JA 8 Points to objects and makes eye contact to share interest		X	
JA 9 Comments on what self or others are doing		X	

SOCIAL PLAY

SKILL	MASTERED	EMERGING ACQUISITION	NOT YET IN REPERTOIRE
SP 1 Engages in social interactive games		X	
SP 2 Plays parallel for five to ten minutes, close to peers with close-ended toys		X	
SP 3 Plays parallel for five to ten minutes, close to peers with open-ended toys			X
SP 4 Shares toys/materials		X	
SP 5 Plays cooperatively for five to ten minutes with close-ended toys			X

Social Play continued on next page

SKILL	MASTERED	EMERGING ACQUISITION	NOT YET IN REPERTOIRE
SP 6 Plays cooperatively for five to ten minutes with open-ended toys			X
SP 7 Takes turns as part of a structured game and sustains attention until completion of the game			X
SP 8 Plays outdoor games with a group until the completion of the activity			X
SP 9 Stops action when requested by a peer			X
SP 10 Ends structured play/game with peer appropriately			X
SP 11 Takes a role in an imaginative play theme and sustains it, both verbally and nonverbally, for up to three to five actions			X
SP 12 Shows others objects and makes eye contact to share interest			X
SP 13 Invites peer to play in a preferred activity			X
SP 14 Approaches peers and appropriately joins in the ongoing activity			X
SP 15 Accepts invitation to play in an activity of peer's choice			X
SP 16 Accepts losing games or getting called "out"		X	
SP 17 Remains appropriately engaged during unstructured times			X
SP 18 Follows changes in play ideas of others and sustains the changes during open-ended play			X
SP 19 Appropriately plays games involving a person being "It"		X	
SP 20 Demonstrates flexibility in following changes in the rules of a game or in accepting novel ideas from peers			X

Social Play continued on next page

SOCIAL PLAY (continued)

SKILL	MASTERED	EMERGING ACQUISITION	NOT YET IN REPERTOIRE
SP 21 Plans a play scheme with a peer and follows it through			X
SP 22 Identifies children who are their friends and can give a simple explanation why		X	
SP 23 Appropriately accepts that others' likes and interests may be different from their own	X		
SP 24 Wins without making bragging comments/gestures		X	

SELF-REGULATION

SKILL	MASTERED	EMERGING ACQUISITION	NOT YET IN REPERTOIRE
SR 1 Demonstrates flexibility with new tasks/activities		X	
SR 2 Appropriately handles denied requests		X	
SR 3 Raises hand and waits to be called before speaking		X	
SR 4 Responds to calming strategies prompted by an adult			X
SR 5 Identifies when upset/frustrated and appropriately asks for a break or a calming item/activity		X	
SR 6 Follows classroom expectations and demonstrates flexibility during transitions	X		
SR 7 Demonstrates flexibility when things are different than planned	X		
SR 8 Demonstrates flexibility when preferred activities are interrupted	X		
SR 9 Responds to feedback/correction without exhibiting challenging behaviors	X		
SR 10 Responds to mistakes made by self or others without exhibiting challenging behaviors	X		

Self-Regulation continued on next page

SELF-REGULATION

SKILL	MASTERED	EMERGING ACQUISITION	NOT YET IN REPERTOIRE
SR 11 Demonstrates awareness of own and other's space		X	
SR 12 Modifies behavior in response to feedback		X	
SR 13 Uses appropriate words and voice tone to turn down requests from others	X		
SR 14 Advocates for oneself without exhibiting challenging behaviors			X
SR 15 Asks for help during novel or challenging activities		X	
SR 16 Waits for help, for requested item, or when directed to for up to one minute without exhibiting challenging behaviors			X
SR 17 Avoids perseveration on a topic or question		X	
SR 18 Uses conversational voice level and tone when speaking	X		

SOCIAL/EMOTIONAL

SKILL	MASTERED	EMERGING ACQUISITION	NOT YET IN REPERTOIRE
SE 1 Recognizes emotions in others and self	X		
SE 2 Gives a simple explanation for the emotional state of self and others when asked		X	
SE 3 Shows empathy toward others			X
SE 4 Expresses negative emotions without exhibiting challenging behaviors	X		
SE 5 Expresses appropriate level of enthusiasm about the actions or belonging of others			X
SE 6 Anticipates how a peer might respond to his behavior and responds accordingly			X

SOCIAL LANGUAGE

SKILL	MASTERED	EMERGING ACQUISITION	NOT YET IN REPERTOIRE
SL 1 Responds to greetings/partings		X	
SL 2 Follows directions involving named adults or peers	X		
SL 3 Initiates greetings/partings			X
SL 4 Addresses peers by name		X	
SL 5 Answers social questions	X		
SL 6 Asks social questions			X
SL 7 Asks concrete questions about an item or information shared by others		X	
SL 8 Requests attention		X	
SL 9 Gains listener attention appropriately			X
SL 10 Responds to initiations from others		X	
SL 11 Answers questions about ongoing activities		X	
SL 12 Shares information about self, family, and major events		X	
SL 13 Answers more than five questions on a preferred topic		X	
SL 14 Makes reciprocal comments			X
SL 15 Shares information about immediate past or future events			X
SL 16 Answers questions, asks questions, or makes comments to maintain conversation for three to four exchanges			X
SL 17 Responds appropriately when a peer changes topic			X

Social Language continued on next page

SOCIAL LANGUAGE (continued)

SKILL	MASTERED	EMERGING ACQUISITION	NOT YET IN REPERTOIRE
SL 18 Directs body and eyes toward social partner when speaking			X
SL 19 Directs body and eyes toward social partner when listening			X
SL 20 Speaks using polite phrases	X		
SL 21 Accepts people who are different	X		
SL 22 Seeks to repair or clarify breakdowns in social interactions			X
SL 23 Converses on age-appropriate topics		X	
SL 24 Uses contextually appropriate language/introduces topic			X

CLASSROOM/GROUP BEHAVIOR

SKILL	MASTERED	EMERGING ACQUISITION	NOT YET IN REPERTOIRE
CG 1 Follows schedule and classroom rules		X	
CG 2 Follows verbal directions as part of classroom routines or activities		X	
CG 3 Recognizes belongings of own, others, and group		X	
CG 4 Keeps toys/materials in designated locations	X		
CG 5 Responds to teacher by looking or coming when directly or indirectly cued		X	
CG 6 Imitates a peer who is leading songs/activities		X	
CG 7 Responds to indirect cueing			X

Classroom/Group Behavior continued on next page

SKILL	MASTERED	EMERGING ACQUISITION	NOT YET IN REPERTOIRE
CG 8 Uses playground equipment appropriately		X	
CG 9 Helps others, both spontaneously and when asked			X
CG 10 Remains in place in a group until called by teacher		X	
CG 11 Prepares for activity by locating area/materials		X	
CG 12 Follows directions during novel activities		X	
CG 13 Gives directions during novel activities		X	
CG 14 Stays in place when walking in line and maintains pace with group		X	
CG 15 Repeats words/actions from a song, book, or play activity			X
CG 16 Accepts that some peers may follow different rules or schedules		X	
CG 17 Asks permission to use others' possessions			X
CG 18 Attends to small-group, teacher-led, hands-on activity for at least ten minutes		X	
CG 19 Sits quietly in circle for at least ten minutes		X	
CG 20 Attends to small-group, teacher-led, listening activity for at least ten minutes			X
CG 21 Responds together with group to teacher or peer leading activity			X
CG 22 Follows basic two- to three-step verbal directions in a group			X
CG 23 Passes items to peers		X	

NONVERBAL SOCIAL LANGUAGE

SKILL	MASTERED	EMERGING ACQUISITION	NOT YET IN REPERTOIRE
NV 1 Reciprocates nonverbal interactions	X		
NV 2 Initiates nonverbal interactions with appropriate adults and peers			X
NV 3 Identifies basic actions without words			X
NV 4 Demonstrates an appropriate level of affection based on history, relationship, and familiarity with the person		X	
NV 5 Follows basic gestures and nonverbal cues		X	
NV 6 Modifies own behavior based on the body language, actions, or eye gaze of others			X

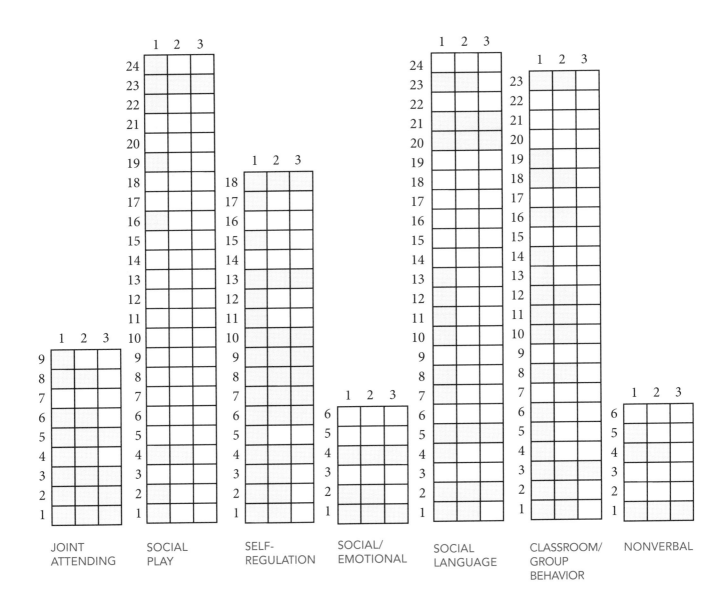

OBSERVATION	DATE	EVALUATOR	OBSERVATION SETTING(S)	LENGTH OF OBSERVATION(S)
1	6/9/2013	Christine Almeida	Social Skills Groups	Two weeks
2				
3				
4				

DATE: _____   STAFF: _____

Activity: Pretend Play (House Area, Dress Up, etc.)

	ETHAN		PAUL		SASHA		AARON		DANIEL	
Independent vs. Prompted	I	P	I	P	I	P	I	P	I	P
Nonverbal Play (e.g., Mixing ingredients to make bread) (SP 11)										
Verbal Play (e.g., "I'm going to make some bread.") (SP 11)										

Activity: Circle Time

	ETHAN		PAUL		SASHA		AARON		DANIEL	
Number of prompts to attend during ten-minute circle (CG 18)										
Independent vs. Prompted	I	P	I	P	I	P	I	P	I	P
Raises hand and waits to be called before speaking (SR 3)										

Activity: Show and Tell

	ETHAN		PAUL		SASHA		AARON		DANIEL	
Independent vs. Prompted	I	P	I	P	I	P	I	P	I	P
Shows others objects and makes eye contact to share interest (JA 7)										
Makes a verbal comment to share (e.g., "This is my favorite toy.") (JA 7)										
Raises hand and waits to be called before speaking (SR 3)										
Addresses peers by name (SL 4)										
Makes reciprocal comments when peer shares (SL 14)										

Activities: Musical Chairs, Follow the Leader, Obstacle Course, etc.

Activity: _____

	ETHAN	PAUL	SASHA	AARON	DANIEL
Number of prompts to maintain space during a ten-minute activity (SR 11)					
Wins without making bragging comments/gestures (SP 24)	Yes No N/A	Yes No N/A	Yes No N/A	Yes No N/A	Yes No N/A

Activity: Turn-Taking Game (Any board game)

	ETHAN		PAUL		SASHA		AARON		DANIEL	
Waits for turn (SP 7)										
Takes and completes turn (SP 7)										
Passes game piece (SP 7)										
Total Independent Steps										
Independent vs. Prompted	I	P	I	P	I	P	I	P	I	P
Ends game appropriately (SP 10)										
Wins without making bragging comments/gestures (SP 24)										

Activity: Charades

	ETHAN		PAUL		SASHA		AARON		DANIEL	
Independent vs. Prompted	I	P	I	P	I	P	I	P	I	P
Raises hand and waits to be called before speaking (SR 3)										
Identifies basic actions without words (NV 3)										

2

BACKGROUND INFORMATION

Chad G. is a 3-year-old boy (40 months) diagnosed with Autism Spectrum Disorder.
Chad might typically be described as "low functioning," and a child for whom social skills might not be a priority.
As part of a neuropsychological profile, Chad presented with cognitive delays and deficits in a variety of skill areas,
including expressive and receptive communication, visual performance, and play. Often times, educators and parents
are more focused on basic language and learning skills with a child with Chad's profile, and place less emphasis on
social skills. Social skills are often not part of formal testing or not something that will be "graded" later and can
therefore seem less important.

Before he began receiving intervention at 30 months, Chad did not use vocal speech and relied on challenging behaviors
to get his wants and needs met. At 3 years and 4 months old, Chad used vocal speech, typically limited to one-word
utterances unless he was encouraged to use a three-word sentence by withholding a preferred item and giving him an
expectant look. Chad's play skills were limited, and his play was often perseverative with trains and stoplights, including
turning his head sideways and laying down on the ground to look closely at the wheels on the track or turning a play
stoplight on its side to watch the colors. When pushed to expand his play, Chad would often continue with known or
preferred play actions (showing inflexibility) and occasionally would revert to challenging behaviors like screaming
or flopping. Chad also engaged in verbal and motor stereotypy by repetitively labeling the objects in a pretend play
scenario (e.g., "Cow says moo. Cow says moo. Cow says moo.") or by repetitively engaging non-functionally with a
piece of the toy. For example, if the toy had a door, Chad might open and close the door repeatedly.

Chad spent the majority of his morning in an inclusion classroom with typical peers but did receive support within
the classroom for one hour each morning from a staff skilled in using Applied Behavior Analysis (ABA) methodology.
For four afternoons a week, Chad participated in one-on-one or small-group intervention using ABA. He was
working on a number of different skills, including sorting, requesting, and labeling. These were important skills to
address, but all the skills work together and parsing them out works for assessment purposes but not in practical,
everyday life when we integrate all our skills all at once. Chad might be able to show certain skills in isolation, but in
everyday life when he will be expected to use all his skills together in school, at the grocery store, at parties, etc., they
will fall apart. Although this is more obvious with Chad, this is true of any child for whom you use the Socially Savvy
Checklist. Often, parents are frustrated when their child does not use skills demonstrated in school or a one-on-one
teaching session in an integrated manner in other settings, like home. Chad is a great example of how neglecting
social skills can actually make acquiring new skills or generalizing old skills more difficult.

RESULTS OF SOCIALLY SAVVY CHECKLIST

Based on the Socially Savvy Checklist, Chad showed a strong need for intervention in the following areas: Joint Attending, Social Play, Social/Emotional, and Social Language. Chad lacked most of the skills within the area of Joint Attending, and we determined our primary emphasis would be on increasing skills in this area, including increasing use of eye contact during social interactions and responding to gestures and eye gaze from others.

When it came to the area of Social Play, Chad had either emerging or absent skills. He showed little interest in play that was not related to his perseverative interests and needed to learn how to engage in simple games and reciprocal activities with adults or peers. Our initial focus in the area of Social Play was to increase Chad's appropriate parallel play and help him learn to participate in structured turn-taking games. Although most skills in the area of Self-Regulation were emerging or absent, we did not identify this area as a priority because Chad exhibited few challenging behaviors at the time of the assessment. Most of the skills within the area of Classroom/Group Behavior were also absent or emerging, but we also did not formally address them. All of the skills in the area of Social/Emotional and most of the skills in the area of Social Language were absent. We determined that in the Social/Emotional area, we would target identifying basic emotions and in the area of Social Language, the target would be responding to and initiating greetings and answering social questions.

IDENTIFICATION OF TARGET SOCIAL SKILLS AND IEP BENCHMARKS

Joint Attending

Skill: *(JA 4)* Uses eye gaze to maintain social interaction
Benchmark: During a variety of structured social activities and games (e.g., passing an object to another person, Red Rover, Simon Says), Chad will make eye contact paired with sharing/passing materials or making the expected response for five consecutive measured opportunities across five different games.

Skill: *(JA 6)* Follows eye gaze to objects
Benchmark: During a variety of close-ended or construction-type activities (e.g., puzzle, blocks, shape sorter), Chad will follow an adult's eye gaze to get and place a piece of the activity (e.g., put specific piece into the puzzle) in 80% of measured opportunities across three consecutive opportunities.

Skill: *(JA 7)* Shows others objects and makes eye contact to share interest
Benchmark: Given the completion of various activities (e.g., puzzles, artwork, picture schedule, daily living skills), Chad will use a complete verbal statement (e.g., "I did it." "Look at my picture.") and look at an adult to request attention for four out of five consecutive opportunities.

Social Play

Skill: *(SP 2)* Plays parallel for five to ten minutes, close to peers with close-ended toys
Benchmark: Chad will play for five to ten minutes with a close-ended toy (e.g., shape sorter, puzzle) close to peers (e.g., within three feet) requiring no more prompts than a typical peer across three toys.

Skill: *(SP 3)* Plays parallel for five to ten minutes, close to peers with open-ended toys

Benchmark: Chad will play for five to ten minutes with an open-ended toy (e.g. blocks, trucks, LEGOs) close to peers (e.g., within three feet) requiring no more prompts than a typical peer across three toys.

Skill: Takes turns as part of a structured game and sustains attention until completion of the game *(SP 7)*

Benchmark: During a simple game with another child, Chad will independently take his turn, pass a game piece, and wait for the other child to take a turn until the completion of the game for four out of five consecutive games.

Social/Emotional

Skill: *(SE 1)* Recognizes emotions in others and self

Benchmark: When presented with a picture of a person exhibiting an emotion, Chad will be able to verbally identify the emotion being displayed (e.g., happy, sad, mad, scared) in 80% of measured opportunities across three consecutive opportunities.

Social Language

Skill: *(SL 1)* Responds to greetings/partings

Benchmark: When presented with a greeting or parting by an adult or peer, Chad will respond with an appropriate verbal greeting/parting ("Hi/Bye") along with eye contact in 80% of measured opportunities across three consecutive days.

Skill: *(SL 3)* Initiates greetings/partings

Benchmark: When entering a classroom or a new activity, Chad will initiate greetings/partings with the adult or peer in that environment in 80% of measured opportunities across three consecutive days.

Skill: *(SL 5)* Answers social questions

Benchmark: Given one of 10 different social questions, Chad will appropriately respond to each social question from a peer or adult for 80% of measured opportunities for three consecutive sessions.

MEASUREMENT

Social-skills intervention with Chad primarily involved following formal teaching plans, and data was collected on each trial or opportunity and recorded as percent of opportunities.

TEACHING STRATEGIES AND RESPONSE

Given Chad's cognitive delays and deficits in a variety of skill areas, including the area of social skills, intervention with Chad occurred in a one-on-one or highly structured group setting, employing detailed teaching plans with specific prompting and reinforcement procedures. For generalization purposes, some social-skills intervention did also occur within the context of a typical preschool classroom, facilitated by a teaching assistant trained in ABA methodology. The following is a brief description of the teaching strategies employed to address each targeted social skill, Chad's general response, and some of the modifications and adjustments that were made based on Chad's progress.

USES EYE GAZE TO MAINTAIN SOCIAL INTERACTION (JA 4)

Specific activities were used as a context to teach Chad to pair eye contact with specific responses. Additionally, a formal program that involved fading a gesture prompt and increasing the complexity of activities was followed. Chad enjoyed passing a ball back and forth to a peer. This was initially taught via direct teaching in a one-on-one setting with an adult (see Turn Taking Lesson Plan in Appendix 1). A peer was added in as Chad became successful. He learned to wait until the peer was ready for the ball by watching the peer's face and body. He would then roll the ball to the peer, who was sitting, like Chad, with his legs apart to catch the ball. Chad had to learn to watch his peer's eyes, not only to share the experience, but also in order to know whether the peer was ready for the ball. This was a wonderful way to work on joint attending and waiting while adding in a nice social component with a peer. The next step was to expand Chad's use of eye gaze to other activities.

FOLLOWS EYE GAZE TO OBJECTS (JA 6)

We introduced a program in which Chad had to complete a close-ended or manipulative activity by following the gesture (e.g., point, head nod) or eye gaze of an adult. For example, a non-interlocking puzzle was used as the first activity, with Chad having to follow an adult's eye gaze to see which pieces to place into the puzzle. Initially, this was extremely difficult for Chad, and we limited this to two pieces, one on each end of the puzzle. His teacher paired eye gaze with moving her entire head in the direction of the target puzzle piece as a form of a gesture until Chad learned to focus on his teacher's head. Gradually, the head movements of his teacher became more subtle, and Chad began to focus more on his teacher's face/eyes. Gradually, the activity involved more puzzle pieces. Once Chad was able to complete a nine-piece puzzle by following the eye gaze of his teacher, his teacher started using simple nonverbal directions such as, "Chad, I want you to come here." or "Chad, pick this up." while gesturing with her eyes to the location where Chad was supposed to go or the object that Chad was supposed to get. Other activities in which Chad was directed to follow eye gaze were also introduced, including stacking blocks and completing a shape sorter. This program transitioned from a structured program (see Follows Gesture/Eye Gaze Lesson Plan in Appendix 1) to being run incidentally throughout the day.

SHOWS OTHERS OBJECTS AND MAKES EYE CONTACT TO SHARE INTEREST (JA 7)

Initially, Chad showed no desire to share objects of interest with others. A structured program was put in place during one-on-one instruction that involved taking turns pointing to a picture in a book, looking at his teacher, and labeling the picture with a carrier phrase (e.g., "Look! It's an airplane!"). Unfortunately, Chad did not find this this activity motivating and required prompts throughout the exercise. To increase his motivation, pictures of things that did motivate Chad (for example, traffic signs) were posted in the hallways at his height, and this program was run during walks and natural transition times. We changed the pictures frequently, and Chad found these walks highly motivating. He learned to label the pictures and share his interests with his teachers. He is just beginning to take walks with another peer to share his interest with that child.

PLAYS PARALLEL FOR FIVE TO TEN MINUTES, CLOSE TO PEERS WITH CLOSE-ENDED TOYS *(SP 2)*

At the outset, Chad had few independent play skills. He was able to complete some close-ended play activities, like a shape sorter, but only if an adult was present. In addition, Chad was not sure what to do when he completed the activity unless an adult set him up with another activity. At the beginning of the year, we provided an activity schedule (See Leisure Activity Schedule Lesson Plan in Appendix 1) for Chad that included one activity he needed to complete around other peers. As Chad became successful with this activity (the adult support was faded out), more activities were added on until Chad could complete five activities. In the coming year, Chad will be working on an activity schedule that includes interactions with peers.

PLAYS PARALLEL FOR FIVE TO TEN MINUTES, CLOSE TO PEERS WITH OPEN-ENDED TOYS *(SP 3)*

Chad's interest in open-ended play was limited at the beginning of the year. In direct teaching, Chad was taught to build various block structures by imitating modeled structured or pictures of block structures. Once he mastered being able to imitate a block structure of up to six blocks from a picture, this was generalized to the block area during Choice Time. Pictures of various block structures were placed in the block area to provide Chad with ideas of what to build if he did not independently build. Chad was not prompted unless he was not actively engaged or if he moved away from his peers for more than fifteen seconds. The time that Chad was expected to play in the block area was systematically increased, with Chad being cued when block time was over. Other open-ended activities were also targeted for direct instruction, including playing with a variety of manipulative materials.

TAKES TURNS AS PART OF A STRUCTURED GAME AND SUSTAINS ATTENTION UNTIL COMPLETION OF THE GAME *(SP 7)*

We put in place a structured turn-taking program that focused on teaching Chad to take a turn, pass materials, and wait. We started with a very simple activity, for example, taking turns using a toy fishing pole with a magnet at the end to catch fish. New games were added one at a time. Chad was initially reinforced after every turn, and this was also systematically faded to Chad being reinforced at the end of the game. Chad worked on turn taking first with an adult, until he no longer required reinforcement to wait for his turn or take his turn appropriately across three games. At that point, Chad started taking turns with a peer. Because the peer was not as quick with turn taking as the adult, reinforcement was reintroduced. Chad currently takes turns with one peer but will be working on increasing his repertoire of games and the number of peers participating in a game (groups of three and four instead of two).

RECOGNIZES EMOTIONS IN OTHERS AND SELF *(SE 1)*

As part of a formal program, Chad was taught to identify emotions in pictures and when displayed by another person. Verbal models of correct responses were quickly faded in these situations, but this did not generalize to Chad identifying his own internal states. To target this, each morning a teacher asked Chad how he was doing and showed him a visual with symbols for happy, sad, sick, and tired. One of the things that prompted us to use this strategy is the realization that Chad was unable to let us know when he was feeling ill. One day he was just "off," and it wasn't until later that his teacher realized that Chad had a high fever. Once Chad was able to communicate how he was doing, he was taught to ask his teacher how she was doing. His teacher would answer, with an exaggerated expression that matched her feeling.

RESPONDS TO GREETINGS/PARTINGS (SL 1)
INITIATES GREETINGS/PARTINGS (SL 3)

We followed a formal teaching program (See Responds to Greetings Lesson Plan in Appendix 1) during structured teaching sessions and incidentally within the classroom to teach Chad to respond to greetings and partings. At first, Chad did not respond to greetings or partings. We began by providing Chad with a reinforcer when he responded to a greeting from an adult, and then moved to a peer providing the reinforcer. As he began to use people's names (e.g. "Hi Anna"), we began to work on initiating greetings.

To target initiating greetings, we included the expectation to greet teachers and peers on a picture schedule. Chad began by initiating greetings to three teachers and then three specific children until he could say "hi" to the whole room. When we started, the pictures of the three specific children were included on his picture schedule, but by the time Chad was initiating a greeting to half the class, the next set of three children could just be pointed out to him. Chad now does very well saying "hi" to just about everyone in the school without the support of visuals or a schedule.

ANSWERS SOCIAL QUESTIONS (SL 5)

We put in place a formal program to teach Chad to respond to targeted social questions (See Social Questions Lesson Plan in Appendix 1). A time delay procedure was used to fade verbal prompts until Chad could independently respond to each target. He mastered, "What is your name?" "How old are you?" and "Where do you live?" At the beginning, Chad would repeat back the question before answering, so we introduced a visual so he could see where his teacher's part ended (the question) and his part began (the answer). This program took much longer than anticipated, but we expect that Chad will learn the next set of target questions more quickly now that he seems to understand not to repeat the question.

OUTCOME OF INTERVENTION

Chad has made many gains over the last year. The biggest are improved eye contact and general awareness of his peers. He no longer moves through space as if others are not part of his world and is aware that he has an obligation to interact with them by looking at them and greeting them. Chad's general play skills have increased, which has opened up a new world of opportunities for social interaction as he becomes increasingly able to play with peers.

Our goals for Chad in the coming year are to help him use his newfound skills to interact and play more with peers than on his own. He will also learn to extend his social skills beyond greeting peers to conversing and sharing interests with them. Chad has made a wonderful start, but there is still much work to be done to help him achieve his social potential.

SOCIALLY SAVVY CHECKLIST SUMMARY REPORT

Child: *Chad G.*   Age: *3.4*

Date of Evaluation: *Sept. 30, 2012*   Evaluator: *Christine Almeida,*
                                                   M.S.Ed., Ed.S., BCBA

The Socially Savvy Checklist evaluates the social skills of preschool and early elementary school children. It provides a picture of a child's social skills in a variety of areas, including Joint Attending, Social Play, Self-Regulation, Social/Emotional, Social Language, Classroom/Group Behavior, and Nonverbal Social Language. Specific skills are identified within each of the seven areas, for a total of 127 separate social skills. Within each section, skills generally move from simpler to more complex and are in the order in which a typically developing child would master them. That is, within each section, the lower numbered skills are simpler or may be prerequisites for later skills.

Any person with firsthand experience or understanding of a child's overall social functioning can complete the Socially Savvy Checklist—this would include, but not limited to, teachers and parents. The evaluator should have observed the child in a social setting for at least a two-week period and ratings should be based on observations of the child in this environment. The Socially Savvy Checklist consists of a four-point rating system: 0 = rarely or never demonstrates this skill; 1 = has demonstrated this skill but only on a few occasions; 2 = can demonstrate this skill but does not do so consistently; 3 = consistently demonstrates this skill; and N/A = not applicable due to setting or because child compensates in other ways. For the purpose of completing the report, skills receiving a score of either 1 or 2 are combined within the category of Emerging Acquisition, a score of 3 is Mastered, and a score of 0 is Not Yet in Repertoire.

The Socially Savvy Checklist helps identify a child's specific strengths and challenges. By evaluating these general areas and specific social skills with fine granularity, teachers and parents can prioritize the specific skills most in need of intervention.

JOINT ATTENDING

SKILL	MASTERED	EMERGING ACQUISITION	NOT YET IN REPERTOIRE
JA 1 Orients (e.g., looks or makes a related response) when an object is presented		X	
JA 2 Repeats own behavior to maintain social interaction		X	
JA 3 Repeats action with toy to maintain social interaction		X	
JA 4 Uses eye gaze to maintain social interaction			X
JA 5 Follows point or gesture to objects			X
JA 6 Follows eye gaze to objects			X
JA 7 Shows others objects and makes eye contact to share interest			X
JA 8 Points to objects and makes eye contact to share interest			X
JA 9 Comments on what self or others are doing			X

SOCIAL PLAY

SKILL	MASTERED	EMERGING ACQUISITION	NOT YET IN REPERTOIRE
SP 1 Engages in social interactive games		X	
SP 2 Plays parallel for five to ten minutes, close to peers with close-ended toys		X	
SP 3 Plays parallel for five to ten minutes, close to peers with open-ended toys			X
SP 4 Shares toys/materials		X	
SP 5 Plays cooperatively for five to ten minutes with close-ended toys			X

Social Play continued on next page

SKILL	MASTERED	EMERGING ACQUISITION	NOT YET IN REPERTOIRE
SP 6 Plays cooperatively for five to ten minutes with open-ended toys			X
SP 7 Takes turns as part of a structured game and sustains attention until completion of the game			X
SP 8 Plays outdoor games with a group until the completion of the activity			X
SP 9 Stops action when requested by a peer		X	
SP 10 Ends structured play/game with peer appropriately			X
SP 11 Takes a role in an imaginative play theme and sustains it, both verbally and nonverbally, for up to three to five actions			X
SP 12 Shows others objects and makes eye contact to share interest			X
SP 13 Invites peer to play in a preferred activity			X
SP 14 Approaches peers and appropriately joins in the ongoing activity			X
SP 15 Accepts invitation to play in an activity of peer's choice			X
SP 16 Accepts losing games or getting called "out"		X	
SP 17 Remains appropriately engaged during unstructured times			X
SP 18 Follows changes in play ideas of others and sustains the changes during open-ended play			X
SP 19 Appropriately plays games involving a person being "It"			X
SP 20 Demonstrates flexibility in following changes in the rules of a game or in accepting novel ideas from peers			X

Social Play continued on next page

SOCIAL PLAY (continued)

SKILL	MASTERED	EMERGING ACQUISITION	NOT YET IN REPERTOIRE
SP 21 Plans a play scheme with a peer and follows it through			X
SP 22 Identifies children who are their friends and can give a simple explanation why			X
SP 23 Appropriately accepts that others' likes and interests may be different from their own		X	
SP 24 Wins without making bragging comments/ gestures		X	

SELF-REGULATION

SKILL	MASTERED	EMERGING ACQUISITION	NOT YET IN REPERTOIRE
SR 1 Demonstrates flexibility with new tasks/activities		X	
SR 2 Appropriately handles denied requests		X	
SR 3 Raises hand and waits to be called before speaking			X
SR 4 Responds to calming strategies prompted by an adult		X	
SR 5 Identifies when upset/frustrated and appropriately asks for a break or a calming item/activity			X
SR 6 Follows classroom expectations and demonstrates flexibility during transitions		X	
SR 7 Demonstrates flexibility when things are different than planned		X	
SR 8 Demonstrates flexibility when preferred activities are interrupted			X
SR 9 Responds to feedback/correction without exhibiting challenging behaviors		X	
SR 10 Responds to mistakes made by self or others without exhibiting challenging behaviors		X	

Self-Regulation continued on next page

SELF-REGULATION

SKILL	MASTERED	EMERGING ACQUISITION	NOT YET IN REPERTOIRE
SR 11 Demonstrates awareness of own and other's space			X
SR 12 Modifies behavior in response to feedback			X
SR 13 Uses appropriate words and voice tone to turn down requests from others			X
SR 14 Advocates for oneself without exhibiting challenging behaviors			X
SR 15 Asks for help during novel or challenging activities			X
SR 16 Waits for help, for requested item, or when directed to for up to one minute without exhibiting challenging behaviors			X
SR 17 Avoids perseveration on a topic or question			X
SR 18 Uses conversational voice level and tone when speaking			X

SOCIAL/EMOTIONAL

SKILL	MASTERED	EMERGING ACQUISITION	NOT YET IN REPERTOIRE
SE 1 Recognizes emotions in others and self			X
SE 2 Gives a simple explanation for the emotional state of self and others when asked			X
SE 3 Shows empathy toward others			X
SE 4 Expresses negative emotions without exhibiting challenging behaviors			X
SE 5 Expresses appropriate level of enthusiasm about the actions or belonging of others			X
SE 6 Anticipates how a peer might respond to his behavior and responds accordingly			X

SOCIAL LANGUAGE

SKILL	MASTERED	EMERGING ACQUISITION	NOT YET IN REPERTOIRE
SL 1 Responds to greetings/partings			X
SL 2 Follows directions involving named adults or peers		X	
SL 3 Initiates greetings/partings			X
SL 4 Addresses peers by name			X
SL 5 Answers social questions			X
SL 6 Asks social questions			X
SL 7 Asks concrete questions about an item or information shared by others			X
SL 8 Requests attention			X
SL 9 Gains listener attention appropriately			X
SL 10 Responds to initiations from others			X
SL 11 Answers questions about ongoing activities			X
SL 12 Shares information about self, family, and major events			X
SL 13 Answers more than five questions on a preferred topic			X
SL 14 Makes reciprocal comments			X
SL 15 Shares information about immediate past or future events			X
SL 16 Answers questions, asks questions, or makes comments to maintain conversation for three to four exchanges			X
SL 17 Responds appropriately when a peer changes topic			X

Social Language continued on next page

SOCIAL LANGUAGE (continued)

SKILL	MASTERED	EMERGING ACQUISITION	NOT YET IN REPERTOIRE
SL 18 Directs body and eyes toward social partner when speaking			X
SL 19 Directs body and eyes toward social partner when listening			X
SL 20 Speaks using polite phrases			X
SL 21 Accepts people who are different			X
SL 22 Seeks to repair or clarify breakdowns in social interactions			X
SL 23 Converses on age-appropriate topics			X
SL 24 Uses contextually appropriate language/introduces topic			X

CLASSROOM/GROUP BEHAVIOR

SKILL	MASTERED	EMERGING ACQUISITION	NOT YET IN REPERTOIRE
CG 1 Follows schedule and classroom rules	X		
CG 2 Follows verbal directions as part of classroom routines or activities		X	
CG 3 Recognizes belongings of own, others, and group		X	
CG 4 Keeps toys/materials in designated locations		X	
CG 5 Responds to teacher by looking or coming when directly or indirectly cued		X	
CG 6 Imitates a peer who is leading songs/activities		X	
CG 7 Responds to indirect cueing			X

Classroom/Group Behavior continued on next page

SKILL	MASTERED	EMERGING ACQUISITION	NOT YET IN REPERTOIRE
CG 8 Uses playground equipment appropriately		X	
CG 9 Helps others, both spontaneously and when asked			X
CG 10 Remains in place in a group until called by teacher		X	
CG 11 Prepares for activity by locating area/ materials		X	
CG 12 Follows directions during novel activities		X	
CG 13 Gives directions during novel activities			X
CG 14 Stays in place when walking in line and maintains pace with group		X	
CG 15 Repeats words/actions from a song, book, or play activity			X
CG 16 Accepts that some peers may follow different rules or schedules		X	
CG 17 Asks permission to use others' possessions			X
CG 18 Attends to small-group, teacher-led, hands-on activity for at least ten minutes		X	
CG 19 Sits quietly in circle for at least ten minutes			X
CG 20 Attends to small-group, teacher-led, listening activity for at least ten minutes		X	
CG 21 Responds together with group to teacher or peer leading activity			X
CG 22 Follows basic two- to three-step verbal directions in a group			X
CG 23 Passes items to peers			X

NONVERBAL SOCIAL LANGUAGE

SKILL	MASTERED	EMERGING ACQUISITION	NOT YET IN REPERTOIRE
NV 1 Reciprocates nonverbal interactions		X	
NV 2 Initiates nonverbal interactions with appropriate adults and peers			X
NV 3 Identifies basic actions without words			X
NV 4 Demonstrates an appropriate level of affection based on history, relationship, and familiarity with the person		X	
NV 5 Follows basic gestures and nonverbal cues			X
NV 6 Modifies own behavior based on the body language, actions, or eye gaze of others			X

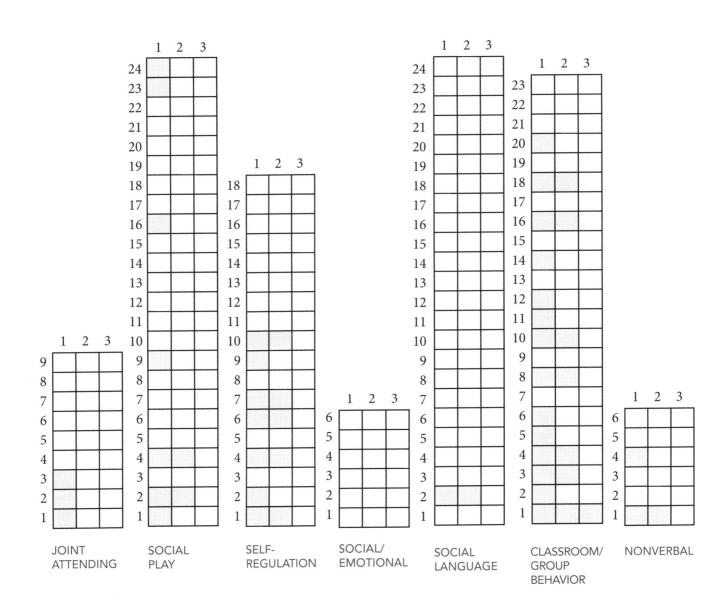

	1	2	3
JOINT ATTENDING			
SOCIAL PLAY			
SELF-REGULATION			
SOCIAL/EMOTIONAL			
SOCIAL LANGUAGE			
CLASSROOM/GROUP BEHAVIOR			
NONVERBAL			

OBSERVATION	DATE	EVALUATOR	OBSERVATION SETTING(S)	LENGTH OF OBSERVATION(S)
1	9/30/2013	Christine Almeida	Integrated Classroom/ Discrete Trials	Two weeks
2				
3				
4				

NAME: *Chad G.* _____ DATE: _____

Instructions: *Teachers/Aides must be familiar with individual program curricula prior to using this data sheet.*

Fill out the form completely at the start of the day by referring to the child's program book. Under "Program," write the program name. Under "Prompt Level," write the prescribed prompt for the session (see the "criterion" section on the curriculum). Under "Discriminative Stimuli," write your prompt or question (i.e., Let's go for a walk). Under "Target Stimuli," write the specific skills being taught (i.e., if you're running body-part ID, the specific body parts being targeted). For numbers 1–10, record per trial data: (+) correct, (-) incorrect, (p) prompted. Vary the programs conducted and do not run 10 trials of the same program consecutively. Under "Total % Accuracy" compute the % for 10 trials. Then transfer data to the summary sheet and graph in the program book.

PROGRAM	PROMPT LEVEL	DISCRIMINATIVE STIMULI (SD)	TARGET STIMULI	1	2	3	4	5	6	7	8	9	10	TOTAL % ACCURACY
Uses eye gaze to maintain social interaction (JA 4)	Two-second delay to Gesture	Holding ball and having eye contact from other person	Passing ball											
Following eye gaze (JA 6)	IND	Use whole head to point out the target stimuli	Puzzle pieces											
Shows others objects and makes eye contact to share interest (JA 7)	FP to point, FVM to label Gesture to look	"Let's go for a walk in the hall and see what we see!" Pictures in the hallway.	Pictures in the hallway; Labels and makes at least one second of eye contact	Point / Label / Look	Point / Label / Look	Point / Label / Look	Point / Label / Look	Point / Label / Look	Point / Label / Look	Point / Label / Look	Point / Label / Look	Point / Label / Look	Point / Label / Look	
Plays parallel with close-ended toys for up to ten minutes (SP 2)	IND	"Time for activity schedule"	Five activities plus reinforcer G= Gets materials P= Plays with materials C= Cleans up materials	G / P / C										
Plays parallel with open-ended toys for up to ten minutes (SP 3)	Least-to-Most prompting	"Time to play with blocks"		# of Prompts (if not engaged or moves away from materials for more than fifteen seconds)										
Greetings (SL 1)	Four-second delay Full Verbal Model	"Hi Chad"	Child responds w/ "Hi +Name" to greet three teachers after they say hi											
Takes turns as part of a structured game and sustains attention until completion of the game (SP 7)	Gesture	Counting, Caribou, Animal Scramble	Novel Games Three different games T=Takes turn C=Comments P=Passes game piece W=Waits for turn	T / C / P / W										
Recognizes emotions in others and self (SE 1)	IND	"Chad, how do you feel today?" at different points in the day	Chad answers with appropriate emotion to match his facial expression											
Answers social questions (SL 5)	IND	"What's your name?" "Where do you live?" "How old are you?"	Name, location, age											

APPENDIX 1:
Lesson Plans

JOINT ATTENDING

Item #	Lesson Plan
JA 4	Uses Eye Gaze to Maintain a Social Interaction
JA 5, JA 6	Follows Gesture/Eye Gaze
JA 8	Joint Attending with Books

SOCIAL PLAY

Item #	Lesson Plan
SP 4	Sharing
SP 5, SP 6	Cooperative Play
SP 7	Turn Taking
SP 11	Reciprocal Symbolic Play
SP 13, SP 14	Inviting a Peer to Play and Joining an Ongoing Activity
SP 17	Leisure Activity Schedule
SP 18	Shifting Play Ideas
SP 21	Cooperative Pretend Play

SELF-REGULATION

Item #	Lesson Plan
SR 14	Advocating for Oneself
SR 16	Waiting

SOCIAL/EMOTIONAL

Item #	Lesson Plan
SE 1	Identifying Emotions
SE 2	Identifying Causes of Emotions

SOCIAL LANGUAGE

Item #	Lesson Plan
SL 1	Respond to Greetings
SL 2	Receptive Identification of Familiar People
SL 5	Social Questions
SL 6, SL 14	Reciprocal Social Questions
SL 8	Requesting Attention
SL 11, SL 15	Answers Questions about Present, Past, and Future
SL 12	Answers Questions about Self, Family, and Major Events
SL 16	Simple Conversation
SL 22, SR 14	Advocating for Oneself

CLASSROOM/GROUP BEHAVIOR

Item #	Lesson Plan
CG 2, CG 22	Follow Classroom Instructions
CG 5	Respond to Name
CG 6	Gross-Motor Imitation from a Peer

USES EYE GAZE TO MAINTAIN A SOCIAL INTERACTION

Skill: *JA 4*

Objective: During a three- to five-minute play session with a teacher with the environment arranged with a variety of highly preferred interactive activities (e.g., tickles, arm shakes, bubbles, big bouncing ball), the child will increase the rate of spontaneously looking at the teacher to at least two instances per minute for four out of five consecutive sessions.

Materials: Highly preferred items/activities, data sheets

General Teaching Strategies: This skill should first be taught in a one-on-one setting. The teacher should set up the environment with a variety of interactive activities (e.g., bubbles, bouncing ball, trampoline) and entice the child with a variety of types of physical play (e.g., arm shakes, tickles). The teacher should engage the child in an interactive activity, stop periodically, and wait expectantly for the child to look. As soon as the child makes eye contact for two to three seconds, the teacher should continue the activity. The teacher can also use gestures or brief continuation of the activities if the child is not spontaneously making eye contact. A variety of activities should be employed, and different activities can be used during any play session.

Targets:

1. Three minutes
2. Four minutes
3. Five minutes

FOLLOWS GESTURE/EYE GAZE

Skill: *JA 5, JA 6*

Objective: The child will follow the eye gaze of a teacher to look at an object in 80% of measured opportunities across three consecutive opportunities.

Materials: Various simple activities (e.g., puzzles, blocks), reinforcers, data sheets

General Teaching Strategies: This skill can first be taught in a one-on-one setting, but can also be taught in a small group (two to four children). Each child should follow the eye gaze of the teacher leading the game to know where to place the material. For example, when completing a puzzle, place the puzzle pieces around the outside of the puzzle frame and say to the child, "Pick up that one," and indicate which puzzle piece by looking at the correct piece. If building a block structure, place several blocks scattered on the floor in front of the child (children), and say, "Put that one over there," and indicate the correct block by looking at it and the correct location by looking at the location. A marble run can also be built this way by scattering the various plastic pieces that make up a marble run on the floor in front of the child (children).

The teacher should use the following prompting hierarchy to have the child respond:

Prompting Procedure: Time Delay

1. Point to material/location paired with eye gaze
2. Eye gaze to material/location paired with point after a two-second delay
3. Eye gaze to material/location paired with point after a four-second delay
4. Eye gaze to material/location

Targets:

1. Non-interlocking puzzle
   a. Two pieces on either end of the outside of puzzle
   b. Four pieces scattered around the outside of puzzle
   c. Six pieces scattered around the outside of puzzle
2. Jigsaw puzzle
   a. Four pieces scattered around the outside of puzzle
   b. Six pieces scattered around the outside of puzzle
3. Blocks
   a. Four blocks scattered around the area in front of child
   b. Six blocks scattered around the area in front of child
4. Marble run
   a. Four pieces of a marble run scattered around the area in front of child
   b. Six pieces of a marble run scattered around the area in front of child

JOINT ATTENDING WITH BOOKS

Skill: *JA 8*

Objective: When looking at preferred books with an adult, the child will point to at least one picture on each page and look at the adult's face until the adult labels the picture for 80% of measured opportunities for three consecutive sessions.

Materials: Simple books, reinforcers, data sheets

General Teaching Strategies: The adult should present a preferred book with no more than five to ten pictures on a page. While turning the pages of the book with a child, the adult should pause on each page for at least ten seconds. The adult should then follow the prompting hierarchy to have the child point to a picture on the page and look toward the adult's face. The adult needs to ensure that the book is of high interest to the child.

The adult should use the following prompting hierarchy to have the child respond:

Prompting Procedure: Most-to-Least

1. Full physical prompt to point to picture and a gesture to look toward adult's face
2. Partial physical prompt at wrist to point to picture and a gesture to look toward adult's face
3. Partial physical prompt at elbow to point to picture and a gesture to look toward adult's face
4. No prompt to point but a gesture to look toward adult's face
5. Independent

SHARING

Skill: *SP 4*

Objective: During naturally occurring situations, the child will share a preferred toy with an adult progressing to a peer in 75% of measured opportunities across three sessions.

Materials: Preferred toys/activities, reinforcers, data sheets

General Teaching Strategies: Initially, opportunities should be set up for the child to share with the adult. When the child has a preferred toy or activity, the adult should say something like, "My turn," or "Can you share with me?" The child should be given five seconds to give the toy/activity and then the prompting hierarchy should be followed to have the child give the toy/activity. As the child progresses, opportunities can be set up during naturally occurring situations in which the child has choices and may pick the same toy or item. For example, at the water table, the adult might provide only one bucket for scooping water and have the child and a peer take turns sharing. The amount of time that the child has to share should be systematically increased following the Targets, initially only requiring the child to share for a couple seconds. When the child has waited the targeted amount of time, he should be reinforced with the item he is waiting for and verbal reinforcement. The adult should use the following prompting hierarchy to have the child give item to the other person:

Prompting Procedure: Most-to-Least

1. Full physical prompt
2. Partial physical prompt
3. Gestural prompt
4. Independent

Targets:

1. Sharing with an adult (two seconds)
2. Sharing with an adult (four seconds)
3. Sharing with an adult (six seconds)
4. Sharing with an adult (eight seconds)
5. Sharing with an adult (10 seconds)
6. Sharing with an adult (15 seconds)
7. Sharing with an adult (20 seconds)
8. Sharing with a peer (four seconds)
9. Sharing with a peer (six seconds)
10. Sharing with a peer (eight seconds)
11. Sharing with a peer (10 seconds)
12. Sharing with a peer (15 seconds)
13. Sharing with a peer (20 seconds)
14. Across three peers
15. Across three environments

COOPERATIVE PLAY

Skill: *SP 5, SP 6*

Objective: Given both close-ended (e.g., puzzle, shape sorter) and open-ended activities (e.g., blocks, trucks), the child will take turns giving and following simple directions with a peer to complete targeted close-ended and open-ended toys for four out of five consecutive opportunities.

Materials: Various close-ended and open-ended activities, reinforcers, data sheets

General Teaching Strategies: Present an activity (e.g., puzzle, blocks) to the child and a peer and direct the children to take turns giving directions. The two children will take turns giving (e.g., "Put this on the top.") or following directions to complete the activity or build a structure. One child will start with the container, pass it to the other, and give a direction. The second child should then follow the direction. After the second child follows the direction, she should pass the container back to the first child and give a direction. This sequence should continue until all of the materials are used. The adult should use the following prompting hierarchies to have the child give and follow directions:

Prompting Procedure (Giving Direction): Time Delay

> 1. Full verbal prompt after two seconds
> 2. Full verbal prompt after four seconds
> 3. Full verbal prompt after six seconds
> 4. Independent

Prompting Procedure (Following Direction): Time Delay

> 1. Full physical prompt after two seconds
> 2. Full physical prompt after four seconds
> 3. Full physical prompt after six seconds
> 4. Independent

Initially, the child should be reinforced after each turn of giving or receiving. When the child moves to the Independent prompt level, reinforcement should be decreased to only at the end of the game/activity.

Targets:

> 1. Puzzle
> 2. Shape sorter
> 3. File folder game
> 4. Blocks
> 5. Marble toy
> 6. Train set

TURN TAKING

Skill: *SP 7*

Objective: During a simple game with a peer, the child will independently take his turn, pass the game piece, and wait for the other person to take a turn until the completion of the game for four out of five consecutive games.

Materials: Turn-taking activity, reinforcers, data sheets

General Teaching Strategies: The adult should set up a simple game with the child and a peer. The game must involve passing an object back and forth (e.g., spinner, box with lotto cards). Data should be recorded for the first five turns during the game. The steps for taking a turn are:

1. Waits for turn
2. Takes and completes turn
3. Passes game piece

At each step, the adult should wait five seconds and then prompt the child according to the prompt hierarchy. No verbal prompts should be used.

Prompting Procedure: Most-to-Least

1. Full physical prompt
2. Partial physical prompt
3. Gesture
4. Independent

Targets:

1. Reinforced after every turn
2. Reinforced after every other turn
3. Reinforced after every three to five turns
4. Reinforced at the end of the game
5. Novel game (three different games)
6. In the classroom

RECIPROCAL SYMBOLIC PLAY

Skill: *SP 11*

Objective: During a play session with a peer, the child will take a role in an imaginative play theme (e.g., restaurant, doctor, firefighter) and sustain for up to three to five actions (verbal or nonverbal) for three consecutive play sessions.

Materials: Toy sets, reinforcers, data sheets

General Teaching Strategies: The adult should present the child and a peer with a set of toys and tell them something like, "It's time to play together." One child should go first and engage in a play action related to the theme. The other child should then engage in a play action that continues the theme. This reciprocal sequence should continue for three to five exchanges. For example, the adult might present a stuffed animal, a pretend medical kit, and a visual depicting "Animal Hospital," and the following exchange might be facilitated:

> Child 1: "Hi, I'm Dr. Smith. What's wrong with your dog?"
> Child 2: "Barky hurt his foot," and hands stuffed dog to other child.
> Child 1: Looks at dog's foot and says, "He needs a shot."
> Child 2: "I can hold him," and holds dog in front of other child.
> Child 1: "This won't hurt too much," while giving dog a shot.
> Child 2: Holds dog, rubbing his head, and says, "It's okay Barky."
> Child 1: "Barky should be okay now."
> Child 2: "Thanks doctor."

The adult should use the following prompting hierarchy to have children engage in reciprocal play:

Prompting Procedure: Time Delay

> 1. Full verbal/physical prompt after two seconds
> 2. Full verbal/physical prompt after four seconds
> 3. Full verbal/physical prompt after six seconds
> 4. Independent

Targets:

> 1. Taking care of baby
> 2. Farm
> 3. Restaurant
> 4. Animal hospital
> 5. Gas station

INVITING A PEER TO PLAY AND JOINING AN ONGOING ACTIVITY

Skill: *SP 13, SP 14*

Objective: Given visuals as needed, the child will verbally invite a peer to join him in a game or play, or ask if he can join an ongoing activity, in four out of five opportunities.

Materials: Various activities, reinforcers, data sheets

General Teaching Strategies:

Invite Peer to Play

Inviting a peer to play should be incorporated within a visual activity schedule (e.g., "Ask Paul to go to blocks with you."), so the child must first be able to independently follow an activity schedule. Next to the pictures of specific activities on the child's activity schedule, put a picture of a peer from the group. The expectation is for the child to look at the schedule, go to the peer whose picture is on the schedule, ask that peer to join the corresponding activity on the schedule, go to the activity with the child, and play for at least three minutes or until a close-ended activity is completed.

Join Peer

This program should be run during Free-Play time and can also be incorporated into an activity schedule or Choice Time schedule. The expectation is that the child always asks to join if he goes to an activity and other children are already there. For example, after making a choice on the choice-board to go to blocks, the child goes to the block area where other children are playing and asks, "Can I help?"

The least amount of physical guidance should be provided from behind to have the child follow the activity schedule or use a choice-board, to approach and look at a peer, and to go to or join an activity. The following prompt hierarchy should be employed to have the child make the verbal response:

Prompting Procedure: Time Delay

      1. Full verbal model
      2. Full verbal model after two seconds
      3. Full verbal model after four seconds
      4. Independent

Targets:

      1. Joining an activity
      2. Inviting a peer to play

LEISURE ACTIVITY SCHEDULE

Skill: *SP 17*

Objective: When given a leisure picture activity schedule with up to five activities, the child will independently complete the picture schedule for four out of five consecutive opportunities.

Materials: Activity schedule book, various activities

General Teaching Strategies: Toys and activities should be organized and clearly labeled on a shelf. The child should be given a visual picture schedule on a strip or in a small book (i.e., one picture per page). There should also be a pouch or designated place to put pictures of completed activities. The following task analysis should be employed to teach the child to follow the picture activity schedule:

1. Point to or look at picture
2. Obtain activity
3. Complete activity
4. Put activity away
5. Remove picture

The adult should use the following prompting hierarchy to have the child complete the activity schedule:

Prompting Procedure: Graduated Guidance

1. Full physical prompt
2. Partial physical prompt (e.g., slightly touch wrist or bumping elbow)
3. Slightly behind one to two feet
4. Behind five feet
5. Behind 10 feet
6. Out of room (looking in every 15 seconds)

Targets:

1. One activity plus reinforcer
2. Two activities plus reinforcer
3. Three activities plus reinforcer
4. Four activities plus reinforcer
5. Five activities plus reinforcer
6. In the classroom
7. On the playground
8. With at least two social components built into schedule

SHIFTING PLAY IDEAS

Skill: *SP 18*

Objective: During structured play activities with a peer, the child will shift play ideas when a peer does (e.g., cars go from driving to flying, doll goes from being a fairy to a princess) in three out of four opportunities across three play sessions.

Materials: Play materials, visual of play ideas/themes, data sheets, reinforcers

General Teaching Strategies: The adult should present the child and a peer with a set of toys and tell them something like, "It's time to play together." The children should also be presented with a visual that provides different play ideas/themes. Every several minutes, one of the children should be directed to pick a different play theme. Both children should then follow along with the selected play idea/theme. For example, the children are playing with some blocks and dinosaurs and pretending to build a house for the dinosaurs, but then the peer says, "Now let's pretend that the dinosaurs are attacking the house." The child should follow along by having a dinosaur pretend to attack the building. The following prompting procedure should be employed to have the child shift play ideas and engage in play related to the specified theme:

Prompting Procedure: Least-to-Most

1. Move toy near the child
2. Put toy in the child's hand
3. Model play action while labeling what you are doing
4. Provide a physical prompt to have the child exhibit play action

If the child is not engaging with the toys for more than fifteen seconds, or is demonstrating play actions not related to the theme, the adult should follow the least-to-most prompt hierarchy, waiting five to ten seconds at each prompt level.

Targets:

1. Blocks (e.g., castle, house, road, bridge, farm)
2. Doll set (e.g., baby is sick, getting baby ready for bed, feeding baby)
3. Farm set (e.g., farmer is feeding animals, animals get out of pen and farmer needs to get them, animals are having a race)
4. Kitchen set (e.g., cooking dinner, restaurant, making birthday cake)
5. House area (e.g., parent and child, siblings, getting ready for a party)

COOPERATIVE PRETEND PLAY

Skill: *SP 21*

Objective: Given a set of pretend play toys, the child will plan a play scheme with a peer and take turns giving and following directions for at least five turns each for four out of five consecutive opportunities.

Materials: Various pretend play sets, visual of different play schemes, reinforcers, data sheets

General Teaching Strategies: Present a set of pretend play toys to the child and a peer, as well as a visual that provides ideas of different play schemes. Have the children use the visual to pick a play scheme. Initially, an adult will need to facilitate the children picking a play scheme. The adult should then direct the children to take turns giving directions, again initially providing adult facilitation to determine who gives directions first. Have the children take turns giving and following directions until they each have had at least five turns to give directions and five turns to follow directions. The adult should use the following prompting hierarchies to have the child give and follow directions:

Prompting Procedure (Giving Direction): Time Delay

1. Full verbal prompt after two seconds
2. Full verbal prompt after four seconds
3. Full verbal prompt after six seconds
4. Independent

Prompting Procedure (Following Direction): Time Delay

1. Full physical prompt after two seconds
2. Full physical prompt after four seconds
3. Full physical prompt after six seconds
4. Independent

Initially, the child should be reinforced after each turn of giving or receiving. When the child moves to the Independent prompt level, reinforcement should be faded to the end of the activity.

Targets:

1. Doll set (e.g., baby is sick, getting baby ready for bed, feeding baby)
2. Farm set (e.g., time to feed animals, animals go to bed, mother animals take care of babies)
3. Kitchen set (e.g., cooking dinner, restaurant, making birthday cake)
4. Stuffed animals (e.g., pet store, animal hospital, zoo)
5. Toy cars and people (e.g., going on a trip, garage/repair shop, car lot)

ADVOCATING FOR ONESELF

Skill: *SR 14, SL 22*

Objective: Given targeted situations in which the child needs help or clarification, the child will use an appropriate functional communication response without exhibiting any interfering behaviors in four out of five measured opportunities.

Materials: Reinforcers, data sheets

General Teaching Strategies: Situations should be set up in which the child needs to make a functional request. In naturally occurring situations, the adult will need to read the child's body language and the ongoing context to determine when it is appropriate to prompt a functional request. Social stories of targeted situations should be developed and reviewed with the child regularly. The adult should use the following prompting hierarchy to have the child make a request:

Prompting Procedure: Time Delay

1. Full verbal model
2. Full verbal model after two seconds
3. Full verbal model after four seconds
4. Independent

Targets:

1. Missing items or materials
2. Novel or challenging activity
3. Direction presented too quietly
4. Complex direction
5. Person in child's space
6. Person taking child's toys/materials

WAITING

Skill: *SR 16*

Objective: During naturally occurring situations, the child will wait without exhibiting challenging behaviors for a preferred toy, edible, or activity with an adult, progressing to a peer, in three out of four opportunities across three sessions.

Materials: Preferred items/activities, reinforcers, data sheets

General Teaching Strategies: During times when the child shows interest in an item via body language (e.g., reaches for the item), the adult should say something like, "It's time to wait." When the child has waited the targeted amount of time, he should be reinforced with the item he is waiting for and with verbal reinforcement.

Prompting Procedure: Least-to-Most

Targets:

1. Waiting for a preferred item from an adult (one second)
2. Waiting for a preferred item from an adult (two seconds)
3. Waiting for a preferred item from an adult (five seconds)
4. Waiting for a preferred item from an adult (eight seconds)
5. Waiting for a preferred item from an adult (12 seconds)
6. Waiting for a preferred item from an adult (16 seconds)
7. Waiting for a preferred item from an adult (20 seconds)
8. Waiting for a preferred item from a peer (four seconds)
9. Waiting for a preferred item from a peer (eight seconds)
10. Waiting for a preferred item from a peer (12 seconds)
11. Waiting for a preferred item from a peer (16 seconds)
12. Waiting for a preferred item from a peer (20 seconds)
13. Waiting for a turn in three games
14. Waiting in a line with peers
15. Waiting for help

IDENTIFYING EMOTIONS

Skill: *SE 1*

Objective: Given six different emotions depicted in cards or expressed by a person, the child will identify the correct emotion when asked, "How does (s)he feel?" or "How do I feel?" in 80% of measured opportunities across three sessions.

Materials: Emotion cards, data sheets, reinforcers

General Teaching Strategies: The adult should present the child with an emotion card or demonstrate a facial expression of an emotion and ask the child, "How does (s)he feel?" or "How do I feel?" The adult should use the following prompting hierarchy to have the child identify the targeted emotions:

Prompting Procedure: Time Delay

1. Full verbal model
2. Partial verbal model
3. Partial verbal after two seconds
4. Partial verbal after four seconds; do not move on to Level 5 until at least 50% of responses are independent for three consecutive sessions
5. Independent

Targets:

1. Happy, Sad, Angry (pictures)
2. Happy, Sad, Angry (in vivo)
3. Scared, Surprised, Tired (pictures)
4. Random (Targets 1–3)
5. Scared, Surprised, Tired (in vivo)
6. Random (Targets 1–5)
7. Silly, Sick (pictures)
8. Random (Targets 1–7)
9. Silly, Sick (in vivo)
10. Random (Targets 1–9)
11. Target 10 across three adults
12. Target 10 across three settings

IDENTIFYING CAUSES OF EMOTIONS

Skill: *SE 2*

Objective: First in pictures and then in naturally occurring situations, the child will be able to verbally identify the emotion (happy, sad, mad, scared) being displayed by herself and others and provide a simple explanation for the emotion (e.g., got a new toy, dropped ice cream, someone took new toy, saw a big dog) in 80% of measured opportunities across three consecutive days.

Materials: Pictures or demonstrations of emotional situations, data sheets, reinforcers

General Teaching Strategies: The adult should present a picture of an emotional situation (e.g., a child on the ground crying near a bicycle that is also on the ground), should act out different situations with dolls or stuffed animals (e.g., two dolls are racing and one wins), or should model different situations (e.g., adult is very carefully coloring a picture and accidentally rips the paper). The adult should use the following prompting hierarchy to have the child identify the targeted emotions and to provide an explanation for the emotion:

Prompting Procedure: Time Delay

1. Full verbal model
2. Partial verbal model
3. Partial verbal after two seconds
4. Partial verbal after four seconds; do not move on to Level 5 until at least 50% of responses are independent for three consecutive sessions
5. Independent

Targets:

1. Happy and Sad (pictures)
2. Happy and Sad (modeled)
3. Mad and Scared (pictures)
4. Mad and Scared (modeled)
5. Random (Targets 1–4)
6. Situations in group

RESPOND TO GREETINGS

Skill: *SL 1*

Objective: Given naturally occurring situations, the child will respond to greetings using the greeter's name ("Hi _____") in 80% of measured opportunities across three consecutive sessions.

Materials: Reinforcers, data sheets

General Teaching Strategies: This skill can be targeted incidentally, but opportunities should also be set up to have peers and adults greet the child. Initially, the program may need to be run in a discrete-trial format. The adult should use the following prompting hierarchy to have the child respond to the greeting:

Prompting Procedure: Time Delay

1. Immediate full verbal model
2. Full verbal model after two-second delay
3. Full verbal model after four-second delay
4. Independent

Targets:

1. Child responds by saying, "Hi"
2. Child responds to three adults, "Hi _____"
3. Child responds to a different set of three adults, "Hi _____"
4. Child responds to three peers, "Hi _____"
5. Generalize to inclusion setting

RECEPTIVE IDENTIFICATION OF FAMILIAR PEOPLE

Skill: *SL 2*

Objective: Given a direction to go to a person and complete an action, the child will approach the correct person and complete the action in 80% of measured opportunities for three consecutive sessions.

Materials: Reinforcers, data sheets

General Teaching Strategies: Adult should ensure that the child is fully attending and provide a direction that involves going to a targeted person and performing an action (e.g., "Give this to Mr. Davis." "Sit next to Susan."). The adult should use the following prompting hierarchy to have the child respond to the direction:

Prompting Procedure: Time Delay

1. Full physical prompt after two seconds
2. Full physical prompt after four seconds
3. Full physical prompt after six seconds
4. Independent

Targets:

1. Three adults
2. Three different adults
3. Three peers
4. Three additional peers

SOCIAL QUESTIONS

Skill: *SL 5*

Objective: Given one of 12 different social questions, the child will appropriately respond to each social question from a peer or adult for 80% of measured opportunities for three consecutive sessions.

Materials: Reinforcers, data sheets

General Teaching Strategies: Adult should ensure that the child is fully attending and then ask a targeted question. The adult should use the following prompting hierarchy to have the child respond to targeted social questions:

Prompting Procedure: Most-to-Least

1. Full verbal model
2. Partial verbal model after two-seconds
3. Partial verbal model after four-seconds
4. Independent

Targets:

1. "What is your name?" "Where do you live?" "How old are you?"
2. "What's your last name?" "Where do you go to school?" "What's your address?"
3. Random (Sets 1–2)
4. "When is your birthday?" "What is your mom's name?" "What is your dad's name?"
5. "Whose class are you in?" "What's your favorite food?" "What's your favorite game?"
6. Random (Sets 1–4)
7. Across three adults
8. Across three peers

RECIPROCAL SOCIAL QUESTIONS

Skill: *SL 6, SL 14*

Objective: Given a turn-taking format and visual cues/topic board, the child will be able to ask social questions or make social comments (e.g., "What is your favorite book?" "I like to play with K'NEX.") and respond to social questions/comments with a related statement or question (e.g., "My favorite movie is Lion King. Do you like Lion King?") for 80% of measured opportunities across three consecutive days

Materials: Set of cards or topic board with visual prompts of questions/comments, reinforcers, data sheets

General Teaching Strategies: The adult should set up a turn-taking game with a set of cards or a topic board with visual prompts of questions or comments to make (e.g., symbol for asking; picture of foods). The child should take turns picking a card or referencing the topic board and then starting a social interaction with another child. The adult should use the following prompting hierarchy to have the child respond to targeted social questions:

Prompting Procedure:

1. Full verbal model
2. Full verbal model after two-seconds
3. Full verbal model after four-seconds
4. Independent

Nonverbal prompts should be provided if the child does not make eye contact.

Targets:

1. Adult in one-on-one setting
2. Peer in dyad
3. Peer in inclusion setting

A. Question-statement ("What's your favorite food?" Child answers: "Cookies.")
B. Question-statement-question ("What's your favorite food? Child: "Cookies. What's your favorite food?")
C. Statement-statement ("I have peaches." Child: "I have apples.")
D. Statement-statement-question ("I have peaches." Child: "I have apples. Do you like apples?")

REQUESTING ATTENTION

Skill: *SL 8*

Objective: Given the completion of various activities (e.g., puzzles, artwork, picture schedule, daily living skills), the child will use complete verbal statements and appropriate voice tone to request attention for completed activities for 80% of measured opportunities across three consecutive sessions.

Materials: Various activities, reinforcers, data sheets

General Teaching Strategies: The adult should set up targeted activities. During naturally occurring situations after completing an activity, the child should say, "I did it." "Look what I made." or some equivalent to request attention. The adult should vary the verbal models provided (e.g., "I did it." "Look what I made." "I made a _____." "I finished my schedule."). The adult should use the following prompting hierarchy to have the child request attention:

Prompting Procedure:

1. Immediate full verbal model
2. Full verbal model after two seconds
3. Full verbal model after four seconds; do not move on to Level 4 until at least 50% of responses are independent for three consecutive sessions
4. Independent

Targets:

1. Finish a close-ended activity (e.g., puzzle, shape sorter)
2. Finish an art project
3. Finish picture activity schedule
4. Finish a daily living skill

ANSWERS QUESTIONS ABOUT PRESENT, PAST, AND FUTURE

Skill: *SL 11, SL 15*

Objective: When asked specific questions about daily activities (e.g., "Who did you sit with at lunch?" "What are we doing in gym?" "What will you do at recess?"), the child will respond with a complete sentence or phrase with the correct verb tense for 80% of measured opportunities across three consecutive days.

Materials: Reinforcers, data sheets

General Teaching Strategies: Throughout day, the adult should ask specific questions about group activities that have either just occurred (e.g., "Who did you sit with at lunch?"), are currently occurring ("What story did the adult read?"), or are going to occur later (e.g., "What are you going to eat for lunch?"). The adult should use the following prompting hierarchy to have the child respond:

Prompting Procedure:

1. Immediate full verbal model
2. Full verbal model after two seconds
3. Full verbal model after four seconds; do not move on to Level 4 until at least 50% of responses are independent for three consecutive sessions
4. Independent

Targets:

1. Ongoing activity
2. Ongoing activity and activity that just occurred
3. Ongoing activity, activity that just occurred, and activity that will happen later

Skill: *SL 12*

Objective: Given targeted questions about self, family, and major events, the child will appropriately respond to each question from a peer or adult for 80% of measured opportunities for three consecutive sessions.

Materials: Reinforcers, data sheets

General Teaching Strategies: The adult should ensure that the child is fully attending and ask the targeted question. The adult should use the following prompting hierarchy to have the child respond to targeted questions:

Prompting Procedure:

1. Full verbal model
2. Partial verbal model after two seconds
3. Partial verbal model after four seconds
4. Independent

Targets:

1. Information about self (e.g., age, birthday, favorite food, favorite toy, favorite color)
2. Information about family (e.g., siblings, pet, mom's job)
3. Information about major events (e.g., vacation, holiday, special event)

SIMPLE CONVERSATION

Skill: *SL 16*

Objective: Given a turn-taking format and visual cues, the child will be able to ask social questions or make social comments to maintain a conversation for at least four complete exchanges for four out of five consecutive opportunities.

Materials: Reinforcers, data sheets

General Teaching Strategies: The adult should set up a turn-taking game with a set of cards, each with a specific topic (e.g., favorite toy, playground, movies). Children should take turns picking a card and then starting a conversation. The adult should use the following prompting hierarchy to have the child respond to targeted social questions:

Prompting Procedure:

1. Full verbal model
2. Full verbal model after two seconds
3. Full verbal model after four seconds
4. Independent

Nonverbal prompts should be provided if the child does not make eye contact.

Targets:

1. Favorite toys, movies, playground
2. Family members, favorite foods, animals
3. Pets, after school, games
4. Books, songs, holidays

FOLLOW CLASSROOM INSTRUCTIONS

Skill: *CG 2, CG 22*

Objective: Given a variety of functional multiple-step directions around the classroom, the child will follow the directions within 10 seconds for 80% of measured opportunities for three consecutive sessions.

Materials: Data sheets, reinforcers

General Teaching Strategies: The adult should present various clear, functional instructions to the child that are generally part of the classroom routine. The adult should use the following prompting hierarchy to have the child respond to targeted directions.

Prompting Procedure: Most-to-Least

1. Full physical prompt from behind
2. Partial physical prompt from behind
3. Gesture
4. Independent

Targets:

1. Put away snack and line up
2. Put on coat and line up
3. Put markers away and go sit down at circle
4. Clean up and sit down at circle
5. Wash hands and get snack
6. Get placemat and sit down for snack

RESPOND TO NAME

Skill: *CG 5*

Objective: Given a variety of cues to look at and attend to the adult, the child will stop an ongoing activity and look toward the adult to listen to a direction from a distance up to ten feet for 80% of measured opportunities for three consecutive days.

Materials: Reinforcers, data sheets

General Teaching Strategies: The adult should call the child's name. The child should turn toward the adult and make eye contact within five seconds. The adult should use the following prompting hierarchy to have the child look.

Prompting Procedure:

1. Gesture
2. Gesture after two seconds
3. Gestural after four seconds; do not move on to Level 4 until at least 50% of responses are independent for three consecutive sessions
4. Independent

Targets:

1. Child sits across the table from the adult
2. Child engages in activity on floor
3. Child is two feet from the adult
4. Child is five feet from the adult
5. Child is 10 feet from the adult
6. Generalize across three adults
7. Generalize across three settings

GROSS-MOTOR IMITATION FROM A PEER

Skill: *CG 6*

Objective: During a structured game like Simon Says, the child will imitate one-step gross-motor actions modeled first by an adult progressing to a peer in 80% of measured opportunities for three consecutive sessions.

Materials: Reinforcers, data sheets

General Teaching Strategies: The adult or child model should stand about five feet away from the child and model a variety of gross-motor actions saying, "Simon says, (action)" The adult should use the following prompting hierarchy to have the child imitate the actions:

Prompting Procedure: Time Delay

1. Full physical prompt
2. Full physical prompt after two-seconds
3. Full physical prompt after four-seconds
4. Independent

Targets:

1. Child imitates the adult from five feet away
2. Child imitates peer from five feet away
3. Child imitates peer in small-group setting as part of "Simon Says" game from five feet away
4. Across three people
5. Across three environments

APPENDIX 2:
Visual Supports

ACTIVITY 1:   Duck-Duck-Animal
ACTIVITY 4:   Charades
ACTIVITY 5:   Who Am I?
ACTIVITY 13: It's All About You!
ACTIVITY 17: Going to the Moon
ACTIVITY 23: Spider Web Questions
ACTIVITY 26: 20 Questions
ACTIVITY 27: Category Game
ACTIVITY 30: Sharing News
ACTIVITY 41: Self-Monitoring Checklist
ACTIVITY 47: Animal Pass
ACTIVITY 48: Conversation Chain

DOG

CAT

FISH

HORSE

SHEEP

PIG

ACTIVITY 1: DUCK, DUCK, ANIMAL (continued)

COW

SNAKE

BIRD

KANGAROO

POLAR BEAR

ELEPHANT

DUCK   GOOSE

ANIMALS:

ELEPHANT

SHARK

FROG

BEE

ACTIONS:

SWIMMING

DANCING

DRINKING

SINGING/PLAYING GUITAR

THROWING

RUNNING

OCCUPATIONS:

FIREFIGHTER

DOCTOR

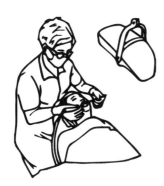

DENTIST

CONSTRUCTION WORKER

CHEF

TEACHER

ANIMALS:

| TIGER | GIRAFFE | POLAR BEAR | STARFISH |

QUESTIONS:

DOES YOUR ANIMAL HAVE:

| STRIPES | SPOTS | A TAIL | FOUR LEGS | WINGS |

DOES YOUR ANIMAL LIVE IN:

| THE OCEAN | THE DESERT | THE POLAR REGION | THE SAVANNA | THE FARM |

ACTIVITY 13: IT'S ALL ABOUT YOU!

HERE ARE POSSIBLE QUESTIONS TO ASK FRIENDS.
WHAT'S YOUR FAVORITE....

 COLOR?	 THING TO DO ON THE PLAYGROUND?	 THING TO DO IN THE SUMMER?	 THING TO DO IN THE WINTER?	TOY?
 ANIMAL?	 SNACK?	 INSTRUMENT?	 TV SHOW/ MOVIE?	 SUPER HERO?
 PLACE TO GO?	 BOOK?	 THING TO DO ON THE BEACH?	 THING TO DO WITH A FRIEND?	 RAINY DAY ACTIVITY?

CATEGORY:

ITEMS:

FRUIT	APPLE	BANANA	CHERRY	PINEAPPLE
VEGETABLES	CORN	CARROT	BROCCOLI	BEANS
TOYS	TRAIN	BUBBLES	BALL	TEDDY BEAR

ACTIVITY 23: SPIDER WEB QUESTIONS

DO YOU HAVE
ANY PETS?

HOW OLD ARE YOU?

WHERE DO YOU
LIKE TO GO?

DO YOU HAVE ANY
BROTHERS OR SISTERS?

WHO IS YOUR
BEST FRIEND?

WHAT DO YOU LIKE
TO DO AT SCHOOL?

WHAT'S YOUR
FAVORITE GAME?

WHAT'S YOUR
FAVORITE FOOD?

WHAT DO YOU LIKE TO
DO ON HOME DAYS?

CATEGORIES:

 ANIMAL

 FRUIT

 VEGETABLE

 SUPER HERO

 DRINK

FEATURES:

IS IT: (USE COLOR BOX)
DOES IT HAVE: (FIRST AND SECOND ROWS)
DOES IT LIVE IN: (THIRD ROW)

 (SPECIFIC COLOR)

 WINGS

 FEATHERS

 FOUR LEGS

 A TAIL

 STRIPES

 SPOTS

 A STEM

 SEEDS

 A TRUNK

 A TREE

 THE OCEAN

 THE SAVANNA

 THE FARM

 THE POLAR REGION

CATEGORY AND EXAMPLES:

DRINK	MILK	WATER	SHAKE	JUICE
FARM ANIMALS	COW	HORSE	SHEEP	PIG
TOYS	BALL	TRAIN	CRAYONS	BLOCKS
FOOD	PIZZA	ICE CREAM	PRETZEL	HOTDOG

QUESTIONS TO ASK:

DID YOU
HAVE FUN?

HOW DID YOU
GET THERE?

WHO DID YOU
GO WITH?

DID YOU EAT
ANYTHING THERE?
DID YOU DRINK
ANYTHING THERE?

WHAT WAS YOUR
FAVORITE PART?

WHO DID YOU
SEE THERE?

ACTIVITY 41: SELF-MONITORING CHECKLIST

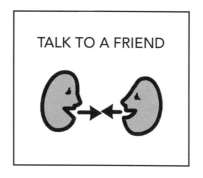

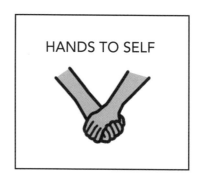

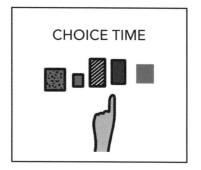

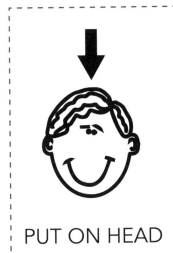

PUT ON HEAD

TRADE WITH
A FRIEND

MAKE ANIMAL
DANCE

MAKE ANIMAL
SLEEP

ACTIVITY 48: CONVERSATION CHAIN

| HOME DAYS | THE BEACH | SUPER HEROES | SUMMER | FALL |

Socially Savvy: An Assessment and Curriculum Guide for Young Children

APPENDIX 3:
Social Stories

(*SL 17*) RESPONDS APPROPRIATELY WHEN A PEER CHANGES TOPIC

(*SL 18*) DIRECTS BODY AND EYES TOWARD SOCIAL PARTNER WHEN SPEAKING

(*SL 19*) DIRECTS BODY AND EYES TOWARD SOCIAL PARTNER WHEN LISTENING

When I am showing listening behavior,

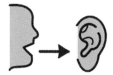

I have my eyes on the speaker

My body is calm and facing forward

My mouth is quiet

When it is my turn to speak, I will make a comment about what the speaker said.

For example, if we are talking about the beach, I will ask a question or make a comment about the beach.

When I have 	something new to 	say, it is 	confusing 	to just say it. 
I have to let people know 	when I want to say something new 			
I can say, 	"I want to tell you about..." 	or I can also say, 	"Guess what?" 	
That way, people know 	I am about 	to talk about 	something new! 	
My parents 	and teachers 	will be so proud of me for 	saying something new the right way! 	I'm doing a great job! 

(*SR 2*) APPROPRIATELY HANDLES DENIED REQUESTS

Some days when my Mom takes me to  ,

I like to go to the  .

I will go to the  when I am in Melissa's 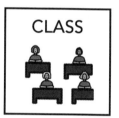 .

It is  if Mom says  .

Some days we do not have  and that is  .

(SR 4) RESPONDS TO CALMING STRATEGIES PROMPTED BY AN ADULT

(SR 5) IDENTIFIES WHEN UPSET/FRUSTRATED AND APPROPRIATELY ASKS FOR A BREAK OR A CALMING ITEM/ACTIVITY

 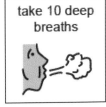  

(*SR 10*) RESPONDS TO MISTAKES MADE BY SELF OR OTHERS WITHOUT EXHIBITING CHALLENGING BEHAVIORS

Sometimes | I don't know | the answer | and I am afraid | to guess.

It is okay | to make a guess! | Making a good guess | is how I learn.

Sometimes, I might be right | Sometimes, I might be wrong.

Either way, | it is okay. | I learned something!

My parents | and teachers | will be so proud of me | for trying and making a good guess! | I did a great job!

Socially Savvy: An Assessment and Curriculum Guide for Young Children

REFERENCES:

[1] Partington, J. *Assessment of Basic Language and Learning Skills.* Behavior Analysis, Inc., 2006.

[2] Sundberg, M. *Verbal Behavior Milestone Assessment and Placement Program (VB-MAPP).* AVB Press, 2008.

[3] McGinnis, E. *Skillstreaming in Early Childhood: A Guide for Teaching Prosocial Skills* (3rd ed.). Champaign, IL: Research Press, 2011.

[4] Maurice, C., Green, G., and Luce, S. C. *Behavioral Interventions for Young Children with Autism.* Austin, TX: Pro Ed., 1996.

[5] Leaf, R., McEachin, J., and Harsh, J. D. *A Work in Progress: Behavior Management Strategies and A Curriculum for Intensive Behavioral Treatment of Autism.* New York: DRL Books, 1999.

[6] McKinnon, K., and Krempa, J. L. *Social Skills Solutions: A Hands-on Manual for Teaching Social Skills to Children with Autism.* New York: DRL Books, 2002.

[7] Gresham, F. M., and Elliot, S. N. *Social Skills Rating System Manual.* Circle Pines, MN: American Guidance Service, 1990.

[8] Charlop, M. H., Schreibman, L., and Thibodeau, M. G. "Increasing Spontaneous Verbal Responding in Autistic Children Using a Time Delay Procedure," *Journal of Applied Behavior Analysis* 18 (1985): 155–166.

[9] Charlop, M. H., Schreibman, L., and Tryon, A. S. "Learning Through Observation: The Effects of Peer Modeling on Acquisition and Generalization in Autistic Children," *Journal of Abnormal Child Psychology* 11 (1983): 355–366.

[10] Charlop, M. H., and Milstein, J. P. "Teaching Autistic Children Conversational Speech Using Video Modeling," *Journal of Applied Behavioral Analysis* 22 (1989): 275–285.

[11] Lonnecker, C., Brady, M. P., McPherson, R., and Hawkins, J. "Video Self-Modeling and Cooperative Classroom Behavior in Children with Learning and Behavior Problems: Training and Generalization Effects," *Behavioral Disorders* 20 (1994): 24–34.

[12] Ganz, J., Earles-Vollrath, T. I., and Cook, K. "Video Modeling: A Visually Based Intervention for Children with Autism Spectrum Disorder," *Teaching Exceptional Children* 43 (2011): 8–19.

[13] Stanfield, J. Circles Curriculum Level 1. www.stanfield.com.

[14] Winner, M. G. *Thinking About You Thinking About Me,* (2nd ed.). Think Social Publishing, 2007.

[15] Gray, C. *The New Social Story Book, 10th Anniversary Edition.* The Gray Center, 2010.

[16] Boardmaker. www.Mayer-Johnson.com.

[17] Carr, S. C., and Punzo, R. P. "The Effects of Self-Monitoring of Academic Accuracy and Productivity on the Performance of Students with Behavioral Disorders," *Behavior Disorders,* 18(4) (1993): 241–250.

[18] Hallahan, D. P., and Kauffman, J. M. *Exceptional Learners: Introduction to Special Education* (8th ed.). Boston: Allyn and Bacon, 2000.

[19] Strain, P. S., Kohler, F. W., Storey, K., and Danko, C. D. "Teaching Preschoolers with Autism to Self-Monitor Their Social Interactions: An Analysis of Results in Home and School," *Journal of Emotional and Behavior Disorders*, 2 (1994): 78–88.

[20] DiSalvo, C. A., and Oswald, D. P. "Peer-Mediated Interventions to Increase the Social Interaction of Children with Autism: Consideration of Peer Expectancies," *Focus on Autism and Other Developmental Disabilities* 17 (2002): 198–207.

[21] Goldstein, H., Kaczmarek, L., Pennington, R., and Shafer, K. "Peer-mediated Intervention: Attending to, Commenting on, and Acknowledging the Behavior of Preschoolers with Autism," *Journal of Applied Behavior Analysis* 25(2) (1992): 289–305.

[22] Strain, P., Kerr, M., and Ragland, E. "Effects of Peer-Mediated Social Initiations and Prompting/Reinforcement Procedures on the Social Behavior of Autistic Children," *Journal of Autism and Developmental Disorders* 9(1) (1979): 41–54.